"This volume contains a wide-ranging set of contributions on evangelical theological education in Australia. It touches on biblical, historical, formational, cross-cultural and educational dimensions of the topic . . . While there is still much work to be done, this collection is a definite milestone along the way."

—Robert Banks
Adjunct Research Professor, Australian Centre for Christianity and Culture, Canberra

"Andrew Bain and Ian Hussey have produced a substantial collection of essays by scholars from the Australian College of Theology (ACT), a major consortium of theological higher education providers in Australia, with an evangelical background. The essays address historical and contemporary matters, traditional Western and modern cross-cultural issues, particular theological and ministry challenges and issues related to the context of the wider community. Though reflecting its base within the ACT, this book will also provide other readers from the theological sector in Australia, and perhaps further afield, with real food for thought as they seek ever more effective approaches to the delivery of high-quality academic programs in theology."

—Diane Speed
Dean and CEO, Sydney College of Divinity

Theological Education

Australian College of Theology Monograph Series

SERIES EDITOR GRAEME R. CHATFIELD

The ACT Monograph Series, generously supported by the Board of Directors of the Australian College of Theology, provides a forum for publishing quality research theses and studies by its graduates and affiliated college staff in the broad fields of Biblical Studies, Christian Thought and History, and Practical Theology with Wipf and Stock Publishers of Eugene, Oregon. The ACT selects the best of its doctoral and research masters theses as well as monographs that offer the academic community, scholars, church leaders and the wider community uniquely Australian and New Zealand perspectives on significant research topics and topics of current debate. The ACT also provides opportunity for contributors beyond its graduates and affiliated college staff to publish monographs which support the mission and values of the ACT.

Rev Dr Graeme Chatfield
Series Editor and Associate Dean

Theological Education

Foundations, Practices, and Future Directions

Edited by
ANDREW M. BAIN
and
IAN HUSSEY

Foreword by
Martin Sutherland

WIPF & STOCK · Eugene, Oregon

THEOLOGICAL EDUCATION
Foundations, Practices, and Future Directions

Copyright © 2018 Wipf and Stock Publishers. All rights reserved. Except for brief quotations in critical publications or reviews, no part of this book may be reproduced in any manner without prior written permission from the publisher. Write: Permissions, Wipf and Stock Publishers, 199 W. 8th Ave., Suite 3, Eugene, OR 97401.

Wipf & Stock
An Imprint of Wipf and Stock Publishers
199 W. 8th Ave., Suite 3
Eugene, OR 97401

www.wipfandstock.com

PAPERBACK ISBN: 978-1-5326-4066-7
HARDCOVER ISBN: 978-1-5326-4067-4
EBOOK ISBN: 978-1-5326-4068-1

Manufactured in the U.S.A.

Contents

Contributors | ix
Foreword by Martin Sutherland | xv
Introduction | xix

Part I: Biblical and Theological Perspectives

1. Theological Interpretation in Theological Education: Teaching Old Testament Studies | 3
   —Kit Barker

2. The Scribe, the Steward and the Inhabiting Word | 17
   —David Starling

3. The Elements of a Theology of Theological Education | 29
   —Martin Foord

Part II: Historical Perspectives

4. Theological Education in Early Christianity: The Contribution of Late Antiquity | 47
   —Andrew M. Bain

5. Models of Western Christian Education and Ministerial Training: Antecedents in the Sixteenth Century | 60
   — Graeme Chatfield

6. American Theological Education at the Beginning of the Nineteenth Century: The Edwardsean Legacy | 74
   — Rhys S. Bezzant

7. A Thematic History of Theological Education in Australia | 88
   —Les Ball

8 The Three (or Four) Identities of the Australian College of Theology, 1891–2016 | 101
— GEOFFREY R. TRELOAR

9 Sydney Missionary and Bible College: A Case Study in Australian Theological Education | 119
— ANTHONY BRAMMALL

Part III: Current Practices

10 Five Years On: The Long-Term Value of Theological Education | 135
—IAN HUSSEY AND ANDREW M. BAIN

11 A Chinese Perspective on Theological Education | 148
—WALLY WANG

12 Women in Theological Education in the ACT in Twenty-First Century Australia | 160
—KARA MARTIN, MEGAN POWELL DU TOIT, JILL FIRTH, AND MOYRA DALE

13 Theological Education for Missional Leadership | 175
—KARINA KREMINSKI AND MICHAEL FROST

14 Developing Genuinely Reflective Ministry Practitioners | 187
—PETER FRANCIS

15 Rethinking Our Approach to Student Formation in Australian Theological Education | 200
—DIANE HOCKRIDGE

16 Theological Education for Cross-Cultural Ministry | 215
—PHILLIP SCHEEPERS

17 Student Attrition in Theological Education: Empirical Research from Australia | 228
—DELLE MATTHEWS

18 The Contributors to Spiritual Formation in Theological Education: What the Students Say | 241
—IAN HUSSEY

Part IV: Future Directions

19 The Utilization of Telecommuting Staff in Australian Theological Education | 259
—NATHAIN SECKER

20 The Current Environment of Theological Education in
    Australia | 274
    —Mark Harding

21 The Challenges for Theological Education in Australia | 287
    —Brian Harris

    Conclusion | 298
    Index | 303

Contributors

Andrew Bain is Vice Principal of Queensland Theological College, Brisbane, where he teaches Church History and Christian Ethics. He is Head of the Department of Christian Thought and History within the Australian College of Theology, a member of the ACT's Academic Board, and has taken an active role in promoting innovation in the ACT as inaugural chair of both the ACT's professional development conference and its coursework units panel. Andrew's PhD was in Latin patristics and he has published in a range of areas in historical theology. He also holds postgraduate qualifications in adult education and management.

Les Ball is Associate Professor of Christian Education and Academic Dean at the Australian College of Ministries within Sydney College of Divinity. He has held numerous positions in Australian theological education over thirty years. His recent research includes the monograph *Transforming Theology* (Mosaic, 2012), presentations at a series of conferences and professional development seminars, and the publication of a work coedited with James R. Harrison, *Learning and Teaching Theology: Some Ways Ahead* (Morning Star, 2014). His current focus is on ways in which new approaches to theological curriculum design can effectively facilitate transition and integration in theological education.

Kit Barker is a lecturer in Old Testament at Sydney Missionary and Bible College. He is the author of a recent monograph on theological interpretation and the Psalms, *Imprecation as Divine Discourse: Speech Act Theory, Dual Authorship and Theological Interpretation* (Eisenbrauns, 2016), and coeditor of the recently published, *Finding Lost Words: The Church's Right to Lament* (Wipf & Stock, 2017). He lives on the northern beaches of Sydney where he serves as an elder at Narrabeen Baptist Church.

Rhys S. Bezzant is Dean of Missional Leadership and a lecturer in Church History at Ridley College, Melbourne. He is the Director of the Jonathan Edwards Center, Australia, and is Visiting Fellow at the Yale Divinity School. He has published *Jonathan Edwards and the Church* (OUP, 2014) and *Standing on Their Shoulders* (Acorn, 2015), has translated *Martin Luther: A Late Medieval Life* (Baker, 2017), and is presently writing a book on the mentoring ministry of Edwards. He also serves as Canon of St Paul's Cathedral, Melbourne.

Anthony Brammall has been teaching at Sydney Missionary and Bible College since 2004, where he is Academic Vice-Principal and a lecturer in New Testament. He is also the editor for SMBC Press. Prior to this he taught Biblical Studies and Greek at Sekolah Tinggi Teologia (STT) INTIM in Makassar, South Sulawesi, Indonesia, where he served as a missionary with CMS. He wrote the centenary history of SMBC, *Out of Darkness*, which was published in 2016.

Graeme Chatfield is Associate Dean and Director of Research for the Australian College of Theology (ACT). He joined the ACT Office in 2009 after teaching for eleven years at Morling College. Graeme has a PhD in Reformation Studies from Bristol University (UK), published as *Balthasar Hübmaier and the Clarity of Scripture: A Critical Reformation Issue* (Pickwick, 2013). His key responsibilities are to foster the research culture of the ACT consortium and to oversee the Department of Teaching, Learning and Research.

Moyra Dale worked in education in the Middle East for two decades. She is an Adjunct Research Fellow at Melbourne School of Theology, and has taught at a number of ACT colleges and at theological colleges in Asia and the US. She holds a PhD in Education and a ThD from the ACT.

Jill Firth is a lecturer in Hebrew and Old Testament at Ridley College, Melbourne, and a Canon of St Paul's Cathedral. She holds an MDiv and PhD from the ACT and an MA in Spiritual Direction from the MCD (now UDiv). She has worked as a missionary and in parish ministry.

Peter Francis is the Principal of Malyon College, Brisbane, where he teaches pastoral studies, missions, and Old Testament survey. After a ten-year career as a high school teacher, Peter served for twenty-three years as a Baptist pastor in a range of locations in Queensland. During this time, he also served as a Regional Consultant with Queensland Baptists for two years.

He has completed a Doctor of Ministry on missional rejuvenation of historic inner-city churches. Over the past thirty years Peter has been involved with numerous short-term missions in places such as PNG, Bangladesh, Thailand, Cambodia, Vietnam, and South America, and has served on various mission boards and committees, including the Far East Broadcasting Company and Global Interaction.

Martin Foord is Senior Lecturer in Christian Thought at Trinity Theological College and is an ordained Anglican minister. His research interests are in systematic and historical theology, especially the doctrine of the gospel, the canon of Scripture, and ecclesiology.

Michael Frost is the Vice Principal (Strategic Development) of Morling College, Sydney, and the Director of the Tinsley Institute, the mission study center at Morling. A part-time lecturer at the college from 1994, he joined the faculty full time when he founded the Tinsley Institute in 1999. Michael teaches a range of subjects across the fields of missiology and evangelism, and has written extensively on a missional paradigm for the church in a post-Christian era. His books include *Jesus the Fool, The Shaping of Things to Come, Exiles, ReJesus, The Faith of Leap, The Big Ideas, The Road to Missional* and *Incarnate*. His latest book is *Surprise the World*. Several of his books have been translated into Spanish, German, Swedish and Korean, which has led to an extensive international speaking ministry.

Mark Harding was the Dean and CEO of the Australian College of Theology from 1996 until 2016. He is currently the Executive Officer of the Australian and New Zealand Association of Theological Schools and of the Council of Deans of Theology.

Brian Harris has served as the Principal of Vose Seminary, Perth, since 2004. He chairs the Academic Board of the Australian College of Theology, and is a director of the ACT. He is also a director of Christian Schools Australia, and a member of the Theological Education Commission of the Baptist World Alliance. He has published several books, including a trilogy with Paternoster, *The Tortoise Usually Wins: Biblical Reflections on Quiet Leadership* (2013), *The Big Picture: Building Blocks of a Christian World View* (2015), and *When Faith Turns Ugly: Understanding Toxic Faith and How to Avoid It* (2016).

Diane Hockridge is a faculty member at Ridley College where she works as the online educational designer. She is currently completing her PhD in education through Macquarie University, researching spiritual formation in online theological education. Diane has worked in a variety of roles in Christian higher education, and in university student ministry.

Ian Hussey is the Director of Post Graduate Studies at Malyon College, Brisbane, where he teaches New Testament, Research Methods and Practical Ministry. He is Chair of the e-Learning panel of the Australian College of Theology and a member of the ACT's Research and Research Studies Committee. Ian's PhD was in Practical Theology. He also holds master's qualifications in theology and management.

Karina Kreminski has been a lecturer in Missional Studies at Morling College since 2015. She oversees the Masters of Missional Leadership program and also the SENT Church Planting Certificate. She wrote her doctorate on the formation of a missional church and practices being an urban missionary in her neighborhood, and her book, *Urban Spirituality: Embodying God's Mission in the Neighbourhood* is soon to be published.

Kara Martin is a lecturer at Mary Andrews College, an ACT Masters graduate, and was Director of the School of Christian Studies in Sydney, and previously was a director of the ACT. She is also Project Leader at Seed Initiatives, and was Associate Dean of the Marketplace Institute at Ridley College.

Delle Matthews has been the Dean of Studies of the Melbourne School of Theology since 2004. She is also Chair of the Academic Quality Committee and a doctoral student of the Australian College of Theology. Her research interests are in student retention, the experience of women in theological education and how faith impacts students' decision making. She was previously a member of Wycliffe Bible Translators Australia serving as a literacy consultant and trainer in Indonesia and Australia.

Megan Powell du Toit is the Publications and Policies Administrator at the ACT and editor of Colloquium, the ANZATS journal. She is currently completing her PhD in theology through Morling College (UDiv). Since attaining her BMin (Hons) though Morling College (ACT) in 2002 she has worked as a Baptist pastor, adjunct lecturer and tutor.

Phillip Scheepers is Vice-Principal of the Reformed Theological College in Melbourne and lectures in Missions and Church History. He is also a Research Associate with Northwest University, Potchefstroom, South Africa. Before accepting his role at the RTC he coordinated the implementation of a church-based theological education program in the Middle East and North Africa under the auspices of Veritas College International. He holds four degrees (BA History, BTh, MTh and DTh) from the University of the Free State in Bloemfontein, South Africa. His doctorate (2003) focused on the history of Islam in South Africa.

Nathain Secker is the Academic Dean of the Timothy Partnership and Training Director of Presbyterian Youth NSW. He has been involved in training people for ministry and in the flexible delivery of theological education since 1997. Holding an MBA from the University of New England and an MHEd majoring in eLearning from Macquarie University, he endeavors to draw connections between pedagogy, educational management, and systems theory for a whole-of-business approach to the delivery of theological education. Nathain is a member of the Australian College of Theology's eLearning Panel and Academic Quality Committee and has recently joined a panel on engaging indigenous students in theological education.

David Starling lectures in New Testament at Morling College, where he serves as the head of the Bible and Theology Department. His PhD studies were at the University of Sydney and his thesis, on Paul's use of exile imagery, was published as *Not My People: Gentiles as Exiles in Pauline Hermeneutics* (BZNW 184; de Gruyter, 2011). Subsequent publications include *UnCorinthian Leadership* (Cascade, 2014) and *Hermeneutics as Apprenticeship* (Baker, 2016), plus two coedited volumes: *Theology and the Future* (T&T Clark, 2014) and *The Gender Conversation* (Wipf & Stock, 2016). Current projects include commentaries on Colossians, Ephesians and 1 Corinthians.

Geoff Treloar has been Director of Learning and Teaching at the Australian College of Theology since 2012. He is also a Visiting Fellow in History in the School of Humanities and Languages at the University of New South Wales and editor of Lucas: An Evangelical History Review. He has written on a range of topics in relation to the history of evangelicalism in the English-speaking world, including his recent volume *The Disruption of Evangelicalism: The Age of Torrey, Mott, McPherson and Hammond* (IVP, 2016).

Wally Wang is the Director of the Chinese-Language Program at Brisbane School of Theology. After obtaining a BSc in Mathematics from Florida State University, he completed an MSc and a PhD in Theoretical Physics from Carnegie Mellon University. After serving as a research associate in Argonne National Laboratory and at UNSW, he went back to Hong Kong and completed an MDiv from China Graduate School of Theology (CGST). After serving as a pastor in the Chinese Evangelical Free Church in Sydney, he returned to CGST and completed an MTh.

Foreword

THEOLOGICAL EDUCATION HAS A long history. It has been variously conceived, variously delivered and variously received. It has always reflected its context and, when alive to its calling, has sought ways to better serve the mission of God. This collection continues that tradition of self-reflection and critique. Some deep historical roots are probed and the outcomes, both across time and in more recent examples, are examined. As one would expect (and, indeed, hope) in a collection like this, there is particular reference to the Australian context. The Australian College of Theology has been a significant player in much of that history. It has exhibited many of the strengths and weaknesses suggested in these essays, but it also remains committed as the contributors are to finding effective models for the future. It is thus very happy to be associated with this volume.

As is evident even to a casual observer, and highlighted in specific detail in these essays, theological education in Australia and across the whole world, is very differently pursued than it was a century or even a few decades, ago. Institutions have come and gone. Some, like the ACT and the (now) University of Divinity, have persisted but in radically altered form. It comes as a surprise to some just how robust theological education is in Australia. In an age when Christian churches feel increasingly marginalized and no longer at the center of public debate, more students than ever are engaging in some version or another of formal theological education. It is wise to ponder this apparent dissonance.

Once understood as the preserve of those training for clerical ministry, theological education is now pursued by many who see (and seek) no particular vocational outcome. One college I have been associated with, in the clearly not identical but nonetheless similar context of New Zealand, changed in two decades from a seminary, training denominational ministry, with some 40 students, almost all in some way aspiring to denominational service, to a general provider with over 300 students, many part-time, of which only 20-30 saw themselves pursuing a clerical vocation. Similar shifts have occurred in other professions. Many study law, for instance, with no expectation or desire to practice as a barrister or solicitor.

Many factors have contributed to this fundamental change. Some are outlined in the essays in this volume. Theological educators in Australasia are subject to a number of tensions. In the colonial era, theological education, regarded as inherently partisan and divisive, was treated with suspicion by bodies governing higher education. Somewhat bruised by this we have spent a hundred and fifty years seeking what we regard as due recognition. If we can't be in the State Universities, then we will set up our own. Failing that, we want at least to have our qualifications recognized. This has been achieved.

Such engagement comes at a price, though not, interestingly, as was long feared, in terms of restriction on what we can teach. Indeed, the freedom of curriculum we enjoy is remarkable. No, the price has been that we have had to lift our game educationally. "Education" has been perhaps the neglected element in the past. We have seen ourselves as custodians of good theology and sometimes assumed that that is enough. The sobering aspect of such mechanisms as accreditation and registration has been that we have had to lift our educational game. This a welcome development, but higher educational quality demands greater resources which the churches have by and large been unable or unwilling to provide. Thus, state funding offers have been welcome and most providers have needed to seek economies of scale. Inevitably, then, we are in a mutually reinforcing process of meeting both educational compliance requirements and student demand.

Educators, particularly theological educators, grumble about such constraints. We need more actively to embrace the opportunity and the challenge that this environment offers. Most other professions have risen to the challenge of higher professional standards, underpinned by more rigorous training. The church and its training arms will gain nothing if, in reaction against hitherto unfamiliar expectations of educational quality we retreat into discussions and models which only echo the fading music of our past. In an age in which Christianity will need to think very deeply about its responses to events and to competing moral codes, we need better not less equipped leaders.

All systems have their problems. Higher Education is not immune, but it does provide opportunity. As participants in a rigorous shared educational environment theological educators have arguably the best opportunity in generations to confidently engage with ideological alternatives, to persuasively present the richness of the plan of God. Our very ways of thinking will need to reflect the grace and character of Christ. Such a task is not easy, but neither is it unprecedented. Christians have done this before. Let us not miss the advantage of the current moment.

I commend this collection of essays on the development, challenges and future of theological education. This level of engagement typifies the hard work we all need to do. If we embrace it, not as a hostilely imposed chore, but as a Spirit-led privilege, we may well succeed.

Martin Sutherland
Dean/CEO
Australian College of Theology

Introduction

ACCORDING TO THE OVERSEAS Council International, "Theological education is central to the Christian mission . . . Where the seminary leads, the church follows."[1] Ferenczi suggests that the theological education received by today's students and tomorrow's leaders determines the future direction of the church. "The education offered by theological schools is directly reflected in the life of the local church. It may be said that the success of an educational institution in transmitting doctrinal and spiritual truth to students is directly proportional to the success of those students in conveying those truths to the people around them."[2]

It is such an awareness that drives those involved in theological education to take so seriously the vocation to which they are called. It is also the awareness that has prompted the development of this volume. Theological education is too important a task to be done without careful and ongoing thought. The imperative to be reflective about how we go about our task as theological educators is amplified dramatically by the changing world in which we live. What may have worked for previous generations may no longer be relevant in our rapidly changing context. Volumes like the one you are currently holding are the manifestation of the serious reflection which your colleagues in theological education have undertaken regarding their practice from the perspective of their particular academic specialization. The fruit that their research has born in their personal practice can be shared in yours as well.

The research reported in this volume emerges from the Australian context. In particular, it largely emerges from academics associated with the Australian College of Theology (ACT). The Australian College of Theology is a consortium of sixteen theological education institutions across

---

1. Quoted in Ferenczi, "The Effectiveness of Theological Education in Ukraine: A Research Project," 179.

2. Ibid., 179.

Australia. There are over 1000 students enrolled in ACT served by over sixty teaching staff. The consortium colleges are from Anglican, Baptist, Presbyterian and interdenominational traditions and serve a wide variety of stakeholders, but all broadly share a commitment to evangelical theology. Most students are being trained for some sort of vocational ministry, but an increasing number are "lay" people looking to improve their skills for ministry.

The headquarters of the ACT is located in Sydney where a number of staff act on behalf of the consortium colleges in maintaining the policy and regulatory requirements of the Australian government with respect to higher education. Students enrolled in a college that belongs to the ACT are eligible for low-interest government loans (called FEE-HELP) to cover the expense of their tuition. The consortium colleges largely depend upon the fee income from students to support their operations as there are few colleges which have endowments or other sources of income. The gradual numerical decline of some parts of the Australian church has meant that some denominations which depend upon colleges for training ministers have reduced their contribution to their colleges. This shortfall has largely been replaced by the income now generated by student tuition fees. The ACT office also coordinates coursework and higher degree research in the consortium colleges.

Students who enroll in ACT degrees and other qualifications (or courses, as they are referred to within the ACT) are usually aged over eighteen and have normally completed their high school education. Degrees are offered at diploma, bachelor, masters and doctoral level. Courses are broken up into "units" (subjects) with eight units composing a one-year full-time diploma and twenty-four units being required for a Bachelor of Theology or Ministry, or a Master of Divinity or Ministry course.

Although the research reported in this volume comes from the Australian context, we are confident that the issues faced by theological education in Australia are shared by those in other contexts as well. As you look through the various contributions you will see that many of the topics and findings are of wider import than just the Australian setting. We hope that you will find the ideas contained in this volume stimulating and thought-provoking in relation to your own practice, and be able to adapt some of them to your particular context.

The approach of this volume is to commence with the biblical and theological groundwork for theological education. No matter what your context, this needs to be the starting point for reflection upon current practices. Kit Barker offers reflections on how an evangelical understanding of what we are teaching should shape how we teach it, especially by drawing on the Old Testament. David Starling then examines three metaphors from the New Testament relating to theological education, and Marty Foord formulates a systematic theology to undergird theological education.

As important as it is to examine the Scriptures for guidance regarding life and practice, it is important to recognize that we are not the first to do so. Church history provides a valuable source of perspective when it comes to interpretation of Scripture and application to Christian practice. Hence, we have included in the volume a number of chapters which survey theological education from a historical perspective. Andrew M. Bain examines some classical approaches to theological education, Graham Chatfield looks at approaches that emerged from the Reformation, and Rhys Bezzant at American theological education at the beginning of the nineteenth century. Moving to Australia, Les Ball surveys the history of theological education in Australia while Geoff Treloar focuses on the history of the ACT and Anthony Brammall focuses on the history of an individual college: the Sydney Missionary and Bible College.

At this point the volume diversifies as it begins to look at an eclectic range of current practices in the ACT. These unique contextual practices provide stimulation for reflection in the particular context of you, the reader. For example, Ian Hussey and Andrew M. Bain have deliberately sought to measure the effectiveness of theological education in the life of ministry practitioners in their chapter. Wally Wang surveys theological education amongst Chinese Australians, particularly focusing on the practices of lecturers. Kara Martin, Megan Powell du Toit, Jill Firth, and Moyra Dale have sought to quantify and understand the experience of theological education for women in Australia. Karina Kreminski and Mike Frost have reported on their own experiment in developing theological education for missional leadership. Peter Francis reports on a model for developing reflective practitioners while Diane Hockridge presents a model for addressing the formation of students right across a theological institution. Phillip Scheepers describes the practice of preparing students for cross-cultural ministry. Delle Matthews reports on her crucial research into student attrition while Ian Hussey reports on what students indicate are the major contributors to their spiritual formation. Finally, Nathain Secker explores the implications of telecommuting academics for the administration of theological colleges.

The final two chapters of the volume seek to describe the current environment of theological education in Australia (Mark Harding) and describe the future challenges that are emerging (Brian Harris).

It is important when reading the Bible to intentionally seek to hear other voices that come from a perspective different to our own. Equally, when we come to reflect upon theological education it is helpful for us to hear the voices of our colleagues from different places and with different experiences. This volume is eclectic by nature. But by being so it will hopefully provide you with dynamic stimulus for your development as a theological educator, for the glory of God.

We are grateful to the ACT for providing funding support towards the costs of readying this volume for publication, and also acknowledge with thanks the assistance of Greta Morris and Megan Powell du Toit in the preparation of the manuscript.

Andrew M. Bain
Ian Hussey
Brisbane, 2017.

Bibliography

Ferenczi, Jason. "The Effectiveness of Theological Education in Ukraine: A Research Project." *Theological Reflections* 7 (2006) 178–205.

Part I

Biblical and Theological Perspectives

I

Theological Interpretation in Theological Education

Teaching Old Testament Studies

Kit Barker

Abstract

Our essential beliefs about what the Old Testament *is* should inform *how* we interpret it and teach it. Thus, the fundamental conviction underlying this chapter is that ontology should determine praxis. While the advent of theological interpretation has helped to clarify the presuppositions and goals of evangelical hermeneutics, the practice of evangelical hermeneutics, particularly with respect to the Old Testament, is often at odds with such beliefs. Broadly, evangelical hermeneutics need to moderate the influence of historical criticism and embrace a consistent and explicit application of our convictions within Old Testament interpretation and pedagogy. Speech act theory is proposed as a helpful means of achieving this objective.

Introduction

IN WRITING ON THE topic of Old Testament perspectives on theological education, it is possible to understand the matter in two ways: 1) What (if anything) does the Old Testament say about theological education? or 2) How should theological education be undertaken in the field of Old Testament studies? My primary interest lies with the latter question, though, of course, the two are fundamentally related. Rather than examine how various texts in the Old Testament might inform our pedagogy, I offer my reflections on how an evangelical understanding of *what* we are teaching should shape *how* we teach it. Put simply, ontology should inform praxis, but I am not convinced that, within evangelicalism, such consistency is always maintained.[1] I believe that recent discussions of theological interpretation provide a helpful platform upon which we can evaluate the relationship between our ontology and praxis.

Ontology

The Presuppositions of Theological Interpretation

The legacy of the Enlightenment has dominated construals of Old Testament ontology. For many within the academy the Old Testament is viewed as varying combinations of history, myth, and political propaganda with no recognition of divine agency. Consequently, the widely accepted hermeneutics of historical criticism are often formed from presuppositions at odds with evangelical convictions.[2] This renders them an inadequate tool for those desiring to engage with Scripture on its own terms. Murray Rae comments,

> Despite the biblical imperative, quite properly insisted on by Kasemann and Pannenberg, to be attentive to God's action in history, it will be argued in what follows that the historical-critical method is incapable of discerning where and how God is at work in the world and that it is unable therefore, to facilitate a faithful reading of biblical texts. This is so, first, because adherence to the standard canons of historical inquiry renders a historical-critical method incapable of reading Scripture on its own terms and of hearing through Scripture the Word of God;

---

1. For an interesting analysis of ontology and pedagogy at bible colleges and seminaries in the North American context see Martin, *Pedagogy and the Bible*, 1–22.
2. Longman, "History and Old Testament Interpretation," 102.

second, because the biblical account of the divine economy requires us to rethink what history is; and third, because God is wholly Other, which is to say that God's being and action cannot be detected through the same methods of inquiry that we use to investigate created realities.[3]

Unfortunately, the influence of higher-critical ontology and praxis has often been met with little critical reflection. Practices in biblical and theological studies will always reflect the broader cultures in which they occur, but as John Goldingay notes, without a critical engagement with this culture we may find that our pedagogy fits our times better than it does the subject of our teaching.

> We need to reflect on the way developments in biblical interpretation are inclined to mirror developments in the study of English literature and the wider critical environment. The literary turn, post-structuralism, post-colonial study, reception history, and so on, did not start as developments within biblical interpretation. They were brought into biblical interpretation from the cultural context. The fact doesn't in itself make them wrong, and those approaches to interpretation make fruitful contributions to our hearing the voice of God in the Scriptures, but the dynamic of the process raises questions about the ease with which we sell our souls to the latest hermeneutical idea. This consideration might suggest another angle on the importance of the question, how do we hear the voice of God from the Scriptures. While hearing may happen in part because approaches that emerge from our context are ones that speak to us, it will also happen because we are not confined to such approaches but are open to ones that correspond to the nature of the text.[4]

The recent "resurgence" of theological interpretation reflects such an attempt to connect our ontology with our praxis. While theological interpretation is defined in a variety of ways, I suggest that Craig Bartholomew's definition in terms of *telos* is most helpful. If we believe that Scripture—and specifically the Old Testament—is the word of God, then the *telos* of theological interpretation must be hearing God's voice.[5] Even so, Bartholomew will note that despite the recent discussions of theological interpretation,

---

3. Rae, "Theological Interpretation and Historical Criticism," 97.

4. Goldingay, "Hearing God Speak from the First Testament," 63. See also Martin, *Pedagogy of the Bible*, 12.

5. Bartholomew, "Listening for God's Address: A Mere Trinitarian Hermeneutic for the Old Testament," 12. See also, Thomas, "The *Telos* (Goal) of Theological Interpretation," 198; Barker, *Imprecation as Divine Discourse*, 5.

there remains little evidence that Old Testament scholars are demonstrating the practice.

> . . . the renaissance of theological interpretation of the Bible is still in its early years, and it remains rare to find scholarship on the Old Testament that embodies the kind of integrated theological hermeneutic that retains critical rigor while aiming throughout to hear God's address.[6]

Divine Rhetoric and Speech Act Theory

If Scripture is the word of God then the best way to describe its canonical genre is divine rhetoric. Scripture is God's communicative act through which he continues to speak. That rhetoric is the best descriptor of this communicative act acknowledges that the information conveyed is intended to be both persuasive and transformative. It is not simply a compendium of truth claims waiting to be arranged and systematized—though it is at least that—but constitutes complex, interpersonal communication intended to impose itself upon readers. It is not abstract or incidental but is inherently self-involving and demanding.[7]

I have found speech act theory to be a valuable tool in clarifying how Scripture, and particularly the Old Testament, can be identified as divine speech.[8] While speech act theory has featured in discussions of biblical interpretation for over thirty years, it has been slow to gain wide acceptance and integration.[9] This is regrettable as I believe it offers a valuable resource for theological interpretation. I am not suggesting that speech act categories are necessary for the task, simply that they bring it greater clarity.

The power of speech act theory is its ability to offer a detailed description of interpersonal communication. In so doing, it provides clarity to both the process and goal of hermeneutics. Most speech act theorists recognize three categories within a communicative act: locution, illocution and perlocution.

> The locution is the words that are uttered or written, the illocution is what the author or speaker is doing with those words, and

---

6. Bartholomew, "Listening for God's Address," 12.
7. See Sloane, "Weeping with the Afflicted"; Evans, *The Logic of Self Involvement*, 14.
8. For those unfamiliar with speech act theory, I have outlined its salient features and discussed its benefits in other places. See, Barker, "Making Sense of *Sensus Plenior*"; Barker, *Imprecation as Divine Discourse*, 66–106.
9. See Briggs, "The Uses of Speech-Act Theory in Biblical Interpretation."

the perlocution is the affect that this produces in the audience. The meaning of a text is the illocution (i.e., what the author was doing with the words, sentences, and text he or she produced).¹⁰

These categories alert interpreters to the fact that meaning is almost always more than a simple assertion. Speech act theory forces readers to ask what the author was *doing* with the text. This will, in most cases, require a description that moves beyond what an author was *asserting* to what an author was asking, demanding, promising, exhorting, etc. To understand the meaning of the text is thus to understand the multitude of speech acts performed through it and to identify those that are primary among them.¹¹

The power of speech act theory is enhanced in the case of biblical interpretation as speech act theory is well equipped to engage with the complexity of Scripture as a multi-authored, divine, and canonical communicative act. It demonstrates the need to establish what illocutions God is performing and how these relate to those of the human author.¹² It also reveals the inherent complexity in interpersonal communication, not only in the multitude of speech acts in any utterance but also that speech acts occur at a variety of textual and literary levels.¹³ Furthermore, it can explain how the canon reshapes the communicative context of the Old Testament, maintaining its function as divine rhetoric.¹⁴ While continuity exists between God's speech acts in their Old Testament canonical context and his speech acts in the same texts as they are situated in the Christian canon, there is also clearly some discontinuity. Speech act theory provides hermeneutic clarity in making assessments about how this new context affirms "original" speech acts, renders others as no longer "in play," and performs new speech acts. Whether one adopts the terminology and taxonomy of the theory is of less importance than engaging with it to gain precision and clarity to our task. Such clarification of how God continues to speak through the Old Testament is of critical importance for those wishing to affirm and to teach the Old Testament as Christian Scripture.

---

10. See Barker, "Lament as Divine Discourse," 57. Of course, there are those who would contest that meaning is a product of authorial intent and action. Those wanting to (ironically) assert the reader as the genesis of meaning will likely point to the perlocution as the locus of meaning.

11. Vanhoozer, *First Theology*, 178; Barker, *Imprecation as Divine Discourse*, 82–90.

12. I am not suggesting that God's speech acts are identical to or coterminous with those of the human author, simply that God's speech acts are based on the locutions and illocutions found in the text.

13. For a detailed discussion of various illocutionary levels, see Barker, *Imprecation as Divine Discourse*, 82–100.

14. Barker, "Making Sense of *Sensus Plenior*."

Praxis: Hermeneutical and Pedagogical Reflections

If this articulation of an evangelical ontology of the Old Testament is accurate, then evidence of it should be found in our hermeneutic and our pedagogy. What follows is my brief attempt at such consistency. Accordingly, to fit with the description of Scripture as divine rhetoric, I have arranged the discussion to reflect the three components of interpersonal communication: history (context), text, and audience.

History

Understanding Scripture as divine rhetoric requires a hermeneutical commitment to the historical context in which the speech acts originally occurred. A sensitivity to the cultural linguistic context is necessary to understand the "language games" being played and the speech acts being performed. The author's/redactor's use of language is discernable to the extent that we can locate it within this context. Readers must attend to the historically situated speech acts of the human author. Thus, responsible reading requires attending to issues of culture, language, geo-politics, and theologies, etc. that form the "background"[15] in which the text resides. Interpretation is not simply a matter of attending to the text but to its historical and cultural context. God's speech acts are only accessible through the speech acts of the human author. Consequently, hermeneutics aimed at discerning the voice of God must remain committed to historical inquiry and employ the wide array of resources available to teachers of the Old Testament.

However, as I stated, a *telos* of hearing God's address in the Old Testament is at odds with much of the historically focused hermeneutics undertaken by the academy over the past two hundred years. The benefits and problems of historical criticism have been discussed at length elsewhere, so only a brief comment here will suffice. While it has been and continues to be necessary for evangelical scholars to engage with historical critical methods, I suspect that we have granted it more influence than it deserves. Its inherent skepticism and vastly differing goals have produced hermeneutics largely unhelpful for theological interpretation. It has of course, resulted in a closer attention to the biblical texts and raised many significant issues that must be addressed. However, any ontology that rejects, *a priori*, notions of a unified text and associated synchronic readings is bound to prove ultimately insufficient for the task of theological interpretation and theological

---

15. John Searle's term for the extra-linguistic, conventional context that allows for speech acts to be performed. See Searle, *Speech Acts*, 12.

education. Goldingay comments on the impotence of historical criticism to produce anything of substantive use.

> ... the attempt to trace the actual history turned out to be a period of fruitless wandering. There are two pieces of evidence for the conclusion that the journey led nowhere. One is that it generated no theology and no insight on the Scriptures' significance for the thinking and life of the world and the church. It generated nothing that would preach. The uselessness for theologians and preachers of nearly all scholarly biblical commentaries written over these two centuries witnesses to the point...
>
> The other evidence that the journey was one of fruitless wandering is the fact that the quest for historical actuality proved futile. No actuality was gained. Two centuries of work by great minds has hardly given birth even to a mouse. The wise assumption is that such study is never going to escape the country of Nod. As far as the Old Testament is concerned, there will never be a critically-justifiable consensus on key questions about the story of Israel's ancestors, about the Exodus, about how Israel became Israel in Canaan, and maybe about David and Solomon and much of the later history. It's actually easy enough to see why it is so. The material in the Old Testament with which historical criticism has to work is not such as can answer the question that historical criticism asks.[16]

Of course, Goldingay is not rejecting the historical nature of reading the Old Testament. In his own words,

> What we require is not a move from a non-theological historical reading of the Scriptures to a non-historical theological reading of the Scriptures. What we require is a move from a non-theological historical reading to a theological historical reading, which will be a fuller historical reading because it articulates the text's own theology.[17]

So, what are the pedagogical implications of a hermeneutic that understands history as tool rather than *telos*? First, Old Testament exegetical courses should be canonically rather than historically shaped. Our own Australian College of Theology units have suffered from this in the past and, in some cases, still do. Prior to 2011, the introductory units in Old Testament were labelled "Formative Old Testament Traditions" and the course structure was arranged by historical epoch rather than canonical form.

---

16. Goldingay, "Hearing God Speak from the First Testament," 60.
17. Ibid., 67.

Currently, the "Exilic Prophecy" unit allows lecturers to choose between Ezekiel, Jeremiah, and Second Isaiah. While there is merit in both understanding Isaiah 40–55 as a literary unit and investigating its intertextuality with Ezekiel and Jeremiah, the ability to focus the entire unit on Isaiah 40–55 appears indebted to historical-critical presuppositions and hermeneutics. For those undertaking theological interpretation, Isaiah 40–55 will have a discreet voice and yet, to understand the "thickness" of its speech acts, it must be considered within the final form of Isaiah and ultimately the Christian canon. Treating these contexts as peripheral to the course ignores our own defining presupposition that the canonical text of Isaiah is divine rhetoric.

Second, the place of historical criticism within Old Testament units should be carefully considered. Many of our students will not serve in ministries where the issues of historical criticism are debated or even understood. It is far more likely that the issues our graduates will face will reflect those of contemporary culture rather than those of past centuries. In our postmodern contexts, postcolonial, ecological, feminist, LGBTQIA, and majority world readings will be far more influential in audiences our graduates encounter. We might ask how well we are equipping students to engage with these approaches to Scripture. Contemporary philosophy and literary theory has moved two steps beyond issues "behind the text,"[18] yet I believe we still grant these issues more time than they are worth.

Lastly, we should continue to model the necessity of historical inquiry in an age that will attempt to loose the text from its historical context. In order to form responsible readers who are prepared to engage with vastly divergent hermeneutics, we must demonstrate the need to understand the "background" of the text and the language games being played. The explicit articulation of a such a hermeneutic will enable the requisite self-awareness for such engagement. Theological interpretation is more than historical inquiry but it cannot be achieved without it.

Text

For those committed to theological interpretation, the text is primary. It is here that the divine speech acts are preserved and communicated. Consequently, final form, synchronic and text-immanent approaches are well suited to the task. While affirming such a focus on the text, I am not endorsing

---

18. For a comprehensive discussion of the shift in hermeneutic focus from "behind the text" to "in the text" and then "in front of the text" see, Thiselton, *New Horizons in Hermeneutics*.

a structuralist ontology. The above discussion of history demonstrates the need to situate the text in its historical context.[19] Speech act theory again proves useful in clarifying the relationship. The meaning of the text is the sum of the speech acts being performed. These are only grasped by understanding how the author was using the text in its context. The goal of interpretation is not uncovering what a text means "in itself," rather, meaning is a product of the public speech acts being performed in accordance with cultural, linguistic conventions.

Speech act theory also demonstrates the need to focus on texts in their fullness, noting that texts are complex and authors perform multiple speech acts at a variety of literary levels. Thus, to understand a unit of text, the broader literary contexts must be examined. In the case of theological interpretation this requires not only a discussion of the text in the literary context of the book where it resides, but also of how that text and book relate to the broader Christian canon. It is only by attending to the speech acts occurring that these higher literary levels, and the ways in which they impact those of the text in question, that the speech acts of this lower-level section are revealed.

If the goal of theological interpretation is to hear God's address (i.e., uncover the divine speech acts), then hearing God's address in an Old Testament pericope is just as important as hearing God's address at the canonical level. The latter will necessarily supervene on the former, but the goal of interpretation is not simply to work toward a canonical and systematic understanding of divine speech; rather, it is also to use this understanding to uncover the fullness of what God is doing in the texts of the Old Testament. In other words, understanding the canonical speech acts is essential to hearing God's address today, but it is not the end of the interpretive process. Understanding the canonical speech acts enables readers to discover how texts in the Old Testament continue to function as God's speech.

This prioritizing of the text should affect our pedagogy in at least the following two ways. Firstly, while ensuring our students have an awareness of and appreciation for other hermeneutics is important, if we are committed to theological interpretation, our focus should be ensuring students are skilled in synchronic and final-form readings. Rhetorical studies align well with the goals of theological interpretation, and assisting students in the identification of rhetorical units (speech acts at various literary levels) is foundational for uncovering the divine rhetoric. Unfortunately, there is a

---

19. For a discussion of the place of history in text-immanent approaches, see Snyman, "A Structural-Historical Approach to the Exegesis of the Old Testament."

distinct lack in Old Testament studies of final-form readings that focus on rhetorical function.[20]

Secondly, to complete the task of theological interpretation in the Old Testament, a discussion of how the text now functions within the Christian canon is essential. While New Testament and systematic units undoubtedly interact with Old Testament texts, I suggest that the inquiry into how the Old Testament now functions is best discussed in the context of the Old Testament units. Specialists in Old Testament studies are best placed to understand how the text functioned in its Old Testament context and this is foundational for understanding how it functions today. This requires that Old Testament lecturers engage with New Testament and systematic studies to explicate their theological interpretations. The alternative is that we leave students with an understanding of what God was doing with the texts "back then" yet leave them little guidance in discerning what God is doing with the texts today. Of course, we could relegate these discussions to the domain of other departments, but I believe it is our responsibility, as teachers of the Old Testament, to explicate our theological interpretation and assist the students in discovering the "application to Christian life and ministry." This suggests the need for interdepartmental collaboration regarding how each of our disciplines and units are working together to produce students skilled in theological interpretation.

Audience

A further benefit for describing the ontology of the Old Testament (and all of Scripture) as divine rhetoric is that it ameliorates the common disjunction between the meaning of the text and its application to an audience. Traditionally, to discern the application of the text, teachers and preachers first discover what the text is saying—perhaps distill a timeless truth or "big idea"[21]—and then attempt to demonstrate how this truth is relevant to their audience. Understanding the text as divine rhetoric—within which is embedded a multitude of speech acts—illuminates a more direct connection between meaning and application. Furthermore, it identifies trans-

---

20. For an excellent example of "the exception that proves the rule" see Renz, *The Rhetorical Function of the Book of Ezekiel*. However, Renz's discussion of rhetoric is limited to that of the human author. For theological interpretation to be successful, a consideration of Ezekiel within the Christian canon is required, as is the differentiation between the implied audience of the book and the new covenant, contemporary audience.

21. For an example of a recent commentary series that provides such a homiletic "big idea" see Sprinkle, *Leviticus and Numbers*.

formation in the reader as the primary goal of theological interpretation. As Heath Thomas states, "theological interpretation reads Scripture to hear God's address, so that the church might be transformed into the image of Christ, for the sake of the world."[22] In as much as it is our responsibility to aid students in hearing God's voice in the Old Testament, it is also our responsibility to aid them in applying the text to their own context(s).[23]

In speech act terms, the illocution is what the author *is doing* with the locution (words uttered or, in this case, written). However, this is not the end of the communicative act. Speech act theory also identifies perlocution as inherent to interpersonal communication. Perlocution is the effect that the illocution has upon an audience. Sometimes the illocution is so strong that a perlocution is automatic and not dependent upon the audience (e.g., when a judge proclaims, "I declare you guilty and sentence you to . . . "). More commonly, speech acts are not this strong and require the audience to respond appropriately for the communicative act to reach a "happy" fulfillment.[24] The inherent need to respond to communication, especially divine rhetoric can be obscured when the text is distilled in the form of an assertion or "big idea." Texts are used to make assertions and the biblical text is no different. Uncovering assertions is necessary for systematizing and clarifying ideas and truths. However, God always uses the biblical text to do more than simply *assert* truth. In fact, the asserting of truths is rarely, if ever, the primary action or meaning of the text. Through these attendant assertions, God *commands, encourages, rebukes, questions, promises, invites*, and *performs a multitude of primary speech acts* that demand readers respond rightly.

Speech act theory highlights the fact that texts are almost always more complicated than simple assertion and that most of the time, assertions are in service to more primary speech acts. Exploring this complexity with students enables them to appreciate the need to uncover the fullness of what God is doing with any given biblical text. Once they move past the often

22. Thomas, H. "The *Telos* (Goal) of Theological Interpretation," 198. See also, Brisben and Klein, "Reading the Old Testament as Story: A Pedagogy for Spiritual Formation," 327.

23. This is reflected in the recently updated learning outcomes for Australian College of Theology Old Testament units. As a result of the unit, students should "Know and understand . . . The relevance of the Exilic Prophets to contemporary ministry," and "Be in a position to: 1. Exegete the text of the Exilic Prophets for personal understanding and for use in ministry context; 2. Integrate perspectives from the Exilic Prophets into biblical interpretation and Christian thinking; 3. Apply the teaching of the Exilic Prophets to situations and issues in contemporary Christianity and society" (http://www.actheology.edu.au/unit/OT423/).

24. Austin, *How to Do Things with Words*, 12–24.

"automatic" and conditioned response of uncovering what the text asserts to be true, they can see that embedded in the meaning of the text are the broad strokes of application. The application (or appropriate perlocution) of the text is directly connected to the illocutions being performed.

We fail in our responsibility as teachers of the Old Testament, if we have not enabled students to understand how God speaks through texts and calls readers to respond. This requires that we commit class or assessment time to moving from text to homiletics, for it is only in this hermeneutic move that the divine rhetoric is fully appreciated.[25] Students need to be able to answer, "What was God doing then and what is God doing now?"[26] As I said earlier, we could leave this solely in the hands of other departments, but this, I believe, would be an abdication of our responsibility.

Conclusion

Pedagogy in theological education should reflect our hermeneutics and our hermeneutics should be consistent with our ontology. Unfortunately, Old Testament education in evangelical contexts has not always demonstrated such consistency. The influence of historical criticism is enduring and requires that we reflect on how it continues to shape our practices.

Recent calls for theological interpretation have clarified the *telos* of evangelical hermeneutics. What remains is the development of hermeneutics that achieve such goals and pedagogy that is explicitly reliant on them. I have found speech act theory a useful tool in this regard as it clarifies the complex nature of interpersonal communication, assigns relative importance to history, text, and audience and is particularly suited to explicating how the Christian canon functions as divine rhetoric.

If we are to teach the Old Testament as divine rhetoric, we need to resist traditional silos in biblical scholarship and education. Clearly, we need to maintain specialization, but our ontology of the Old Testament (and of Scripture) requires that we train students in the identification of divine

---

25. Over the past few years I and some of my colleagues have included homiletic components in our exegetical units. In my second and third-year exegetical units I now include an in-class sermon and discussion. In the Exilic Prophecy unit I have also included a second major assessment where students are required to: 1. Divide the book of Ezekiel into rhetorical units; 2. Choose one smaller rhetorical unit within these for a focused exegetical discussion; 3. Provide a brief homiletic outline of the text including a discussion of how the implied audience of the book relates to the intended audience of their sermon.

26. For a discussion of speech act theory and homiletics, see Chan, *Preaching as the Word of God*; Kuruvilla, *Privilege the Text*.

rhetoric. For this to occur, as Old Testament lecturers we must engage in canonical, systematic and homiletic practices.

Bibliography

Austin, John L. *How to Do Things with Words*. 2nd ed. The William James Lectures 1955. Oxford: Clarendon Press, 1975.

Australian College of Theology. http://www.actheology.edu.au/unit/OT423/.

Barker, Kit. *Imprecation as Divine Discourse: Speech Act Theory, Dual Authorship, and Theological Interpretation*. Journal of Theological Interpretation Supplement 16. Winona Lake: Eisenbrauns, 2016.

———. "Lament as Divine Discourse." In *Finding Lost Words: The Church's Right to Lament*, edited by G. Geoffrey Harper and Kit Barker, 55–65. Eugene: Wipf & Stock, 2017.

———. "Making Sense of *Sensus Plenior*: Speech Act Theory, Dual Authorship, and Canonical Hermeneutics." *Journal of Theological Interpretation* 3, no. 2 (2009) 227–39.

Bartholomew, Craig. G. "Listening for God's Address: A Mere Trinitarian Hermeneutic for the Old Testament." In *Hearing the Old Testament: Listening for God's Address*, edited by Craig G. Bartholomew and David J. H. Beldman, 3–19. Grand Rapids: Eerdmans, 2012.

Bartholomew, Craig. G. and Heath A. Thomas. *A Manifesto for Theological Interpretation*. Grand Rapids: Baker, 2016.

Briggs, Richard. "The Uses of Speech-Act Theory in Biblical Interpretation." *Currents in Research* 9 (2001) 229–76.

Brisben, David and Amelia Klein. "Reading the Old Testament as Story: A Pedagogy for Spiritual Formation." *Christian Education Journal* 3, vol. 9, no. 2 (2012) 326–41.

Chan, Sam. *Preaching as the Word of God: Answering an Old Question with Speech Act Theory*. Eugene: Pickwick, 2016.

Evans, Craig. *The Logic of Self Involvement: A Philosophical Study of Everyday Language with Special Reference to the Christian User of Language about God as Creator*. London: SCM, 1963.

Goldingay, John. "Hearing God Speak from the First Testament." In *The Voice of God in the Text of Scripture*, edited by Oliver D. Crisp and Fred Sanders, 59–77. Grand Rapids: Zondervan, 2016.

Kuruvilla, Abraham. *Privilege the Text: A Theological Hermeneutic for Preaching*. Chicago: Moody, 2013.

Longman III, Tremper. "History and Old Testament Interpretation." In *Hearing the Old Testament: Listening for God's Address*, edited by Craig G. Bartholomew and David J. H. Beldman, 96–121. Grand Rapids: Eerdmans, 2012.

Martin, Dale B. *Pedagogy of the Bible: An Analysis and Proposal*. Louisville: Westminster John Knox, 2008.

Rae, Murray. "Theological Interpretation and Historical Criticism." In *A Manifesto for Theological Interpretation*, edited by Craig G. Bartholomew and Heath A. Thomas, 94–109. Grand Rapids: Baker, 2016.

Renz, Thomas. *The Rhetorical Function of the Book of Ezekiel*. Leiden: Brill, 1999.

Searle, John. *Speech Acts: An Essay in the Philosophy of Language.* London: Cambridge University Press, 1983.

Sloane, Andrew. "Weeping with the Afflicted: The Self-Involving Language of the Laments." In *Finding Lost Words: The Church's Right to Lament,* edited by G. Geoffrey Harper and Kit Barker, 162–74. Eugene: Wipf & Stock, 2017.

Snyman, S. D. "A Structural-Historical Approach to The Exegesis of the Old Testament." In *Words and the Word: Explorations in Biblical Interpretation and Literary Theory,* edited by David G. Firth and Jamie A. Grant, 51–74. Nottingham: Apollos, 2008.

Sprinkle, Joe M. *Leviticus and Numbers.* Grand Rapids: Baker, 2015.

Thiselton, Anthony C. *New Horizons in Hermeneutics: The Theory and Practice of Transforming Biblical Reading.* Grand Rapids: Zondervan, 1992.

Thomas, Heath. "The *Telos* (Goal) of Theological Interpretation." In *A Manifesto for Theological Interpretation,* edited by Craig G. Bartholomew and Heath A. Thomas, 197–217. Grand Rapids: Baker, 2016.

Vanhoozer, Kevin J. *First Theology: God, Scripture and Hermeneutics.* Downers Grove: IVP, 2002.

2

The Scribe, the Steward, and the Inhabiting Word

DAVID STARLING

Abstract

Indicating what the New Testament has to speak into the enterprise of theological education is no easy task. This chapter is conscious of the complexities involved in the assignment, but undertakes nonetheless to offer three New Testament images that ought to inform the shaping of contemporary theological education. These perspectives serve to remind that theological education must be oriented toward the life of the church and and its God-given mission in the world, captivated above all things by Christ and Scripture, and conducted within relational contexts that foster personal formation and transformation.

Introduction

THE ORIGINAL INVITATION THAT I received to contribute to this volume asked me to write a chapter entitled "New Testament Perspectives on Theological Education." This filled me with a mixture of enthusiasm and uncertainty. I love the New Testament, and my working life is devoted to teaching it; and I am an enthusiast for theological education, with some deeply-held convictions about what it is and how it ought to be approached. But bringing those two enthusiasms together is trickier than it might at first sound. There was, after all, no such thing as "theological education" (in the sense in which we use those words) during the time in which the New Testament authors were writing,[1] so how could they have had "perspectives" on it? And even if they did, was my job simply to describe their various views, or was it to construct some kind of "New Testament" synthesis and offer a series of views expressing the consensus of the New Testament authors on issues relating to the topic?

My initial uncertainties were, of course, somewhat greater than they needed to be. There may not yet have been, within the time of the New Testament, a systematically-constructed "theology" along the lines that writers such as Origen attempted to write in the succeeding centuries, or institutions analogous to the pagan philosophical schools in which a theology of that sort might be taught, but the Christianity of the New Testament era was not without its *theologia*, in the broader sense of that word,[2] and the early Christian movement, from its very beginning, included deliberate arrangements for teaching and learning the faith and the way of life that went with it.[3]

Nor does the diversity to be found within the New Testament take a form that would make a project like this chapter impossible. The New Testament writers shared a common allegiance to Jesus as Lord, a common trust in the truth and power of Old Testament Scripture, a common involvement in the interconnected communities of the first-century Christian movement, and a common endowment of the Spirit. The various perspectives from which they wrote and the various contexts which they addressed do not cancel out the deep coherence and unity of the New Testament—or indeed the Bible—as a whole.

Some healthy caution is still in order. It would be a mistake to assume that "theology" and "education" in the first century meant the same thing as "theology" and "education" in the twenty-first, or to rush too quickly into producing a single, synthesized set of "New Testament" perspectives that look suspiciously similar to my own passions and prejudices, dressed up with a few convenient Bible verses. The New Testament writers must be allowed to speak in their own voices, addressing the original contexts in

---

1. On the emergence of institutionalized forms of theological education within the early church, see especially Markschies, *Christian Theology and Its Institutions*, 1–190.

2. Cf. Wright, *Paul and the Faithfulness of God*, 1–74; Starling, "'Nothing Beyond What is Written'?", 8.

3. Cf. Wilkins, *The Concept of Disciple*; Judge, "The Early Christians as a Scholastic Community," 532–51.

which they wrote, before we can hear them authentically in our own. But hear them we must. The institutions that we build for the sake of theological education and the curriculum that we teach within them are always at risk of becoming (and frequently do, in fact, become) captive to the cultural assumptions, local traditions and market forces of the time we live in. Theological education can all too easily be reduced to a body of information to be crammed, a set of skills to be mastered, or a product to be sold to the greatest possible number of consumers.

Into that world, the voices of the New Testament speak with a power that is doubly liberating. First, if we have ears to hear, they speak to us with the power of their very strangeness, from a time and place that differ from our own, blowing through the staleness of our minds and our classrooms with what C. S. Lewis memorably described as "the clean sea breeze of the centuries."[4] And second, more importantly, they speak with the truth and power of inspired Scripture to reshape our thinking and convert our imagination. We did not write these texts, and if we hear them properly then we will be hearing a voice that is not our own, with the power to change who we are and what we do.

Three Images

This chapter focuses on three New Testament images—Matthew's image of "the scribe . . . trained for the kingdom of heaven" (Matt 13:52), the image in Titus 1:7–9 of the overseer as "God's steward," and the image in Col 3:16 of the Christian congregation as a community of mutual, wise instruction, inhabited by the word of Christ—exploring each within its original context, then discussing the implications of the three for our contemporary task of shaping the curriculum, aims and strategies of theological education.

The three images are not chosen entirely at random. They are linked by a common focus on the people of God, on the work that the word of God does within the life of his people, and on the role that is played by the human servants and speakers of that word. They also share a common metaphor—visible on the surface of the text in Matt 13:52 and Titus 1:7, and buried within the implicit metaphor that Paul's language evokes in Col 3:16—of the church as God's household, called by the gospel of the kingdom into a community whose common life is ordered and shaped by that gospel. And as *images*—of the church, and of the ministry of the word within it—they

---

4. From his essay "On Reading Old Books," written as a preface to Athanasius, *The Incarnation of the Word*.

have a particularly powerful part to play in refreshing our imagination and reshaping the basic assumptions on which we operate.[5]

"The scribe . . . trained for the kingdom of heaven" (Matt 13:52)

When Jesus asked his disciples who the crowds thought he was, the various answers that they gave ("John the Baptist . . . Elijah . . . Jeremiah . . . one of the prophets"; Matt 16:14) all had in common the assumption that Jesus's activity was best understood in prophetic categories. The message of the kingdom that he proclaimed, the miracles that he performed, the way in which he called his disciples—all of these had striking similarities with the ministries of Elijah and the prophets who come after him.[6] But Jesus's ministry was not one-dimensionally prophetic in its character.[7] He not only proclaimed the kingdom to the crowds and called the nation to repentance; he also gathered together a community of disciples, teaching them the wisdom of the kingdom and forming them to be leaders and servants and teachers within his church.[8]

This dimension of the ministry of Jesus and the role of his disciples is particularly noticeable in Matthew's gospel. It is memorably summed up in the image that Jesus uses in Matt 13:52 of a "scribe . . . trained for the kingdom of heaven," who, "like the master of a household . . . brings out of his treasure what is new and what is old." The immediate context of the saying (following after Jesus's question to his disciples in 13:51, "Have you understood all this?" and their answer, "Yes"),[9] suggests that the "scribes" he has

---

5. See especially the insightful comments of Paul Minear on the images of the New Testament and the communal imagination of the church in Minear, *Images*, 16–27.

6. See especially the classic discussion of the prophetic nature of Jesus's ministry in Hengel, *The Charismatic Leader*.

7. Nor, of course, was the ministry of the Old Testament prophets one-dimensionally "prophetic" in the stereotypical sense of that word. Isaiah, for example, gathered "disciples" (*limmûdîm*) to whom he passed on a "teaching" (*tôrāh*; Isa 8:16), and, on occasion at least, was capable of casting his teaching in the form of a parable of the wisdom of YHWH (e.g. Isa 28:23–29).

8. These activities are presented by Matthew as having been in part, at least, an expression of Jesus's messianic vocation; it is as "the Messiah, the Son of the living God" (Matt 16:16) that he builds his church (16:18), gives to Peter (and, by extension, the disciples) the keys of the kingdom (16:19), and begins to teach the disciples about the paradoxical nature of his kingship (16:21–28; cf. 20:24–28). On the didactic dimension of Jesus's ministry, see especially Judge, "Scholastic Community," 532–35, and Witherington, *Jesus the Sage*, 147–208.

9. Note the "therefore" (*dia touto*) that connects v. 52 with v. 51.

in mind are, in the first instance, his disciples,[10] and that he aims for them to become "trained" (*mathēteutheis*) in the things of the kingdom so that they can fulfill the role among his people of the "master of the household" (*anthrōpos oikodespotēs*) pictured in the second half of the verse.

In Second Temple Jewish understanding, a scribe was not merely a bureaucrat or a copyist, but an interpreter of Scripture and a teacher of wisdom. The ideal scribe, according to the depiction in Sir 38:34b—39:11, devoted himself to the study of the Scriptures in all their varied forms—"law" (38:34b, probably used as an overarching category), "prophecies" (39:1), "sayings" (v. 2), "proverbs" (v. 3) and "parables" (vv. 2, 3)—deriving from them "wisdom" and "counsel" that he used in the service of God's people (39:4-11).[11] The many harsh things that Jesus has to say within Matthew's gospel about the "scribes and Pharisees" who were Israel's official teachers are not intended to convey the message that the role of "scribe" itself is an unnecessary or unhelpful one; within the mission of Jesus, the scribes of Israel are not to be made redundant but "trained for the kingdom of heaven" (13:52; cf. 23:34).

The "train[ing]" that Jesus is referring to in Matt 13:52 clearly involves the time that his disciples spend listening to his parables and asking him questions about their meaning (cf. Matt 13:10-12, 36), but it is not limited to that; it involves what they "see" (literally as well as metaphorically), not just what they hear (13:16-17). What they see in Jesus includes both the signs that mark him out as the Messiah (11:4) and the example of costly, persecuted faithfulness that they are to emulate (10:24); the vocation of the disciple is both to listen to the teacher and to become like the teacher, reflecting his character and participating in his mission. And if the "treasure" that the disciples are to accumulate and draw upon is to include both "what is new" and "what is old," then they will need to focus their learning not only on the new things of Jesus's kingdom proclamation but also on the old things of Israel's Scriptures (cf. 4:4; 5:17-19; 9:13).[12]

Out of this training—sustained, devoted reflection on the Scriptures and the words of Jesus, focused attentiveness to Jesus's person and work,

---

10. The role that Jesus envisages for the "disciples" he is addressing in vv. 51-52 (cf. vv. 10, 36) within the metaphorical household of his people suggests that the saying may be using the word in the slightly narrower sense that it can sometimes carry within Matthew's gospel (e.g. 19:23, 25; cf. 19:28), to refer to the twelve, or perhaps a slightly larger inner circle that includes them. Cf. Osborne, *Matthew*, 543-44, who takes "disciples" here in Matt 13 to be referring to "the apostolic band."

11. Cf. Witherington, *Matthew*, 7-9.

12. On the hermeneutical relationship between the "new" words of Jesus and the "old" words of Scripture within Matthew, see Starling, *Hermeneutics as Apprenticeship*, 93-104.

and personal involvement in his service—emerges wisdom. Within the context of a saying about a "trained . . . scribe," the metaphorical "treasure" in the second half of the verse is—primarily, at least—a reference to the "treasuries of wisdom" (*thēsaurois sophias*; Sir 1:25; cf. Prov 2) given by God to his people. This will include, of course, the personal treasures stored up in the memory of the individual scribe, but will also draw upon the collective memory of God's people, as scribe learns from scribe and sage from sage, and all learn from the Lord himself, the giver of all wisdom (Sir 1:1).

Nor is the wisdom of the scribe to be used merely for the scribe's own personal advantage; the treasures of the *anthrōpos oikodespotēs*, the master of the household, are resources to be drawn upon for the good of the household as a whole. Within that household, the discipled scribe serves as a conduit and exemplar of the wisdom of God—the new, precious, demanding wisdom of the kingdom of heaven, that does not abolish the old wisdom of Israel's Scriptures but fulfills it.

"God's steward" (Titus 1:7)

Although the primary and immediate reference of Jesus's words in Matt 13:52 is to the inner circle of his disciples, whom he has been teaching in the preceding paragraphs, the explicit generality of the saying—"every" scribe—hints at a broader applicability and a continuing application within the timeframe of Matthew's original readers and beyond. The role of Jesus's first disciples as eyewitnesses to the gospel events and foundational apostles within his church is represented by Matthew as something unique and non-transferable, but their function as wisdom teachers within the community of Christ's people is one, according to the implications of the imagery in Matt 13:52, that requires successors in each generation.

What is implicit in Matt 13:52 becomes explicit elsewhere in the New Testament—for example in the opening chapter of Titus, where Paul gives his delegate instructions for the appointment of "elders in every town" (1:5), who will be able "both to preach with sound doctrine and to refute those who contradict it" (1:9). As in Matt 13:52, so in Titus 1:7, this ministry is pictured as taking place within a metaphorical household,[13] in which the *episkopos* (NRSV: "bishop"; NIV: "overseer"),[14] according to Paul, is to serve

---

13. See especially the discussion of estate stewardship as a "controlling metaphor" in the Pastoral Epistles, in Tomlinson, "The Purpose and Stewardship Theme," 67–83.

14. Given the relationship between v. 5 and v. 7 within the logic of the paragraph ("appoint elders . . . someone blameless . . . for a bishop, as God's steward, must be blameless"), the term "bishop" appears to be functioning interchangeably with "elder"

as "God's steward" (*theou oikonomos*).¹⁵ Just as the whole church must have, in Jesus's original disciples, "scribe[s] . . . trained for the kingdom of heaven," so also, in every town, local communities of believers must have faithful overseers who will serve like stewards in a household, preserving, defending and teaching the "trustworthy . . . word" that has been passed on to them.

If this work is to be done faithfully and effectively, those who serve in this role must have both "a firm grasp of the word that is trustworthy in accordance with the teaching" (1:9) and a character of blamelessness, humility and self-control (1:7–8). Here (as is also the case in the similar passage in 1 Tim 3:1–7), the list of virtues and dispositions that are chosen for emphasis reflects not only an assumption that the church's overseers will be exemplars of generically Christian behavior but also a particular focus on the character attributes that are required in those who exercise authority within a community ("not . . . arrogant or quick-tempered or addicted to wine or violent or greedy for gain; but . . . hospitable . . . prudent . . . and self-controlled").

These two requirements—a "blameless" character and "a firm grasp of the word"—are closely connected within one another. The word itself is "trustworthy" (1:9; cf. 3:8; 1 Tim 1:15; 3:1; 4:9; 2 Tim 2:11), just as those who minister it must be (cf. 2 Tim 2:2). The doctrine that is to be preached to the congregation is not only true but "sound" (*hygiainousa*), i.e. healthy and life-giving in its effects, both in the culture of the congregation and in the character of the minister (cf. 1 Tim 4:6).

The bond connecting truth with virtue is love: the overseer must be not only a person who knows what is true and does what is good, but one who is a "lover" of goodness (1:8), with a deep, affectionate commitment to the truth of the gospel and the vision of the good that it teaches. Cold virtue and dispassionate orthodoxy are not enough; the goal, as Paul puts it elsewhere, in his charge to Timothy, is "love that comes from a pure heart, a good conscience, and sincere faith" (1 Tim 1:5).¹⁶

---

or perhaps, more precisely, to refer to the same person but with a slightly greater foregrounding of his function of oversight (*episkopē*) within the congregation. Cf. Towner, *The Letters to Timothy and Titus*, 685–6; Mounce, *Pastoral Epistles*, 390.

15. The term *oikodespotēs*, used in Matt 23:52, can refer either to the master of a household or to the steward who oversees its affairs on the master's behalf (cf. "*oikodespoteia*," LSJ). The term *oikonomos*, however, is always used to refer to a steward and never to the master of the house.

16. Note also Paul's portrait of the false teacher in 2 Tim 3:2–3 as a person of misdirected loves.

"The word of Christ . . . in you" (Col 3:16)

In both Matt 13:52 and Titus 1:7, the household metaphor lies on the surface of the text, and the ministry of the word within the church is pictured as taking place through the work of an *anthrōpos oikodespotēs* ("master of a household") or *oikonomos* ("steward"). In Col 3:16, however, the metaphor is buried within the language Paul uses to express his desire that the word of Christ might "dwell" (*enoikeitō*; NJB: "find a home") within the community of believers, and the picture is not of a householder or steward ministering the word to the congregation, but of all the congregation members ministering the word to one another.

The word that makes its home within the congregation is present on many lips and in diverse forms, as the congregation members "teach and admonish one another in all wisdom,"[17] and as, with grateful hearts, they "sing psalms, hymns, and spiritual songs to God."[18] Of particular interest is the way in which the language Paul uses in 1:28 to describe his own ministry as an apostle ("It is he whom we proclaim, warning everyone and teaching everyone in all wisdom") is echoed in the language he uses in 3:16 to describe the Colossians' ministry to one another; his goal, it seems, is not merely a community that is shaped by the ministry of wise leaders, but a community that is itself pervasively wise, inhabited by the word of Christ in such a way that the speech and conduct of all its members become vehicles for God's wisdom (cf. 4:5–6).

The wisdom that Paul conveys in his preaching, and which he hopes to see the Colossians conveying to one another in their mutual teaching and admonition, is both comprehensive ("all" wisdom; 1:28; 3:16) and

---

17. In the syntax of the original, the phrase "in all wisdom" could be taken as modifying either "let the word of Christ dwell . . . in you" (e.g., KJV) or "teach[ing] and admonish[ing] one another" (e.g., NRSV, ESV, NIV). The decision of most English versions to opt for the latter is supported by the way in which the ideas of warning, teaching and wisdom are linked in the similar language of 1:28 ("warning everyone and teaching everyone in all wisdom").

18. A further, more difficult, question raised by the syntax of the verse is whether the "psalms, hymns and spiritual songs" should be read as the means through which the congregation members teach and admonish one another (e.g., NIV) or as the content (or better, perhaps, in view of the dative cases of the three nouns, the form) of what they sing to God (e.g., NRSV, ESV). The NIV's rendering of the verse has the advantage of corresponding more closely to the way in which the congregation's singing is presented as functioning within the parallel passage in Eph 5:19, where the psalms, hymns and spiritual songs are spoken "among yourselves" (*heautois*). Nevertheless, the fact that Col 3:16 pictures the congregation members not merely "speaking" to one another (cf. Eph 5:19; *lalountes*) but "teach[ing] and admonish[ing] . . . in all wisdom" (cf. the language of Col 1:28) suggests something more is involved than merely the singing of songs, and tips the balance in favor of a rendition of the verse along the lines of the ESV or NRSV.

Christocentric ("it is *he* whom we proclaim"; 1:28, emphasis added). The fact that Paul can assert in the same breath that the content of his proclamation is "Christ" (1:27–28) and that he warns and teaches with "all wisdom" (1:28) is a reflection of his conviction that "Christ himself" is "God's mystery" (2:2) and that "all the treasures of wisdom and knowledge" are hidden in him (2:3). Negatively, Paul's assertions imply a sharp negation of the "plausible arguments" (2:4), "empty deceit" and "human tradition" (2:8) that might lead the Colossians in other directions. Positively, they imply a boundless, integrative, all-embracing wisdom that seeks to understand all things in their relation to Christ (cf. 1:15–23), and to shape the life and speech of the Christian community—including their missionary interaction within the surrounding culture—accordingly (cf. 4:5–6).

Theological Education Today

How might these three New Testament images—the discipled scribe, the faithful steward, and the inhabiting word—inform the way in which we seek to shape the curriculum for theological education in our own time and the institutions within which we teach it?

First, and perhaps most obviously, they draw our attention to the church as the "household" within which theological wisdom makes its home. The wisdom that we learn in Christ is vast and all-encompassing in the scope of its interests, and the conversations it participates in include—potentially, at least—all the conversations of human life. But it is not without a home; it is (as Paul puts it in Eph 3:10) "through the church" that God has chosen to make his richly-varied wisdom known in the world. Any attempt to construct a version of "theological education" that is abstracted from the life of the church and its mission in the world, selling it in the marketplace as a free-floating educational commodity, will inevitably end up falsifying the subject it claims to teach.[19]

This does not mean that the sole purpose of theological education is to train the church's ordained ministers. It is certainly true (as Matt 13:52 and Titus 1:7 imply) that the household of the church requires its "scribes" and "stewards," and that their particular vocation requires the kind of specialized formation that equips them to be a source of wise instruction and godly example for the whole church.[20] But it is also true (as Col 3:16 makes clear)

---

19. See especially Hauerwas, "How I Think I Learned to Think Theologically."

20. I leave to one side the question of whether the New Testament category of "elders"/"overseers" ought, in our context, to be regarded as coterminous with the membership of a full-time, formally-educated ministry profession.

that the wisdom of God ought to be in the minds and on the lips of all the church's members. If there are good reasons to create seminaries that serve the church by helping with the formation of its pastors, there are also good reasons to give careful and continuing thought to how—within and beyond the local church—Christians who labor in other vocations can be strengthened and deepened in theological understanding. In both cases, however, Christian theological education remains faithful to its subject only when the institutions within which it is taught work in active partnership with the church, in which the knowledge of God has its proper home.

A second way in which the three New Testament images that we have examined within this chapter inform our thinking about theological education is as reminders of the deep biblical foundations and the clear Christological center that must be present if the curriculum we teach is to foster the authentically Christian wisdom that the church requires. In two out of the three passages (Matt 13:52 and Col 3:16), the language of wealth and abundance is used ("treasure . . . new and . . . old"; "richly"; cf. Col 2:3: "all the treasures of wisdom and knowledge") to stress the extent and the preciousness of the gift that is given to us in Scripture and the message of the gospel. In the third (Titus 1:7–9), a similar idea is conveyed through Paul's reminder of the "trustworthy" nature of the gospel word and the "sound" (i.e., health-giving) function of the doctrine that accords with it. There is something tragically shortsighted about models of theological education that attempt to cut corners by skimping on the amount of attention that is paid to the text of Scripture and the disciplines by which that text is read and pondered and integrated into an overarching vision of life. There are riches here, and riches that are indispensable for the church's health and life.

Third, and finally, the three New Testament images on which this chapter has focused direct our attention toward the relational context in which effective theological education must take place, and the formative and affective dimensions that it must include. In an age of ever-expanding technological possibilities, and an economic context that places increasing pressure on education providers to maximize the efficiency with which they equip their graduates with marketable competencies, these things cannot be taken for granted. They are not easily quantified or cheaply accomplished, but they are essential nonetheless. The scribe of Matt 13:52 must not only be informed and equipped but "discipled" (*mathēteutheis*)—language which, in the context of Matthew's gospel, implies something more than merely access to a body of information and mastery of a set of skills. The overseer of Titus 1:7–8 must not only know the word but "grasp" it firmly; God's steward must not only be able to teach about what is good but must be a "lover" of goodness. The word of Christ that inhabits the congregation, as it is pictured in Col 3:16, must be present not merely as accurate information but also in the deeply relational forms of wise instruction, faithful admonition, and joyful, thankful singing.

There is room, of course, for a wide diversity of creative ways in which the academic, practical and relational dimensions of the ministry formation process might be shared between churches, families, theological colleges, mission societies, denominational bodies, and other formal and informal communities of learning.[21] It would be a mistake to think that the institutions in which formal theological education takes place can (or should) take care of the whole process of forming men and women for ministry. But it would be a mistake, too, to think that they can contribute usefully to that process if the way in which they approach the task is evacuated of relational content, personal example and contagious affection. Theology must be caught as well as taught, if it is to be characterized by the love and faithfulness that its subject requires.

In all three of these ways, therefore—as reminders of the orientation toward the church and its mission in the world that the content of theological education requires, the biblical foundations and Christological center that make it true and life-giving, and the relational, affective dimensions that it must retain—the images of the New Testament speak a vital word into our contemporary discussions about the shape and strategies of theological education. May God give us a vision for the future for our discipline that is deeply and authentically informed by them.

Bibliography

Athanasius. *The Incarnation of the Word of God*. Translated by R.P. Lawson. London: Geoffrey Bles, 1944.
Hauerwas, Stanley. "How I Think I Learned to Think Theologically: The Post-Christendom Church and the Future of Theology." In *Theology and the Future: Evangelical Assertions and Explorations*, edited by Trevor H. Cairney and David I. Starling, 99–114. London: T&T Clark, 2014.
Hengel, Martin. *The Charismatic Leader and His Followers*. Translated by John Riches. Edinburgh: T&T Clark, 1981.
House, Paul R. *Bonhoeffer's Seminary Vision: A Case for Costly Discipleship and Life Together*. Wheaton: Crossway, 2015.
Judge, E. A. "The Early Christians as a Scholastic Community." In *The First Christians in the Roman World: Augustan and the New Testament Essays*, edited by James R. Harrison, 526–52. Tübingen: Mohr Siebeck, 2008.

---

21. Cf. the stimulating and provocative range of possibilities discussed in House, *Bonhoeffer's Seminary Vision*, ch. 6.

Liddell, Henry George, Robert Scott, and Henry Stuart Jones. *A Greek-English Lexicon*. 9th ed. Oxford: Clarendon, 1996.

Markschies, Christoph. *Christian Theology and Its Institutions in the Early Roman Empire: Prolegomena to a History of Early Christian Theology*. Waco: Baylor University Press, 2015.

Minear, Paul S. *Images of the Church in the New Testament*. 2nd ed. Louisville: Westminster, 2004.

Mounce, William D. *Pastoral Epistles*. WBC. Nashville: Nelson, 2000.

Osborne, Grant R. *Matthew*. ZECNT. Grand Rapids: Zondervan, 2010.

Starling, David I. *Hermeneutics as Apprenticeship: How the Bible Shapes Our Interpretive Habits and Practices*. Grand Rapids: Baker, 2016.

———. "'Nothing Beyond What Is Written'? First Corinthians and the Hermeneutics of Early Christian Theologia." *JTI* 8 (2014) 45–62.

Tomlinson, F. Alan. "The Purpose and Stewardship Theme Within the Pastoral Epistles." In *Entrusted with the Gospel: Paul's Theology in the Pastoral Epistles*, edited by Andreas J. Köstenberger and Terry L. Wilder, 52–83. Nashville: B&H, 2010.

Towner, Philip H. *The Letters to Timothy and Titus*. NICNT. Grand Rapids: Eerdmans, 2006.

Wilkins, Michael J. *The Concept of Disciple in Matthew's Gospel as Reflected in the Use of the Term Μαθητής*. NovTSup. Leiden: Brill, 1988.

Witherington, Ben. *Jesus the Sage: The Pilgrimage of Wisdom*. Minneapolis: Fortress, 1994.

———. *Matthew*. SHBC. Macon: Smyth & Helwys, 2006.

Wright, N. T. *Paul and the Faithfulness of God*. London: SPCK, 2013.

3

The Elements of a Theology of Theological Education

Martin Foord

Abstract

Theological education, given its object, would reasonably be expected to be shaped by the theological beliefs and assumptions of those who provide it. This chapter offers a proposal for how this might be done systematically. Firstly, a foundation is laid upon the gospel, and then the word gifts and relevant offices provided for in the New Testament. Next, a theological rationale for theological education is developed along biblical lines, as any theology of theological education must have the purpose or end in view. Finally, the nature, elements and content of theological education are discussed, in light of the foundation and the ends which have been identified.

Introduction

THEOLOGICAL EDUCATION IS COMMONPLACE in contemporary Christianity.[1] In many denominations prospective pastors must undertake theological

---

1. I am grateful to Allan Chapple, Andrew Reid, and Don West who read early

education for employment in a church. Yet, theological education comes in many shapes and sizes. How do we judge whether a particular kind of theological education is truly Christian? Moreover, is not the local church the best place to train those whose goal is to serve in the local church? Can the theological college be justified from Scripture itself, or is it a once-helpful tradition that no longer has a place in the modern world? This chapter seeks to propose the elements of a theological education.

Theology examines Scripture topically; it discovers what the Bible says about particular topics (or doctrines). Systematic theology attempts to learn how Scripture arranges its topics: how important a topic is, and in what way biblical topics relate to each other. So, a theology of theological education would attempt to discover and elucidate the topic of theological education from Scripture. If this topic is not explicitly addressed by Scripture, a theology of theological education would examine related topics it to see if it could be justified as a so-called "good and necessary" consequence of Scripture.

The Ground for Theological Education

An evangelical understanding of theological education must begin with the gospel itself (evangeliology). The gospel declares that God has *accomplished* full salvation in the death and resurrection of Christ. But Christ's salvation needs *application*. This is the concern of the doctrine of salvation (soteriology). Christ applies his accomplished cross-work as priest and king in his session at the right hand of the Father. He does this by pouring out his Holy Spirit, who draws people into a relationship with the Father. But Christ also applies his accomplished salvation through his Spirit by growing his people. And the means he uses to grow believers is the church (ecclesiology).

It is the nature of church *ministry* that determines the nature of theological education. In Scripture, church ministry or service (διακονία) is the task of serving fellow believers so that the church strengthens (1 Cor 12:4–6; Eph 4:12).[2] The NT calls this work the "building" (οἰκοδομή, οἰκοδομέω) of the church (1 Cor 14:3–5, 12, 26). Ministry (or building) is for all believers because the church is Christ's body and each member is needed for its growth (Eph 4:16). Hence, Christ in his session equips all church members with the Holy Spirit so that they serve in a variety of ways for the "common

---

drafts of this paper and gave indispensable feedback.

2. In 1 Cor 12:4–6 the words "gift" (χάρισμα), "service" (διακονία), and "working" (ἐνέργημα) are all used for the same activity of serving church members for the common good.

good" (1 Cor 12:7–11). This is the classic reformation doctrine of the priesthood of all believers.[3]

Word Gifts

However, despite all believers being involved in ministry, there is a kind of ministry that the NT distinguishes from all others:

> Now you are the body of Christ, and each one of you is a part of it. 28 And God has placed in the church first of all apostles, second prophets, third teachers, then miracles, then gifts of healing, of helping, of guidance, and of different kinds of tongues (1 Cor 12:27–28, NIV).

Paul's list of gifts (or ways of serving) here is not intended to be exhaustive. It is simply a "sampling of members that God has placed in the church body."[4] But this gift list differentiates the first three gifts from all others by ordering them "first," "second," and "third." The explicit numbering of only the first three ministries indicates something significant about them.[5] What they have in common is *proclamation*. For ease, I will call them word gifts.

The significance of word gifts is teased out in a passage central to the reformers' doctrine of ministry, Ephesians 4:11–12:[6]

> So Christ himself gave the apostles, the prophets, the evangelists, the pastors and teachers, 12 to equip his people for works of service, so that the body of Christ may be built up . . . (Eph 4:11–12, NIV).

Here again is a list of people who have proclamation in common. But notice the purpose of these word ministries. They are to "equip" or "prepare" (καταρτισμός) all other church members to exercise their own ministries (or "works of service").[7] So, the word gifts are to train the rest of the church in how to exercise their own gifts. The result is that all believers engage in ministry and in this way the body of Christ grows as a whole. The ordering here is crucial. The word gifts "have an enabling function."[8] The rest of the

---

3. First defended by Martin Luther in his Appeal to the German Nobility of 1520.

4. Garland, *1 Corinthians*, 598.

5. Thiselton, *The First Epistle to the Corinthians*, 1014–15.

6. See, for example, Bucer, *Common Places of Martin Bucer*, 83. Then there is the influential Heinrich Bullinger, *Decades* 5.3, 105.

7. For a cogent defence that the three prepositional phrases in this verse are not coordinate see Thielman, *Ephesians*, 277–80; Best, *Ephesians*, 398.

8. Best, *Ephesians*, 398.

church will not properly exercise their gifts without the word gifts preparing them to do so. To be sure, all believers have a word ministry to each other (Eph 4:15; Col 3:16; Heb 5:12). But not all have word gifts. The latter are a specific group who minister the very same word at a different level.

What are these word gifts? Firstly, there is the "apostle." An apostle is one sent to deliver a message on behalf of their sender (John 13:16). The vital point about an apostle is *who* sends them. The apostles to whom Paul refers in Eph 4:11 are those personally sent by Christ himself (John 20:21; Gal 1:1); they are "apostles of Christ" (Rom 1:1; 1 Pet 1:1; 2 Cor 11:13; Jude 17). Other people in the NT are called "apostles" who are not sent by Christ; they had been sent by a church to deliver that church's message (Phil 2:25; 2 Cor 8:23). They are not apostles of Christ.

The "apostles" of Eph 4:11 (and 1 Cor 12:28) are those personally sent by Christ as recipients of his direct teaching (John 14:26; Gal 1:11–12) and eyewitnesses of his resurrection (Acts 1:8; 1 Cor 9:1; 15:5–11).[9] Their unique ministry was to deliver Christ's teaching to the world on his behalf once-for-all time (John 17:20; 2 Pet 3:2; Jude 3). Therefore, Christ especially equipped them with the Holy Spirit to deliver his teaching in all truth (John 14:26; 16:7; 1 Cor 2:13).[10] The apostles *of Christ* are an exclusive group confined to the first century, Paul himself being the "last" one sent (1 Cor 15:8).

The "prophets" of Eph 4:11 (and 1 Cor 12:28) and NT prophecy in general is greatly contested and there is not the room here to enter the debate. But a few definite points can be made.[11] Prophecy is some kind of God-given revelation (1 Cor 14:30) proclaimed to people (1 Cor 14:3). Its effects include the strengthening, encouragement, and comfort of believers (1 Cor 14:3) as well as the conviction of sin in unbelievers (1 Cor 14:24). A revelation may arise through the so-called ordinary means (such as human reflection on Scripture) and thus is not necessarily ecstatic:

... And if on some point you think differently, that too God will make clear to you (Phil 3:15, NIV).

Indeed, it seems that all believers are able to prophesy (1 Cor 14:1, 24, 31) but not all are "prophets" (1 Cor 12:29). And, importantly, non-apostolic NT prophecy is clearly under the authority of apostolic teaching (1 Cor 14:37). Indeed, non-apostolic NT prophecy is fallible and needs evaluation (1 Cor 14:29).

---

9. See, for example, Rabanus Maurus, *Expositio* 4:11.

10. Bullinger, *Decades* 1.2, 61–64.

11. Amidst the massive literature on this subject I am particularly indebted to Carson, *Showing the Spirit*, 108–17, 160–65.

The next word gift is the "evangelist" (εὐαγγελιστής). The word only occurs in three NT verses (Acts 21:8; Eph 4:11; 2 Tim 4:5) from which we get no clear definition. However, the cognates "to preach the gospel" (εὐαγγελίζω) and "gospel" (εὐαγγέλιον) help shed some light on this gift. In the OT, the announcer of the "gospel" is depicted as one who ran distances to deliver news that the enemy's king has been destroyed (2 Sam 18:19, 31; 1 Kgs 1:42; 1 Chr 10:9; Nah 2:1).[12] So, in Isaiah 52, when God will bring future salvation in the Messianic age the gospel announcer with "beautiful feet" will run distances to declare: "Your God reigns" (Isa 52:7). Paul uses this verse in Rom 10:15 to speak of the gospel being preached to those who have not heard it. This work appears to be exemplified by "Philip the evangelist" (Acts 21:8) who "travelled about, preaching the gospel in all the towns until he reached Caesarea" (Acts 8:40). Hence, the evangelist, it seems, especially preaches the gospel to those who have not heard it. Despite many in the Christian tradition who have held that evangelists were confined to the first century, there is no clear evidence in Scripture to support this.[13]

Finally, Eph 4:11 mentions "pastors" and "teachers." Some have argued that "pastors" and "teachers" are "one order of ministry" because they are governed by one article.[14] Others see them as two distinct gifts.[15] This is not the place to resolve the question because its outcome does not affect our conclusions. Suffice to note that the person called a "pastor" (ποιμήν) in the NT leads the "flock" (Christ's church) like a shepherd. It involves keeping watch over God's people, modeling godliness, and teaching (Acts 20:28–29, 32; 1 Pet 5:2). And whilst all believers are called to teach each other (Rom 5:14; Col 3:16; Heb 5:12) there is a particular figure in the NT named the "teacher" (Rom 12:7; 1 Cor 12:28). At the very least teaching involves passing on and explaining the "tradition" or "teaching" which Christ delivered to the apostles (Acts 15:35; Gal 6:6; 1 Tim 4:6, 11, 13, 16; 6:1–2; 2 Tim 2:2; Titus 2:1, 7).[16]

---

12. See particularly Seccombe, *The Gospel of the Kingdom*.

13. Various names believed evangelists were confined to the first century such as, Bullinger, *Decades*, 4:108–9; Beza, *The Christian Faith*, 91–92; Bannerman, *The Church of Christ*, 235–44. However, opposed to this is a figure like Bucer who says: "Tales [Evangelistae] hodie quoque inveniuntur," Martin Bucer, *Praelectiones Doctiss In Epistolam*, 107.

14. Bruce, *The Epistles to the Colossians, to Philemon, and to the Ephesians*, 348.

15. Wallace, *Greek Grammar Beyond the Basics*, 284; Thielman, *Ephesians*, 275; Bullinger, *Decades*, 4:106.

16. Best, *Ephesians*, 391; Thielman, *Ephesians*, 276.

Leadership Office

A second theological concept related to church ministry is office. Gift and office are distinguished in the NT. Gift is a *ministry* given by Christ that is exercised in the power of the Spirit to build believers (1 Cor 12:7-11; Eph 4:7-12). Office, on the other hand, involves the *appointment* of one with pastoring and teaching gifts to an *official position* which is recognized by fellow believers (Acts 14:23; Titus 1:5). One person may possess both gift and office (such as an apostle). But gift and office must be distinguished even where they may not be separated.

In the NT, the church's leadership office is the "elder" (πρεσβύτερος) or "overseer" (ἐπίσκοπος) which appear to be identical (Acts 14:32; 20:17, 28; Titus 1:5, 7; 1 Pet 5:1-4). In Hebrews, there seems to be common recognition of a similar (if not identical) office named the "leader" (ἡγούμενοι) (Heb 13:7, 17). For ease, I will call the office of elder, overseer, or leader the leadership office.

The leadership office involved three main tasks with Jesus as the supreme model. The first task was to "lead" or "govern" believers (1 Tim 5:17) but like a father over a family (1 Tim 3:4-5), a shepherd over the flock (Acts 20:28), and a slave serving others (John 13:14-17). Secondly, the leader was to teach God's people the apostolic tradition (1 Tim 3:2; Heb 13:7) which also involved refuting error (Titus 1:9). Finally, the leader was to model the Christian life for all believers (1 Tim 4:11; Titus 2:7; Heb 13:7). The leader's own lifestyle was their most powerful teaching illustration. Given this the leader was to be exemplary in character (1 Tim 3:2-7; Titus 1:6-8). Hence, the leader was to keep watch over their own life even before their flock's (Acts 20:28; 1 Tim 4:16).

The Rationale for Theological Education

Thus far, we have seen that in the church today there exist word gifts, and that some who possess these gifts are appointed to the leadership office. We have also seen that the word gifts are to equip the rest of the church to serve. Theological education would concern the training of those who will exercise word gifts and those who will be appointed to a leadership office. But do they need theological education? The answer is yes because of the nature of word gifts and leadership office.

The Need to Train for Word Ministries

If the word gifts and leadership office involve proclamation, then one cannot proclaim what one does not know. The ministries of pastor and teacher and the leadership office particularly involve teaching God's people. But one cannot teach without a thorough knowledge of the "teaching" Christ delivered to the church (through the apostles). This logic is captured by Paul himself when he says to Timothy:

> And the things you have heard me say in the presence of many witnesses entrust to reliable people who will also be qualified to teach others (2 Timothy 2:2, NIV).

Timothy himself was to guard "the good deposit [παραθήκη]" that he had heard from Paul (2 Tim 1:13). Yet Timothy was also to "entrust" this same deposit to others. But not just anyone. Timothy was to entrust it to "reliable" people, who could "teach others." In sum, we see in the NT evidence for a special focus on training those who have a specific teaching role.

Biblical Examples of Training

Not only does the NT explicitly discuss the need to train those with word gifts it also includes examples.[17] The supreme example is Jesus' training of the apostles. Whilst he had many followers, Jesus chiefly focused on twelve disciples giving them intensive instruction over several years (Matt 5:1; 11:1; Mark 9:31). He was, after all, a "Rabbi." Jesus imparted to his disciples a body of teaching showing how it fulfilled the OT (Luke 24:45–49; John 17:6–9; Acts 1:1–5). Christ's disciples, compared to the average follower of Jesus, needed extra focused time to learn and assimilate the tradition they would deliver as apostles to the church.

Another example of concentrated training was Paul's time in Ephesus. There he taught, not simply at a weekly church gathering, but daily in the Hall of Tyrannus for two years (Acts 19:9–10). Paul likely taught during the five-hour siesta period of the day (11am–4pm) when the hall was not formally used.[18] Dunn says of this time:

> For Paul to have lectured for two years in the same setting indicates an extensive range of subjects, texts and traditions covered during the period. We have to envisage a large syllabus covering the exposition of many Scriptures, instruction in the Jesus

---

17. I owe the ideas in this section to David Seccombe.
18. Schnabel, *Acts*, 792, note 45.

tradition, and elaboration of characteristic Pauline themes that we know of from his letters.[19]

Here is an intensive and sustained teaching program which had a great effect. As Eckhard Schnabel says, "The significance of Paul's being able to teach uninterrupted for two years cannot be emphasized enough."[20] Paul's educational regime resulted in the entire "province of Asia" hearing the "word of the Lord" (Acts 19:10). The province of Asia appears to have been reached through Paul's coworkers. It probably included Epaphras who founded a church in Colossae without Paul. It also included Philemon (from Colossae), Aristarchus (from Macedonia), Gaius (from Corinth), as well as Tychicus and Trophimus, and perhaps Stephanas, Fortunatus, and Achaicus (from Corinth).[21] In other words, Paul's teaching agenda included the training of word ministers who then helped expand Paul's mission.

The Nature of Theological Education

The nature of theological education is determined by the nature of word gifts. One on hand, they are gifts, which need recognition and confirmation. But on the other hand, they focus on the word, which needs to be learned. Let us now turn to what a training program might look like for those who will exercise word gifts and leadership office in the church. There are three vital elements to it: preparation, education, supervision.

Preparation

Christ himself, not humans, gives word gifts to the church (Eph 4:7, 11). Therefore, those who come to exercise these ministries will no doubt naturally manifest the abilities and fruit initially without formal training. It is these early signs that indicate who may need to be trained. This is the nature of a spiritual gift.

Ideally practitioners already exercising word gifts should be watching for believers who evidence word gifts, as Timothy and Titus were to do (Titus 1:5–9; 1 Tim 3:1–7; 2 Tim 2:2). And those who manifest early signs of word gifting ideally need the opportunity to test, confirm, and foster their abilities for word gift ministry. Something like an apprenticeship program under those doing word gift ministry is an excellent way of achieving this.

19. Dunn, *Beginning from Jerusalem*, 769.
20. Schnabel, *Acts*, 793.
21. Ibid., 794.

It helps clarify a person's fitness for this work as well as show their need for further theological education.

Education

Once a person's giftedness for word ministry is trialed and nurtured there follows the need to learn God's word thoroughly. If word ministry focuses on proclamation, one cannot proclaim what they do not know. However, true knowledge of God goes beyond the mere rational accumulation of information: "to know this love that surpasses knowledge" (Eph 3:19). Growth in a knowledge of God must include growth in love and zeal. Any kind of theological education that reduces love and zeal is nothing less than pernicious. But what is to be taught?

In the New Testament, the word gifts (particularly pastor and teacher) and leadership office are to be competent to proclaim the "good deposit" or "sound teaching" (2 Tim 1:13-14) that has been passed on from Christ through the apostles once-for-all. This deposit now exists in the NT writings (John 20:31; 21:24; 1 Cor 2:13; 1 Tim 5:18; 2 Thess 2:15; 2 Pet 3:16; Rev 22:6, 18-19).[22] Hence, training must focus on the understanding and ability to apply these writings.

But the apostolic message (in the NT) was itself a fulfillment of the OT (e.g. Matt 5:17-18; Luke 24:27, 44-47; John 5:39; 10:35; 1 Cor 15:3-4). Indeed, the NT itself speaks of the OT as God's inspired words—all of it (2 Tim 3:15–17). The OT and NT are two parts of one whole. Those who exercise word gifts cannot be competent in the NT without being competent in the OT (and *vice versa*).

Therefore, training for the word gift ministries must attend to the Bible *as a whole*. Paul did say to the Ephesian elders about his time teaching in the Hall of Tyrannus:

> For I have not hesitated to proclaim to you the whole will of God (Acts 20:27, NIV).

Paul did not simply focus on one small area of God's plan, whether it be the Jesus tradition, apocalyptic, wisdom, or the eighth-century prophets but the entire counsel of God.

If Paul's purpose was to deliver the whole will of God, then a theological education should do the same. Put another way, a theological education should lay a theological *foundation* upon which more specialized theological levels can be built. There is no use constructing the second and fifth stories

---

22. For a classic treatment of this see Bullinger, *De Scripturae Sanctae*.

of a building if the foundation has not been fully laid. Thus, a theological education is more like training in medicine than arts. In arts, the student can pick and choose their subjects. Not so a medical student. They cannot specialize without a basic knowledge of the entire human body, not simply the arm or leg. For medical students, a foundation must be laid before they specialize. The same goes for theological education. One cannot study the specialty of church planting without knowing firstly what the church is and how to derive this from Scripture. What might be included in a theological foundation? To this we now turn.

Bible Skills

The nature of Scripture itself, its supreme authority and form of genres, demands that a word minister not only learn the content of Scripture, but also how to read and interpret Scripture rightly. Skills in bible reading and interpretation enable the student to evaluate past traditions. It is not enough merely to receive a tradition. The current generation must test it anew. And this requires requisite skills in reading and interpreting Scripture as the highest authority. What are these skills?

The first skill is *exegesis*, or how to read meaning rightly from the Scriptural text, both Old and New Testaments. It includes a general understanding of language and how it conveys meaning. Words have meaning in context, and the fundamental unit of context is the individual book of Scripture. Hence, exegesis entails the study of individual books of the Bible as units.

But exegesis properly done requires the biblical languages.[23] If God has chosen to reveal himself at a particular moment in history using specific languages, then surely we should respect that choice. Without knowledge of the biblical languages we lose moorings with the very sources word ministers are to teach. Translations of Scripture only go so far. The Reformation is a stark reminder of what happens when the church loses knowledge of Scripture's original languages. It may not be necessary for some word gift ministries, those such as evangelists, youth leaders, or children's workers, to know the original languages. But if a central task of the pastor and teacher is to instruct God's people in God's word, they need expertise in at least New Testament Greek, and for those who can, Old Testament Hebrew.

The second essential skill is a facility with *biblical theology*. The phrase "biblical theology" has many meanings. However, I use it in a particular

---

23. Harman, "The Place of the Biblical Languages," 91–97; Jensen, "Maturing the Mind," 114–17.

sense that concerns Scripture as one whole.[24] Biblical theology recognizes that Scripture contains one fundamental narrative from Genesis to Revelation. And that this narrative has a series of main themes and subthemes that develop through the story line all reaching fulfillment in Christ's person and work.

Biblical theology enables the student to *apply* Scripture to the present. Whereas exegesis shows what a biblical text *meant*, biblical theology shows what it *means*. For example, an Old Testament text about Israel's king being victorious over his enemies, is now understood to be fulfilled in God's true king Christ and his defeat of the ultimate enemies of sin, death, and the devil (1 Cor 15:25-28). Understood in this light, Biblical theology includes hermeneutics, the science of interpretation.

The third biblical skill relates to *systematic theology*. Systematic theology presents the contents of Scripture in another form, that of topics (or doctrines). Where biblical theology concerns Scriptural themes temporally, systematic theology concerns Scriptural themes atemporally. Biblical theology is diachronic; systematic theology is synchronic. For example, a biblical theology of sin will present this theme as it unfolds through the biblical storyline. A systematic theology of sin will simply summarize what all of Scripture says about sin. Biblical theology and systematic theology are complements; they cannot exist without the other.

Scripture itself demands the discipline of systematic theology. The New Testament encourages believers to know their faith topically (Heb 6:1-2). And these topics can be summarized into a whole, which must entail some kind of systematization (Jude 3; 2 Tim 1:14; Rom 6:17; 16:17). Scripture itself demonstrates how its key topics are related (e.g. Gal 2:21; 5:6; 1 Cor 15:13-17). Indeed, some topics are more important than others and not knowing which take precedence will muddle priorities (Matt 22:34-40; 23:23; 1 Cor 15:1). An evangelical systematic theology will set the gospel at the center (1 Cor 15:3).

If systematic theology is concerned with Scripture's arrangement of biblical topics then it must focus on the principal topics. Hence, subjects like ethics and pastoral care, which are both branches of systematic theology, will be covered in a theological education seeking to be true to Scripture because of their importance to word ministry. It is thus artificial to call systematic theology theoretical and pastoral care practical.

A theological education must also engage with the *Christian tradition*. The contemporary Christian should interact with our Christian heritage.

---

24. I will be using it in the sense set out in works like Chapple, *God's Plan for Salvation*; Dumbrell, *The Search for Order*; Dumbrell, *The End of the Beginning*; Gibson, *Interpreting God's Plan*; Goldsworthy, *Christ-Centered Biblical Theology*.

The church is universal not only in place but time (Matt 16:18). A knowledge of church history prevents repetition of past mistakes and helps glean wisdom for the present. Contemporary believers have much to learn from how past Christians have done mission, suffered under totalitarian regimes, and attempted to create a Christian society. If Christ promised to be present with his people "always, to the very end of the age" (Matt 28:20) then a basic knowledge of the *entire* history of the church is vital.

An indispensable subset of church history is historical theology. The current church is not the first to read Scripture. Christians have been wrestling with the Bible and its topics for two millennia and it would be foolish to ignore what has been learnt. God has raised up those with word gifts in past generations to equip us in the present (Eph 4:11). It would be arrogant to study physics without learning from the discoveries of Isaac Newton and Albert Einstein. The same goes for the study of Scripture. We would be unwise to ignore the past breakthroughs of the Cappadocian Fathers, Luther, Calvin, and Owen, as well as the great statements codified in controversy, like the Apostles' Creed (against Gnosticism) and the Nicene Creed (against Arianism).

A student must gain a knowledge of God, but they must also learn how to *communicate* it. Paul was keen to become like the people he ministered to, whether Jews, those under the law, those without law, or the weak (1 Cor 9:19–23). He sought to understand the people group he worked within to communicate most effectively to them. People do not exist in a cultural vacuum. Hence, theological education should help students to understand the culture in which they find themselves through the tools of worldview and cultural analysis so that they can be good students of the people group they hope to serve.

The learning of God's word is about taking hold of the good deposit. But this needs to be put to use, and *pastoral skills* seek to do this. It is one thing to know what Scripture says about death; it is another to interact with the bereaved and perform a funeral. A student may know how to understand a psalm. But they also need to know how to communicate its meaning effectively. Pastoral skills focus on putting the good deposit to work in the lives of people.

The Training Context

The local church would be an ideal context for theological education. There, word gift ministries would be seen in action. A theological education that lays a foundation as described above will require teachers with competency in various areas like exegesis, church history, and theology. Unfortunately, the average local church cannot provide this, hence the need for an institution that does.

Who should teach in theological education? If students are being prepared for word gift ministry, then theological educators should be word gift ministers themselves, with requisite experience. This ensures that what they teach (whether languages, church history, or theology) will always have an eye on, and be applied to, coalface ministry. It is a terrible mistake to use teachers whose desire is simply to do academic theology without reference to real-life ministry.

Moreover, those who teach theology are to display an exemplary life before the students. It is essential that students get to know their teachers personally to see what a life above reproach looks like up close. For it is this that legitimates a true Christian teacher, as Paul says to Timothy:

> But as for you, continue in what you have learned and have become convinced of, *because you know those from whom you learned it* . . . (2 Tim 3:14, NIV, italics added).

Simple competence with the Scriptures is not enough. Paul's own life embodied the message he taught so much so that he could say:

> Whatever you have learned or received or heard from me, or seen in me—put it into practice (Phil 4:9, NIV).

Paul urged Timothy:

> Don't let anyone look down on you because you are young, but set an example for the believers in speech, in conduct, in love, in faith and in purity (1 Tim 4:12, NIV).

And to Titus:

> In everything set them an example by doing what is good. In your teaching show integrity, seriousness . . . (Titus 2:7, NIV).

In other words, Christian education is not simply imparting information but also illustrating it with one's life.

The appropriate context for theological learning is in Christian community. As Paul exhorted the Colossians:

> Let the message of Christ dwell among you richly as you teach and admonish one another with all wisdom through psalms, hymns, and songs from the Spirit, singing to God with gratitude in your hearts (Col 3:16, NIV).

Growing in a knowledge of God is a collective activity. Relationships with fellow students are thus critical to preparation for word ministry. Friends teach, encourage, and rebuke each other; they encourage each other as they sing together to God with gratitude in their hearts; they pray with each other for growth in grace. And friendships formed during theological education should be aimed to last a lifetime with those also in word ministry.

If theological education needs teachers who model godliness and a community that builds faithfulness, then theological education is best done in something like a theological college. It should never be done completely online. There may be certain benefits to online learning, but these cannot replace day-to-day relationships with teachers and students.

Supervision

The completion of theological study does not necessarily conclude the training of those for word ministry. As with many vocations the student needs a time of supervision as they begin a ministry appointment. It is one thing to learn about preaching in a theological education and deliver several sermons a year. It is quite another to preach regularly week in and week out. It is one thing to learn about the right principles of divorce and remarriage at college; it is another to experience those embroiled in marital struggles. This transition is best done under the care and direction of those with experience. Word ministry is not only taught but also caught.

Conclusions

I have argued that theologically the nature of church ministry demands the need for theological education. And the kind of theological education required arises from the character and function of word gifts and leadership office. Because these ministries involve both gift and word, then theological education includes three fundamental moments: preparation where word gifts are tested and fostered; education which trains people in both the learning and using of God's word to serve people; and supervision when the knowledge and skills learnt are more formally put into practice.

Bibliography

Bannerman, James. *The Church of Christ: A Treatise on the Nature, Powers, Ordinances, Discipline, and Government of the Christian Church*. Vol. 1. Edinburgh: T&T Clark, 1868, 235–44.

Best, Ernest. *A Critical and Exegetical Commentary on Ephesians*. Edinburgh: T & T Clark, 1998.

Beza, Theodore. *The Christian Faith*. Translated by James Clark. East Sussex: Focus Christian Ministries Trust, 1992.

Bruce, Frederick Fyvie. *The Epistles to the Colossians, to Philemon, and to the Ephesians*. New International Commentary on the New Testament. Grand Rapids: Eerdmans, 1984.

Bucer, Martin. *Common Places of Martin Bucer*, edited by David F. Wright. The Courtenay Library of Reformation Classics. Abingdon: Sutton Courtenay, 1972.

———. *Praelectiones Doctiss In Epistolam D. P. Ad Ephesios, Eximij Doctoris D. Martini Buceri, Habitae Canatbrigiae in Anglia*. Basileae: Apud Petrum Pernam, 1562.

Bullinger, Heinrich. *The Decades of Heinrich Bullinger*. Translated by H. I. Vol.4, 4 vols. The Parker Society. Cambridge: The University Press, 1852.

———. *De Scripturae Sanctae Authoritate, Certitudine, Firmitate Et Absoluta Perfectione*. Zurich: Christoffel Froschouer, 1538.

Carson, Donald A. *Showing the Spirit: A Theological Exposition of 1 Corinthians, 12–14*. Homebush West: Lancer, 1988.

Chapple, Allan. *God's Plan for Salvation*. Sydney South: Aquila, 2013.

Dumbrell, William J. *The End of the Beginning: Revelation 21–22 and the Old Testament*. Wipf & Stock, 2001.

———. *The Search for Order: Biblical Eschatology in Focus*. Wipf & Stock, 2001.

Dunn, James D. G. *Beginning from Jerusalem*, Christianity in the Making 2. Cambridge, U.K.; Grand Rapids, Mich.: Eerdmans, 2008.

Garland, David E. *1 Corinthians*. Baker Exegetical Commentary on the New Testament. Grand Rapids: Baker, 2003.

Gibson, Richard, ed. *Interpreting God's Plan*. Adelaide: Openbook and Paternoster, 1997.

Goldsworthy, Graeme. *Christ-Centered Biblical Theology: Hermeneutical Foundations and Principles*. IVP Academic, 2012.

Harman, Allan M. "The Place of the Biblical Languages in the Theological Curriculum." *Reformed Theological Review* 50.3 (1991) 91–97.

Jensen, Peter. "Maturing the Mind: Intellectual Attainment and Theological Education." *Reformed Theological Review* 55.3 (1996) 114–17.

Maurus, Rabanus. *Expositio In Epistolam Ad Ephesios*. PL 112:430B.

Schnabel, Eckhard J. *Acts*. Zondervan Exegetical Commentary on the New Testament. Grand Rapids: Zondervan, 2012.

Seccombe, David. *The Gospel of the Kingdom: Jesus' Revolutionary Message*. Whitefield, 2016.

Thielman, Frank. *Ephesians*. Grand Rapids, Mich.: Baker, 2010.

Thiselton, Anthony C. *The First Epistle to the Corinthians*. New International Greek Testament Commentary. Grand Rapids: Eerdmans, 2000.

Wallace, Daniel B. *Greek Grammar Beyond the Basics: An Exegetical Syntax of the New Testament*. Grand Rapids: Zondervan, 1996.

Part II

Historical Perspectives

4

Theological Education in Early Christianity
The Contribution of Late Antiquity

Andrew M. Bain

Abstract

Late antiquity can sometimes be seen as a time in which various negative practices and trends began to emerge within Christianity, particularly when the period is viewed from the standpoint of contemporary evangelicalism. This chapter argues that many of the characteristic emphases of theological education in this era, such as it was at the time, have substantial positive value for all contexts including for evangelical theological training today. In particular, the ever-present concern of late patristic authors for the central importance of character and deep immersion in Scripture is considered, and a case made that even some features of theological formation in the period that are commonly regarded in a negative light today continue to point to much that is constructively relevant today.

Introduction: Christian Theological Education and the Ancient Context

IN SPEAKING OF THEOLOGICAL education in the ancient world, we are looking at a very different phenomenon to that known today, or even that found in a time such as the High Middle Ages located roughly halfway between then and now. It was a time long before universities—even on a model very different to our own—were born, let alone stand-alone seminaries or the concept of formal vocational training for a particular function had emerged. That said, the idea that key roles in society might require some kind of carefully-considered preparation was present in at least some contexts in the ambient culture. This is illustrated most famously in the ideal by Plato's program for the preparation of guardian-rulers, and in practice by such social institutions as the *cursus honorum* typically followed by members of the Roman elite aspiring to high public office. Well-established educational assumptions and practices, such as forms of schooling and expectations of courses of "canonical" reading, existed in relation to teaching and training the young and those wishing to be well educated in some sense.[1]

What is notable about Christian theological education in antiquity is how relatively little it reflected these contextual norms and practices. We might point to the emergence of Christian catechetical schools in the second century and beyond as evidence that the developing Christian religion sought to institutionalize its pedagogy in ways that mirrored that of pagan society. Certainly, there are some parallels that could be drawn between these institutions in the main centers of learning and their philosophical equivalents. However, the catechetical schools as institutions, being mostly located in selected major urban centers (and more commonly in the Greek East than the Latin West) and in practice open to persons of some means and often prior learning, were not a viable or easily accessible option for most Christians in the Roman Empire. Also, Christian approaches to the practice of catechesis were also consciously different to Greco-Roman practices that might be seen to be parallel to them.[2] The vast majority of the clergy do not appear to have attended the catechetical schools, or received any other formal training that we might recognize as such in any modern sense.[3] In the post-Constantinian world of late antiquity which is the focus of this chapter, the church was firstly faced with the need to produce far

---

1. For a brief overview, see Muir, "Education, Roman," and for a fuller account see Harris, *Ancient Literacy*, chapters 7 and 8.
2. Hoek, "The 'Catechetical' School of Early Christian Alexandria."
3. Cf. Young, "Christian Teaching," 466–67.

larger numbers of clergy than ever before in the fourth century. Then in the fifth century (in the Latin West, at least) the church still had to produce large numbers of clergy in a context of major political and social upheaval in which literacy levels and old educational models were in severe decline.[4] In this context, it appears that very few clergy, let alone the general Christian population, had the benefit of training in such institutions as catechetical schools. By the later fourth century many clergy had spent some time in monastic contexts which appear to have been deemed as helpfully formative for many, but in practice most training probably occurred on the job.[5] As a result, the later patristic authors have very little to say that directly addresses the question of the shape and content of "theological education," at least in any formal or institutional sense. Their commentary in relation to those considering or being considered for clerical office is largely comprised of reflection on the suitability at the level of the character of potential candidates. The catechetical writings that we have incorporate material delivered to those considering baptism—who were at varying and often later stages of their Christian life—and not with vocational training.[6] They did not give much explicit consideration to questions of what we might term curriculum or method.

However, this is not to say that Christian thinkers in late antiquity were unconcerned with theological education broadly considered, or that we cannot identify some key emphases in their thought regarding this area. Those receiving catechetical instruction, particularly in the shorter form delivered by the clergy, were of a range of backgrounds, ages and faith-stages.[7] This very diversity both distinguished the training involved from that typically received in the ambient culture, and highlighted its importance as a key moment at which the clergy could give focused formal input to those committed to learning more deeply about the Christian faith. How it was practiced can tell us something of how Christianity in late antiquity understood its general values of Christian education. More substantially, the advice given by various authors to those considering the pastoral office or in their early years in it, together with their reflections on the key elements of the clergy's role, also has some important points to highlight for us in relation to theological education.

---

4. Gonzales, *The History of Theological Education*, 14.
5. Rowdon, "Theological Education in Historical Perspective," 76.
6. Johnson, "Christian Initiation," 704.
7. Cyril, "Catechetical Lectures," Protocatechesis, 4–6, 15. Cf. Hoek, "The 'Catechetical School' of Early Christian Alexandria," 65–66.

The Overriding Goal: The Formation of Christian Character

In considering the literature explicitly on the pastorate in late antiquity, a striking and fundamental feature of it, is its near-total concern with matters of personal character and godliness. Three of the best-known examples of the genre, Chrysostom's "Treatise Concerning the Christian Priesthood," Ambrose's "On the Duties of the Clergy," and Gregory the Great's "Pastoral Rule," all typify this approach, saying nothing directly about educational prerequisites, and only very occasionally offering remarks about training more broadly. Whether they are discussing questions of suitability, preparation, or the practice of formally-recognized ministry, matters of character are critical and receive almost all of the attention given in all cases, even though there is also a clear recognition alongside this of the centrality of the task of preaching the word. Besides mirroring the approach of the Pastoral Epistles in this regard, these authors believed that the most critical factors relating to "success" in ministry, and those most clearly providing reasons for failure, were questions of character rather than deficiencies in biblical or practical training, and therefore they attended above all to the former. Concentrating on humility as an antidote to pride, and avoiding the love of money and ambition, are themes that received particular emphasis.[8] In the case of Augustine at least, this concern is consciously driven by his anthropology and his doctrine of sin in the life of the believer: Augustine pointedly reminds us that even—especially—well-known leaders will continue to struggle with sin.[9] In a similar vein, Cyril of Jerusalem reminds those undergoing his catechetical instruction that the fundamental truths he is setting before them will remain important whatever their station in the church in the future, precisely because of the dangers presented by sin in its concrete expressions and temptations.[10]

For this reason, whereas in today's functional age matters of ready applicability in training are emphasized, one gains the impression in reading the patristic literature that functional training in how to perform the tasks of a pastor was considered "the easy part" which could be passed over lightly relative to questions of character and godliness. We might be tempted in our turn to move quickly past what the authors of this time taught on this point, perhaps regarding it as driven by the needs of an age

---

8. E.g. Chrysostom, "On the Priesthood," 4.1; Ambrose, "Duties of the Clergy," 1.2.5.

9. A common theme for Augustine; see Brown, *Augustine*, 140–1 for some examples.

10. Cyril, "Catechetical Lectures," Protocatechesis, 11.

where the post-Constantinian church was rapidly growing in wealth and public profile, leading to strong temptations for Christian leaders in certain areas. However the problems of pride, ambition and love of money do not appear to be unique to the Mediterranean world of the fourth century; that we see the same concern regarding addiction to material wealth still raised with immediate practical urgency by Gregory the Great in the very different economic circumstance of the late sixth century should remind us in our own varied contexts that such temptations are perennial.[11] For this reason, the central importance of Christian character formation and growth in godliness in Christian leadership for the later patristic authors, should not be passed over lightly as an all-too-obvious point, but as a pointed reminder of the fact that theological education for both leadership and the Christian life must at every turn seek to form the character biblically. Whatever theological teachers and learners are doing, there lies the importance of always relating it to spiritual growth and progress in godliness. It is also important to remember that whatever our training model might be, there is always the risk that we may fail to hit this target through simply regarding it as an obvious matter that can be assumed alongside all else that we do. For example, those committed to a traditional residential model may drift into assuming that personal formation "happens" straightforwardly through the very fact of biblical teaching occurring alongside the consistent close personal proximity of those partaking in it. In other contexts, those committed to online delivery may unwittingly slip into effectively outsourcing personal formation to the local context of the student and not take sufficient responsibility for promoting and assisting integration between the delivery of formal theological education and personal spiritual growth.

The Ongoing Challenge of Learning in Leadership

Late-patristic perspectives would also push against any tendency to assume that theological education is ever complete, whether after ordination, or elevation to the episcopacy, or completion of a course of reading or other training. Their emphasis on humility demands a recognition of the importance of ongoing learning. As Ambrose expresses it, all including even the leading bishops must remember that if you would teach, you must learn and be willing to learn, for "there is one true Master."[12] The experienced priest has, and continues to have, largely the same spiritual needs and challenges as the members of his congregation according to Nazianzen, and therefore

---

11. Gregory the Great, "The Book of Pastoral Rule," 1.3, 8–9.
12. Ambrose, "Duties of the Clergy," 1.1.3.

in the learning of spiritual wisdom should be considered in the same way.[13] Likewise according to Chrysostom, even the very gifted preacher must continue unceasingly to study and work hard at their task, as otherwise their skills would atrophy and their preaching will fall short of the high expectations that their congregations have of them.[14]

A right understanding of Christian leadership sees that the skills required for the pastorate are difficult to learn and to maintain and develop: more difficult than those needed for any other vocation, since the understanding and application of the Scriptures to the full variety of spiritual conditions found in a congregation is the most difficult of skills.[15] This implies that theological training, at least for this group of Christians, in whatever form it takes will necessarily involve serious effort. Regarding the understanding and teaching of the Scriptures, Augustine points out that virtually no Christians gain an immediate grasp upon the truth of Scripture without serious effort to learn, and to learn from human teachers regarding proper interpretation of the Bible: humble application to the task of learning over time is essential.[16] In the context of much training occurring for junior clergy "on the job" in late antiquity, those in question are well-advised to not seek to overextend themselves while inexperienced and with much still to learn, lest they harm themselves or others in the process.[17] In modern terms we might express this as underlining the importance of younger or emerging Christian leaders being self-aware in regard to their capabilities and the areas where they are still at the early stages of pedagogical development.

The Foundation of Theological Learning: The Scriptures

Turning to the content of what is to be learnt by those advancing into the ranks of the clergy, a very consistent emphasis on the Scriptures as the foundation and center is evident in late antiquity, exemplified in Chrysostom's brief statement introducing his discussion of the skills required of a pastor: "it should be our ambition that the Word of Christ dwell in us richly."[18] The personal experience of Ambrose upon unexpectedly finding himself a bishop is instructive: he immersed himself in Scripture and particularly in

13. Nazianzen, "Orations," 2.82.
14. Chrysostom, "On the Priesthood," 5.5.
15. Nazianzen, "Orations," 2.51.
16. Augustine, *On Christian Doctrine*, Preface, 3–6.
17. E.g. Nazianzen, "Orations," 2.47–49.
18. Chrysostom, "On the Priesthood," 4.4.

the best-known and most learned contemporary interpreters of Scripture he was able to access from the Greek East where he believed the best exegetes of his time to reside. It is also apparent in the advice offered by leading pastors for the time. For example, as we read Chrysostom discussing the skills needed to be a priest, speaking, a capacity to argue, skill in responding to heretics and in uprooting sin, all of these capabilities are in his view only made possible through a thorough knowledge and personal appropriation of Scripture.[19] Likewise, what is needed to critique and respond to heretics is not primarily knowledge of heresies or skill in general argumentation, but a knowledge of the Bible as the safe "middle path" through the various dangerous and misleading alternatives on either side, which provides the standpoint from which to correctly understand and judge all manner of views expressed by people.[20] This also ensures that the wise pastor avoids the problem of attacking one particular heresy so strongly yet without sufficient care for the measured biblical position, that the door is opened to an opposite kind of error: for often "the way of orthodoxy is narrow and hemmed in by threatening crags on either side, and there is no little fear lest when intending to strike at one enemy we should be wounded by the other."[21] Either this same concern, or the related fact that the fourth and fifth centuries were a time in which biblical interpretations of key texts were vigorously contested, led Augustine to emphasize the importance of continually seeking the Spirit's illumination as one's knowledge of the Scriptures grows.[22] In today's world where the complexity of theological debate and the variety of biblical interpretations and the challenges to biblical orthodoxy are as varied as ever, the advice given by Chrysostom and Augustine in this regard remains critically important for theological educators and students alike.

By the late fourth century, the Bible is not only authoritative in a theological sense, but within the Christian culture that has developed it has taken on a normative role analogous to that which the great pagan classics had held within pagan society for the previous half-millennium. Augustine's *On Christian Doctrine* handles the biblical text in this manner, even though the author urges Christian readers to approach Scripture with a different attitude and modified exegetical methods relative to study of the pagan classics.[23]

19. Chrysostom, "On the Priesthood," 4.3–5.
20. Ibid., 4.4.
21. Ibid.
22. See Matthews, "Knowledge and Illumination," 180, for some examples and associated discussion.
23. Brown, *Augustine*, 260–1; Young, "Christian Teaching," 467.

The Place of Pagan Learning

However, theological education, particularly for Christian leaders, while very heavily centered around study of the Scriptures, is not necessarily to exclude all study of non-Christian thought. For example, Basil and Gregory Nazianzen both imply that there is continuing value of pagan education so that Christian pastors can relate and function effectively in relation to other educated people in their context.[24] The practical value of being well-versed in the pagan heritage is demonstrated at the extreme and at great length by Augustine in the first half of his *City of God*,[25] where for page after page the anti-Christian claims of the educated Roman are systematically dismembered. The key is to use pagan contributions with Christian ends in mind and while fully cognizant of any spiritual dangers involved. Augustine's approach to both the reading and the teaching of the Scriptures in *On Christian Doctrine* is an instructive example: interpretative and rhetorical techniques can and should be borrowed from non-Christian sources where these serve the goals of right understanding and effective preaching.[26] However the aim is not to produce classical rhetoricians who happen to be Christian, but rather those who know how to use the treasures of the classical world to serve the goals of Christian preaching.[27] On this point, the key distinction to have learnt is to avoid mere intellectual curiosity and instead be motivated by the love of God.[28] In this regard, the characteristic patristic emphasis upon humility performs a further important function, keeping intellectual pride in check as the Christian engages with the seductive riches of pagan thought, while enabling and encouraging continued learning as the existing limitations of personal understanding are highlighted.[29] As the contemporary church continues to respond to the ever-changing challenge of contextualization, the approach modeled by Augustine and others on working through how to effectively utilize the best resources that the secular world has to offer with appropriate biblically-guided caution alongside personal humility, represents a vital example to follow.

---

24. See Young, "Christian Teaching," 468.

25. Augustine, *The City of God*, 1–10.

26. E.g. Augustine, *On Christian Doctrine*, 4.2.3. Cf. Brown, *Augustine*, 261; Thompson, "Augustine and Contemporary Theological Education," 42–44.

27. Augustine, *On Christian Doctrine*, 2.40.60–61; see Young, 475 on a similar implication in Basil.

28. Augustine, *Of True Religion*, 4.7.

29. Young, "Christian Teaching," 482.

Learning in the Monasteries of Late Antiquity

The emergence of monasteries as key locations for theological learning is a notable feature of the late patristic period, and one which would be of great importance for the succeeding centuries. However, it is important to avoid anachronistically reading medieval developments in this area back into our period or associate the rise of a monastic model too closely with events supposed to herald the beginning of the Middle Ages. For example, Rowdon presents monasticism and the theological education derived from it as being triggered by the so-called "barbarian invaders."[30] Such a view is not sustained by the raw facts. Monasticism and monastic learning took on major importance in the Greek East over the course of the fourth century, a time and place in which Germanic migrations and incursions were only intermittently of major importance, and continued to grow in significance in the centuries afterward where the movements of these peoples were largely irrelevant to the shaping of Byzantium and its Christianity. In the Latin West, where these wider political and demographic developments were of much more decisive importance, the causal link is also far from apparent: for example, Jerome founds his monastery and Augustine his monastic community in the mid-380s and mid-390s respectively, in times of relative political stability and well before the sack of Rome in 410 and the other major disruptive events which occurred over the years and decades that followed.

Within a volume such as this produced within an evangelical context, these facts are important to note, because they disrupt a common evangelical narrative. The account in question tends to present the move to a monastic model as a degeneration associated with the beginning of the medieval period and all of its historically negative associations in the Protestant mind. For example, Gonzales writes of growing ignorance among the clergy and Christians more generally due to a move from the early catechumenate system to new circumstances dominated by monasticism, in which "what was earlier expected of most Christians and offered to them was now reserved for a smaller group of particularly devout Christians."[31] Although in the early medieval period it might be argued that theological literacy was lower among Christians and their clergy than in say the first three centuries after Christ, the emergence and operation of the monastic model in late antiquity at least should be viewed more positively than it sometimes is. Compared with the pagan educational models of antiquity, the early mon-

---

30. Rowdon, "Theological Education in Historical Perspective," 77.
31. Gonzales, *The History of Theological Education*, 30 (see also 14).

asteries opened up the opportunity for study and reflection to people from a much wider range of social backgrounds: for example, Augustine's own monastic community incorporated members from both learned and relatively unlearned backgrounds, and the guidance he offered he intended to be appropriate for both kinds of people.[32] The example of Augustine's community also highlights that the formation provided by this emerging kind of context was often very effective in supporting the development of Christian leaders, given the number of key long-serving African bishops and other clergy who were products of this particular institution. Likewise, the fact that many of the leading bishops of the mid-late fourth century and beyond in the Greek East underwent substantial formation within the monasteries—and what these Eastern contexts had to offer was valued by outsiders such as Jerome—also suggests that they were highly effective nurseries for Christian leaders at the time.

The monasteries offered two particular benefits in terms of training in late antiquity. The first was *community*, the opportunity for those eager to progress in the Christian faith to spend substantial time with likeminded Christians, enabling keen and often able Christians to sharpen one another thoroughly. Related to this, the emphasis of some Christian leaders in the period on the importance of self-reflection and self-knowledge for all Christians to develop, and particularly pastors, could be promoted and extended within the monastic settings of the time. The second benefit concerned the *Scriptures*: at least in this period, the monasteries provided a context in which participants could spend several months or years being saturated with the Bible, more than would be possible at other times of their lives. The result was Christian leaders with characteristics seen most famously in Augustine, Chrysostom, and the Cappadocians: people whose sermons and writings (and so presumably also their conversations) are so Scripturally-soaked that biblical references, allusions and applications seem to come at almost every turn, with well-developed habits of sharing the struggles and joys of their Christian lives with others. The second of these two characteristics also led to a well-developed ability to be able to speak to and discuss matters of personal-biblical application and pastoral interest in their sermons and letters, seen at its very best in the sharp advice often given by Chrysostom and the psychological insight of Augustine. Both of these characteristics are critical for pastoral ministry—and for other Christians ministering to one another—not only in late antiquity but in all ages. It may not be appropriate or desirable in other times and places to promote them through a reinstatement or reinvention of the monastic models of late

---

32. Brown, *Augustine*, 263–64.

antiquity. However, the very effectiveness of the leaders of this period in using these models to promote key personal capabilities and characteristics for ministry serves as a reminder that our own models of theological education today must also actively seek ways of serving the same ends.

Conclusion: Theological Learning in Late Antiquity and Theological Education Today

It is common, particularly in contemporary evangelical contexts, to regard late antiquity as a fateful time when various first steps were taken in directions that would ultimately prove problematic, or at least irrelevant and unhelpful for today's world where the global South is numerically dominant within Christianity and Western churches are located in a post-Christian culture.[33] However on closer inspection the thinking and practices of late antiquity regarding theological education broadly conceived ought to be more positively regarded, and point to some vital imperatives that are perennially important. The narratives discussed above regarding monasticism are an example of this. More broadly, the perspective late antiquity offers on theological education as well as other matters can sometimes be dismissed as being the key time in which "Christendom" emerged with its problematic legacies for churches in post-Christian contexts today, such as "cloistered" theological training undertaken without sufficient regard for or connection to the ambient culture or the real-life settings of most students, let alone as relevant. Against this, we might observe that leaders such as Chrysostom and Augustine lived and wrote (and with renowned effectiveness) in a time when Christianity was still challenged by a number of non-Christian religious menu-options and in which the influence of pagan philosophical currents was still quite strong, strong enough for a busy bishop such as Augustine to devote his most substantial single work to the rebuttal of these challenges, and for warnings against the still very real temptation of certain other religions to feature in the preaching of Chrysostom in an imperial capital. As we have noted above, at least in the late fourth century, theological formation in the monasteries and elsewhere was not characterized by a turning inward and away from pagan learning so much as a desire to relate critically to it. The standpoint from which this relating activity was to occur,

---

33. Ma, "Theological Education and Missional Formation," 3–5, provides a typical example of this perspective in summary form. The conclusion of Gonzales, *The History of Theological Education*, also advances similar assumptions in the context of a very well-known recent evangelical treatment of theological training's history.

and indeed all Christian teaching and learning, was that of the Christian Scriptures.

For the kind of theological formation valued and offered in late antiquity was as we have seen strongly Bible-based and heavily focused on relating the Scriptures first to one's own life and character and secondly to the lives of others as they walked the road of godliness. It was also very commonly undertaken in the context of ongoing local ministry, or even on-the-job, and at least in some cases was characterized by thoughtful, scripturally-guided critical interaction with and constructive use of pagan ideas and materials. While substantial shifts did occur in relation to theological education in late antiquity, the key developments which we have considered above do not seem to have caused the problems sometimes cited, at least directly, and key leaders at the time appear to have placed great emphasis on combating the peculiar challenges of the post-Constantinian order such as temptations to greed and pride among emerging Christian leaders. Indeed, the churches of late antiquity appear to have done well given their circumstances. They produced a far larger number of clergy than in previous centuries, with the formation which did occur incorporating key features which would be valuable in any time and place including contemporary evangelicalism: a single-minded emphasis on the vital importance of godly character formation within theological education and development, training and growth that is Scripture-soaked and centered, ready applicability of all that is learnt to the practice of the Christian life, and the importance of lifelong learning for both faith and ministry.

Bibliography

Ambrose. "On the Duties of the Clergy." In *St. Ambrose: Select Works and Letters*, edited by Philip Schaff and Henry Wace, 1–89. Translated by H. de Romestin, E. de Romestin, and H. T. F. Duckworth. New York: Christian Literature Company, 1896.

Augustine. *Of True Religion*. Edited by Louis O. Mink and translated by John H. S. Burleigh. Philadelphia: Westminster John Knox, 1953.

Augustine. *On Christian Doctrine*. Translated by D. W. Robertson, Jr. Upper Saddle River, N.J.: Prentice Hall, 1958.

Augustine. *The City of God Against the Pagans*. Edited and translated by R. W. Dyson. Cambridge: Cambridge University Press, 1998.

Chrysostom, John. "Treatise Concerning the Christian Priesthood." In *Saint Chrysostom: On the Priesthood, Ascetic Treatises, Select Homilies and Letters, Homilies on the Statues*, edited by Philip Schaff, 33–83. Translated by W. R. W. Stephens. New York: Christian Literature Company, 1889.

Cyril of Jerusalem. "The Catechetical Lectures of S. Cyril, Archbishop of Jerusalem." In *S. Cyril of Jerusalem, S. Gregory Nazianzen*, edited by Philip Schaff and Henry

Wace, 1–157. Translated by R. W. Church & E. H. Gifford. New York: Christian Literature Company, 1894.
Farley, Edward. *Theologia: The Fragmentation and Unity of Theological Education*. Philadelphia: Fortress, 1983.
Gonzales, Justo L. *The History of Theological Education*. Nashville: Abingdon, 2015.
Gregory the Great. "The Book of Pastoral Rule of Saint Gregory the Great, Roman Pontiff, to John, Bishop of the City of Ravenna." In *Leo the Great, Gregory the Great*, edited by Philip Schaff and Henry Wace, 1–72. Translated by J. Barmby. New York: Christian Literature Company, 1895.
Harris, William V. *Ancient Literacy*. Cambridge, MA and London: Harvard University Press, 1989.
Hoek, Annewies van den. "The 'Catechetical' School of Early Christian Alexandria and Its Philonic Heritage." *The Harvard Theological Review* 90, no. 1 (1997) 59–87.
Johnson, Maxwell E. "Christian Initiation." In *The Oxford Handbook of Early Christian Studies*, edited by Susan Ashbrook Harvey and David C. Hunter, 693–710. Oxford: Oxford University Press, 2008.
Ma, Wonsuk. "'Life' in Theological Education and Missional Formation: A Reflection for a New Christian Era." *Transformation* 33, no. 1 (2016) 1–15.
Matthews, Gareth B. "Knowledge and Illumination." In *The Cambridge Companion to Augustine*, edited by Eleonore Stump and Norman Kretzmann, 171–85. Cambridge: Cambridge University Press, 2001.
Muir, J. V. "Education, Roman." *Oxford Classical Dictionary*. http://classics.oxfordre.com/view/10.1093/acrefore/9780199381135.001.0001/acrefore-9780199381135-e-2347.
Gregory Nazianzen. "Select Orations of Saint Gregory Nazianzen." In *S. Cyril of Jerusalem, S. Gregory Nazianzen*, edited by Philip Schaff and Henry Wace, 203–434. Translated by C. G. Browne and J. E. Swallow. New York: Christian Literature Company, 1894.
Thompson, Mark D. "Augustine and Contemporary Theological Education—A Conversation with *On Christian Teaching*." In *The Church of the Triune God*, edited by Michael P. Jensen, 29–54. Sydney: Aquila, 2013.
Rowdon, Harold H. "Theological Education in Historical Perspective." *Vox Evangelica* 7 (1971) 75–87.
Young, Frances. "Christian Teaching." In *The Cambridge History of Early Christian Literature*, edited by Frances Young et al., 464–84. Cambridge: Cambridge University Press, 2004.

5

Models of Western Christian Education and Ministerial Training

Antecedents in the Sixteenth Century

Graeme Chatfield

Abstract

The sixteenth century was and continues to be foundational for Protestantism in many ways, and theological education is no exception to this. This chapter explores developments in Christian education and ministerial education which emerged from the Reformation and associated developments, in relation to three basic approaches which emerged at this time: university, seminary, and vernacular models, with the trajectories of each of these being discussed in relation to the historical context and key figures of the Reformation.

Introduction

WESTERN SOCIETY IS CURRENTLY experiencing major disruption. Models of business, government, technology, and education are all scrambling to adjust to constantly changing patterns as the kaleidoscope of our world is continually re-tweaked. It should come as no surprise to theological educators that the known models of theological training are being caught up in this disruption.

This chapter seeks to provide a description of sixteenth-century models of Christian education and ministerial training, many features of which remain recognizable in the twenty-first century. The Reformers of the sixteenth century agreed that all the people in any way related to their churches should receive a Christian education that would prepare them as good Christian citizens and that an elite of the most promising male students should continue into ministerial training. Christian education happened not only in formal settings such as schools, but more generally through catechetical instruction conducted by the head of families or parish priests. The more advanced training of those destined for the priesthood would be undertaken usually at universities or seminaries. However, these general models could vary significantly, frequently reflecting the local context in which they were established. Beyond the university and seminary models, a potential third model was tried, the vernacular model. However, since it did not have support from established political forces, it did not take recognizable institutional form in the sixteenth century.

Twenty-first-century theological educators are familiar with both the university model and seminary model of ministerial education, and are aware of their links to the Reformation. The university ministerial training model of the Reformers developed from the late medieval university model which utilized Latin as the language of theology and the texts of scholastic theologians as the texts for instruction. The Reformers modified that late medieval model by insisting that knowledge of Greek and Hebrew was essential to understanding and expositing the text of Scripture. They also replaced the theological works of the scholastic theologians with the text of Scripture in Greek and Hebrew, and the scholastic theologians' methods with a variety of new methods. At the universities of the Reformers, theology continued to be one field of study among others, notably, law and medicine. In short, in the universities controlled by the magisterial reformers there was a significant curriculum review.

The seminary model, developed out of the church-associated schools, shared several features with the Reformers' university models: the essential knowledge of the biblical languages and the Scriptures in those languages as the essential text for study. However, the seminary model differed from the university model in some significant ways. Theology was the only field of study at a seminary and an explicit goal of training was the preparation of preachers who would preach in the vernacular based on the correct exegesis of a biblical passage. Seminaries were also not able to offer degrees recognized as the equivalent of a university degree. Until the twentieth century institutions following the university and seminary models only accepted male candidates.

A prototype of the vernacular model of ministerial training existed in the sixteenth century. Twenty-first-century Christian educators are familiar with a developed form of the vernacular model from the late nineteenth century, the Bible college (e.g. Moody Bible Institute). In the sixteenth century, there were those who were familiar with both the university and seminary models who advocated that the vernacular text of Scripture was sufficient for both Christian education and ministerial training, and that the academic disciplines associated with the theological methods being taught by the magisterial reformers were only another form of sophistry used to exclude people from their rightful role in determining the meaning of Scripture.

Sixteenth-Century Christian Education

Christian education was a concern of both Renaissance humanists and those who would become known as magisterial reformers. By the close of the fifteenth century education had grown to encompass a mixture of cathedral schools, monastics schools, and schools associated with the Brethren of the Common Life, all providing preliminary education for entry to universities. Amongst historians of education Erasmus of Rotterdam is something of a hero. He is presented as an enlightened person who argued not only for curriculum reform but a change in the way teaching occurred; from brutal enforcement of rote learning set medieval text to affirming encouragement of exploring a "classics" curriculum at times even through play.[1] Many features of Erasmus' reform agenda were applauded by nineteenth and twentieth-century educationalists.[2] However, his concerns were not restricted to only establishing a "classical" education, nor was he intent on removing Christian ideals from the curriculum as are some educationalists of the present day. While his popular writings targeted scholasticism as a theological method to be overthrown, and the worldly excesses of the Roman Catholic church dignitaries as something to be deplored, he vigorously advocated his "philosophy of Christ" to all people, continuing to popularize the idea of the imitation of Christ, a concept he had imbued during his own

---

1. Erika Rummel suggests Erasmus's "On Education for Children," "reflects Erasmus' own priorities in its firm depreciation of mechanical rote-learning, its lively insistence on the educative power of play in the instruction of the young, and in the emphatic rejection of corporal punishment." Rummel, *The Erasmus Reader*, 65.

2. Gangel and Benson, *Christian Education: Its History and Philosophy*, 129–130.

education with the Brethren of the Common Life. His passion for returning to the original text of Scripture and its translation into the vernacular became his model for disseminating the text to common people to encourage the development of a pious life.

While Erasmus produced *On Education for Children* (published in 1529) primarily as a rhetorical defense of the value of education, in it he does provide an outline of his program for Christian education. He makes clear to his readers that fathers have responsibility to the community and to God to provide an education in holiness for their children; failure to do so will bring down God's judgement on the negligent.[3] Education, Erasmus insists, begins from birth: "As soon as a child is born, he is ready for instruction in right conduct and, as soon as he is able to speak, he is ready for learning his letters."[4] Learning languages other than the child's vernacular should also be an essential part of education. Erasmus contends that if "a German boy could learn French in a few months quite unconsciously while absorbed in other activities"[5] he should equally be able to learn Greek and Latin. He reprimands those who delay beginning instruction in Greek and Latin till a child is at least sixteen years old.[6] The curriculum for the young should be based on the "fables of the ancient authors," their comedies, and "brief pointed aphorisms, which include almost all proverbs and sayings of famous men," [7] as a source of moral education. As well as grammar and rhetoric, for those who show signs of aptitude, music, arithmetic and geography can be added to the curriculum. This syllabus Erasmus described as "a liberal education."[8] An obvious omission in this curriculum is any reference to the place of Scripture or catechisms.

While Erasmus also contributed to the curriculum debates in the universities of his day he did not engage in the struggle to reform the theological curriculum at any specific university. His legacy to educationalists is more in the realm of establishing what would become after the Enlightenment the curriculum of a classical education.

This broad agenda for reform of Christian education was also evident in the works of Martin Luther, Ulrich Zwingli, and in the second phase

---

3. "Parents also cause harm to society when they, in so far at least as it lies within their power, present the community with a citizen who constitutes a real threat. They also sin against God, for God gave them children to be raised in the ways of religion." Erasmus, "On Education for Children," 75.

4. Ibid., 86.

5. Ibid.

6. Ibid., 87.

7. Ibid., 95.

8. Ibid., 65.

of the Reformation, John Calvin.[9] Among these magisterial reformers the place of Scripture in Christian education was paramount.[10] All agreed that the text of Scripture was essential to a revised curriculum for education of the young, and that catechisms should be used to provide the framework for all people, especially the young undertaking formal education, so they could articulate true doctrine.[11] However, their social and political contexts saw them develop quite distinct models for both general Christian education and ministerial training.[12] It was in regard to ministerial training that their proposed models differed most dramatically, leading to the development of two foundational models of ministerial training among Protestants that continue in the early twenty-first century. Yet for both Luther and Zwingli their work reforming Christian education provided opportunity for

---

9. Luther, "To the Councilors of All Cities in Germany That They Establish and Maintain Christian Schools, (1524)," LW 45, 341–78; "Instructions for the Visitors of Parish Pastors in Electoral Saxony 1528," LW 40, 263–320; "Sermon on the Duty of Sending Children to School, 1530"; Zwingli, "On the Education of Youth," 96–118; "John Calvin: Catechism, 1538," 1–38, and "The Ecclesiastical Ordinances, 1541," 71–6.

10. Concerning the necessary books in a school library Luther wrote: "the Holy Scriptures in Latin, Greek, Hebrew and German and any other languages in which they might be found," in Bornkamm, *Luther in Mid-Career*, 141–42. "But a man cannot rightly order his own soul unless he exercises himself day and night in the word of God. He can do that most readily if he is well versed in such languages as Hebrew and Greek . . . I do not think that Latin should be altogether neglected. For an understanding of Holy Scripture it is of less value than Hebrew and Greek, but for other purposes it is just as useful,": Zwingli, "Of the Education of Youth," 108.

11. "The deplorable conditions which I recently encountered when I was a visitor constrained me to prepare this brief and simple catechism or statement of Christian teaching. Good, God, what wretchedness I beheld! The common people, especially those in the country, have no knowledge what ever of Christian teaching, and unfortunately many parish pastors are quite incompetent and unfitted for teaching": "Luther's Small Catechism (1529)," 61. Noll suggests Zwingli's "Sixty-Seven Theses" acted like a catechism in Zurich, even though it did not follow the more normal pattern of question and answer. Interestingly, Calvin's first catechism (1536 in French, 1528 in Latin translation) also did not follow the question and answer format, though his 1541 version had reverted to this format as it was considered easier for people to follow. John I. Hesselink, *Calvin's First Catechism*, 2. Hesselink observes "It [1538 Catechism] was intended primarily for the instruction of the youth of Geneva," but the revised editions (French 1541, Latin 1545) were required because the 1538 edition was "too difficult for children." *Calvin's First Catechism*, 40–41.

12. For Luther's fullest description of his model of Christian education, see "Instructions for the Visitors." Zwingli's "On the Education of Youth" does not have the detail of Luther's proposal. Potter notes that Zwingli's educational reforms remained localized, and focused on producing ministers for Zurich and its environs. He does note that the pattern Zwingli established in Zurich was copied in Strassburg and Basel, with parallels in Puritan England and Scotland. Potter, *Zwingli*, 223.

the expression of an emphasis on vernacular Bible training for both general Christian education and ministerial training.

The University Model

Luther worked within the context of Electoral Saxony and an existing university, albeit, a very recently established university (1502).[13] Here, endeavoring to secure the support of Elector Frederick the Wise, without whose support he thought no reform was possible, Luther participated in effecting a change in what was taught in the "department" of theology, while simultaneously advocating the establishment of a state-controlled system of general education.[14]

University education had been undergoing a slow evolution during the later medieval period. Paris University, arguably among the most influential universities of the period underwent a shift in governance, with power and authority shifting from ecclesial to civil authorities, and academic authority concentrating in the hands of the upper echelons of the university, the doctors.[15] In theology, it had also been diversifying; in 1521 "at least eight theological schools were identified" at Paris University.[16] What was evident at Paris University was identifiable at Wittenberg University.

Luther began his theological studies at Erfurt, being exposed to teachers sympathetic to the theology of the *via moderna* (as epitomized in the theology of Gabriel Biel) rather than the *via antiqua*, typically represented by the work of Thomas Aquinas and Duns Scotus. Prior to Luther's arrival at Wittenberg in 1508, under the influence of its new rector who had recently arrived from the University of Erfurt, Wittenberg University dramatically changed its rules and allowed lecturers to follow the *via Gregorii* (representative of the *via moderna*) as well as the already established two schools of the *via antiqua* (i.e. *via Thomae* and *via Scoti*).[17] By 1517 with the publication of his *Disputation Against Scholastic Theology*, Luther had moved beyond the *via moderna* he knew from Erfurt to advocate the soteriology of the *schola Augustiniana moderna* (as the *via Gregorii* had become

---

13. Elector Frederick the Wise established the University of Wittenberg in 1502. Martin Luther joined the faculty in 1508.

14. Lindberg, *The European Reformations*, 127. For a general discussion on curriculum reform in the sixteenth century see Hamilton, "On the Origins of the Educational Terms," 3–20.

15. Ibid., 7.

16. Alister McGrath, *The Intellectual Origins of the European Reformation*, 69.

17. Ibid., 110–11.

more exactly defined), as had the majority of the faculty of theology at the University of Wittenberg.[18]

Not only had the University of Wittenberg adopted a new approach to theology, it also adopted a new text for teaching theology. Luther's use of Scripture as the primary text for teaching theology through exposition of set books shifted the ground from other approaches that relied on the works of recognized scholastic theologians.[19]

From Wittenberg came the model of Protestant university-based ministerial training where Scripture was central to the curriculum and training of ministerial candidates who were part of a department of theology. Theology was only one of several fields of study.[20] Variants to this model developed over the sixteenth and subsequent centuries. Residential colleges associated with a university had existed for centuries prior to the Reformation and were often associated with a specific theological school.[21] By the late seventeenth century in English universities a residential college would be associated with a particular confessional statement, yet supply faculty to a university-wide department of theology. In the Australian context, generally universities did not have a department of theology, and the faculty associated with the halls of residence were associated with the university in other ways as the department of theology did not exist. Confessional theology was taught at independent denominational seminaries established for that purpose.

The Seminary Model

From Zurich, the first recognizable institution of the seminary model arose. Zwingli's context was Zurich, a major canton of the Swiss Confederation which in 1499 had asserted its claim to self-rule from the Holy Roman Empire.[22] Here he worked cautiously to win the support of the elected officials of the various councils that made up the government of Zurich before moving to advance controversial theological ideas and reform existing practices. At the Great Minster where he was people's priest, Zwingli reorganized the ex-

---

18. Ibid., 120.

19. Bernhard Lohse, *Martin Luther*, 28–30.

20. The other principal fields of study in a sixteenth-century university were typically law, medicine and philosophy.

21. Hamilton, "Origins of Educational Terms," 7.

22. Potter summarizes the Swiss Confederacy in the middle ages as: "Very poor, simple, rough and self-confident, the Swiss of the later middle ages lived in a bewildering world of local, disorganized semi-anarchy." Potter, *Zwingli*, 3.

isting school for training ministers into two schools, "a grammar school for boys and a theological college for the training of ministers."[23] Potter claims it was the so-called *Prophezei*, the seminary for training ministers, that was Zwingli's original contribution to ministerial education. Gangel and Benson claim: "It was a genuine community of scholars in which lecturers and students joined together to seek out truth. The atmosphere exemplified New Testament community and respect for student as well as content." They go on to assert the *Prophezei* to be "a solid foundation for effective contemporary theological education."[24] A feature of Zwingli's ministerial training not recognized by Gangel and Benson was his commitment to communication of the word of God in the vernacular. For Zwingli, the exposition of the biblical text using the biblical languages and Latin was not the end of learning for those in the *Prophezei*.

> Every morning, except Sundays and Fridays, at seven in the summer and at eight in the winter, the preachers and students met in the cathedral choir. After the opening prayer, the Old Testament was read in Latin from the Vulgate. Then it was read in Hebrew and expounded in Latin; after that it was read in Greek from the Septuagint and expounded in Latin. Finally what had been done in Latin, the language of the educated, was expounded in German, the language of the people. The leaders changed in the course of time and increasingly it was Zwingli who preached in the final part, which was attended by the general public'.[25]

Such was the process of education in Zwingli's "seminary."

For Zwingli, the "prophet" had "a higher status and greater responsibilities within the Christian community than the simple evangelist or preacher,"[26] something akin to Calvin's view of the role of teachers in the Geneva Academy. The model of the *Prophezei* was copied in Strassburg and Basel,[27] and Calvin spent considerable time in Strassburg 1539–1541, where he most likely became acquainted with this model of Christian education and ministerial training. Gangel and Benson suggest that the "broad features" of the Zurich *Prophezei* "were taken and modified to fit many other contexts, most famously the Geneva Academy."[28] Calvin's context precipitated one significant modification to Zwingli's model, that is, train-

23. Ibid., 220.
24. Gangel and Benson, *Christian Education*, 144–45.
25. Stephens, "Huldrych Zwingli: The Swiss Reformer," 34–35.
26. Potter, *Zwingli*, 223.
27. Ibid., 223.
28. Gangel and Benson, *Christian Education*, 145.

ing missionary ministers, in this case French students trained to return to Reformed churches in France.[29]

From the beginning of negotiations between Calvin and the Genevan magistrates, a difference in purpose for the Geneva Academy was evident. For Calvin, the intention was to "establish a model institution for the training of a learned ministeriate, the motivating force for many native Genevans was to improve local educational provision at all levels."[30] This initial tension was heightened when after the death of Calvin in 1564 Theodor Beza became the key figure among the Reformed leaders in Geneva. Beza had advocated adding law and medicine to the faculties of the Geneva Academy as early as 1559, and by 1565 with the support and interest of the Small Council, law lectures had commenced, and a lecturer in medicine appointed.[31] For the Small Council of Geneva, training a confessionally uniform ministeriate was only one of their concerns; they wanted to "raise Geneva's profile in the early sixteenth-century educational world, and thus to attract more wealthy and noble students to the Academy."[32] By 1581 the Small Council had instituted changes to the governance of the Geneva Academy that gave it greater control of the affairs of the academy, citing the governance practices of Berne, Strassburg and the University of Basel. They permitted the seal of the Small Council to be affixed to matriculation statements so Geneva Academy graduates' statements would look "like other universities," and by 1584 were requiring matriculating students to pay fees, and take an oath of obedience to the magistrates that no longer included a doctrinal statement.[33] Between 1592–1599 the Small Council sought to have France and the United Provinces recognize the awards of the Geneva Academy as equivalent to degrees.[34] By the first decade of the seventeenth century arts and Greek had become "preliminary subjects, operating at a lower level than theology or law," effectively adopting a "university model of an arts faculty through which all students had to pass before they could go on to higher study in theology or law."[35]

Even in the sixteenth century those in ministerial education had to contend with the challenge of defining the purpose for the existence of their institutions, as well as the influence of secular authorities that paid the bills,

29. Maag, *Seminary or University?*, 29.
30. Ibid., 9.
31. Ibid., 26–27.
32. Ibid., 3.
33. Ibid., 51–52.
34. Ibid., 80–81.
35. Ibid., 79.

and student aspirations for attending their institution. In this regard, the sixteenth-century experience of Christian education and ministerial training is not too far removed from the twenty-first-century experience, except that a Christian worldview was a given in the sixteenth century.

The Vernacular Model

The "vernacular" model became a focus of debate in Wittenberg from 1521 as the exchanges between Martin Luther and his colleague Andreas Bodenstein von Carlstadt clearly demonstrate.[36] Luther was concerned that his early statements on the priesthood of believers were being misrepresented as social and religious egalitarianism by the Zwickau prophets and Thomas Müntzer, and of Carlstadt naively attempting to establish this at the Orlamünde church. One aspect of Luther's position Carlstadt took exception to was the necessity of "prophets" in the church being experts in the biblical languages.[37] For Carlstadt, Luther's original teaching on the priesthood of believers had an anti-elitism implication; priests should earn their living through working like others rather than off the offerings of the congregation, they should wear the same clothing as the common people and not clothing that indicated status above the common people, and they should communicate the gospel in the vernacular relying on the Holy Spirit to communicate the truth being conveyed.[38] Luther was appalled by Carlstadt's interpretation of his views, and countered that while a person might use the vernacular to preach for pious outcomes in the congregation, it was absolutely necessary to know Latin, Greek and Hebrew if the priest was to

---

36. Luther, "To the Councilmen," 363–65; Carlstadt, "Several Main Points," 339–77.

37. Luther, "To the Councilmen," 363. "A simple preacher (it is true) has so many clear passages and texts available through translations that he can know and teach Christ, lead a holy life, and preach to others. But when it comes to interpreting Scripture, and working with it on your own, and disputing with those who cite it incorrectly, he is unequal to the task: that cannot be done without languages. Now there must always be such prophets in the Christian church who can dig into Scripture, expound it, and carry on disputations. A saintly life and right doctrine are not enough. Hence, languages are absolutely and altogether necessary in the Christian church, as are prophets or interpreters; although it is not necessary that every Christian or every preacher be such a prophet."

38. Carlstadt, "Several Main Points,": on common dress and working, 369–71; on the necessity of the Holy Spirit to illuminate understanding the truth of the gospel, something the people of Orlamünde knew and experienced from Carlstadt's preaching, compared to the preachers imposed on them by the Elector of Saxony, 357–61.

exposit the Scriptures accurately, the real basis for teaching the truth of the gospel.

The issues between Luther and Carlstadt were well known in Zurich, where several young members of Zwingli's *Prophezei* were in communication with Carlstadt and Thomas Müntzer and took their side against Luther.[39] The issue of communicating the word of God based only on a vernacular translation was taken up by their associate Balthasar Hubmaier in his disputes with Zwingli over the nature of baptism. Hubmaier urged that the Bible in the vernacular was sufficient for proclamation of the whole gospel; the assurance of the Holy Spirit's presence in the congregation of the rebaptized ensured the true gospel was being heard and received. Hubmaier insisted that Zwingli, and other magisterial reformers, with their reliance on biblical languages and literary methods were darkening with sophistry what was the clear message of the gospel; the German translation was basis enough to know the truth.[40]

However, Hubmaier did not exclude those learned in the biblical languages having a role in determining the meaning of Scripture. He advocated a congregational hermeneutic where such people were included yet not with the authority beyond the congregation.[41] He sought to put this idea into practice in Nikolsburg in 1527 to 1528 where he established an Anabaptist church with the support of the lords of Lichtenstein.[42] It was from this same Anabaptist church that some members would leave over a dispute regarding the use of the sword and establish the first Hutterite community, a community noted for its radical approach to Christian education and for training those who would be pastors of their communities.

Clearly, the "vernacular model" for Christian education and ministerial training was attempted during the sixteenth century. However, without the support of civil authorities, it was forced to the margins of society in groups identified with the Radical Reformers.

That the idea of Christian education and ministerial training based on using a vernacular text of Scripture did not die out with the triumph of the university and seminary models is evidenced by the periodic resurfacing of the issue across the centuries. By the late nineteenth century, the social

---

39. "Greble to Muntzer, Zurich, September 5, 1524," 284–92.

40. "Therefore I want every Christian church and congregation to judge and discern. How blind, how blind! Why do they distress the godly, simple Christians at this point with such invented, sophistic glosses and additions." Hubmaier, "On the Christian Baptism of Believers," 113. For extended discussion of the issue of the clarity of Scripture see my *Balthasar Hubmaier and the Clarity of Scripture*.

41. Hubmaier, "Theses Against Eck," 49–57.

42. Hubmaier, "A Form of Christ's Supper," 394–95.

context in which Christian education and ministerial training took place had changed significantly enough to allow an institutional version of the vernacular model to be established, the Bible school movement. Independent of the existing university and seminary models, lay men and women as well as trained clergy established institutions where they focused on the Bible in the vernacular, and taught "evangelistic methods, and other practical skills useful to students who planned to become missionaries, evangelists, pastors, Sunday school teachers and Christian workers of other kinds."[43]

> Nothing was inherently wrong with learning Latin, Greek, and Hebrew, and with reading classical literature; many of the training school founders had themselves received classical educations. But it was not appropriate for recruits to the mission fields; it took too long and sometimes dulled their zeal.[44]

Brereton notes, however, that the rhetoric of the founders did not always match reality, and rudimentary Greek, Latin, or Hebrew could be found in curriculums, but only where a willing teacher could be easily recruited.[45]

The same debates that motivated the Bible school movement are also evident among some Christians in Australia at the turn of the twentieth century. The New South Wales Baptists debated the nature of Christian education and ministerial training. This was especially evident in the debates regarding the establishment of their own ministerial training college—one group advocating the continued necessity of facility in the biblical languages and preferably a university level education for ministerial training utilizing the latest methods in academic scholarship, while the other group, suspicious of the "new learning" in the academy, advocated a Bible in the vernacular and the instruction of the Holy Spirit was all that was needed for ministerial training.[46]

The outcome of the ongoing tension between the vernacular model and seminary model played out in the United States over the next century. Brereton notes a progression in the Bible school movement: initially skepticism towards the academy was the most common position, but over time there emerged a tendency to actually become part of the academy. By the 1940s some Bible schools began to offer degrees, added liberal arts subjects to the curriculum, and eventually sought accreditation through government

---

43. Brereton, *Training God's Army*, xvii.
44. Ibid., 62.
45. Ibid., 63.
46. Chatfield, "Approaches to Ministerial Training among New South Wales Baptists: Initial Lines of Enquiry," 39–62.

agencies,[47] some even becoming Christian liberal arts universities. In the early twenty-first century, some heirs of the Bible college movement in Australia are following a similar path.

The sixteenth-century Christian educators adapted new learning, skills and technologies that enabled the development of new models in Christian education and ministerial training. That capacity to adapt to their changing context while continuing to proclaim the unchanging message of the gospel is a model their twenty-first-century heirs could do well to emulate.

Bibliography

Bornkamm, Heinrich and Karin Bornkamm, eds. *Luther in Mid-Career, 1521–1530*. Translated by E. Theodore Bachmann. Philadelphia, PA: Fortress, 1983.

Brereton, Virginia L. *Training God's Army: The American Bible School, 1880–1940*. Bloomington, IN: Indiana University Press, 1991.

Calvin, John. "The Ecclesiastical Ordinances, 1541." In *Registres de la Compagnie des pasteurs de Geneve au temps de Calvin*, edited by J. F. Bergier and R. M. Kingdon, n. p. 2 vols. 1962–4. Registres I. Translated by G. R. Potter and M. Greengrass, *Jean Calvin*, 71–76. London: Edward Arnold, 1983.

———. "John Calvin: Catechism, 1538." In *Calvin's First Catechism: A Commentary: Featuring Ford Lewis Battle's Translation of the 1538 Catechism*, edited by I. John Hesselink, 1–38. Columbia Series in Reformed Theology. Louisville, KY: Westminster John Knox, 1997.

Carlstadt, Andreas. "Several Main Points of Christian Teaching Regarding Which Dr. Luther Brings Andreas Carlstadt Under Suspicion Through False Accusation and Slander, 1525." In *The Essential Carlstadt. Fifteen Tracts by Andreas Rudolff-Bodenstein Von Karlstadt*, edited and translated by E. J. Furcha, 339–77. Classics of the Radical Reformation. Vol. 8. Scottdale PA: Herald, 1995.

Chatfield, Graeme. "Approaches to Ministerial Training Among New South Wales Baptists: Initial Lines of Enquiry." *The Pacific Journal of Baptist Research* 2.1 (April 2006) 39–62.

———. *Balthasar Hubmaier and the Clarity of Scripture. A Critical Reformation Issue*. Eugene, OR: Pickwick, 2013.

Erasmus, Desiderius. "On Education for Children/*De pueris instituendis*." In *The Erasmus Reader*, edited by Erika Rummel, 65–100. 2nd ed. Toronto: University of Toronto Press, 1990.

Gangel, Kenneth O. and Warren S. Benson. *Christian Education: Its History and Philosophy*. Chicago: Moody, 1983.

Grebel, Conrad. "Grebel to Muntzer, Zurich, September 5, 1524." In *The Sources of Swiss Anabaptism: The Grebel Letters and Related Documents*, edited by Leland Harder, 284–92. Classics of the Radical Reformation. Vol. 4. Scottdale, PA: Herald, 1986.

Hamilton, David. "On the Origins of the Educational Terms Class and Curriculum." In *New Curriculum History*, edited by B. Barker, 3–20. Rotterdam, Boston and Taipei: Sense, 2009.

---

47. Brereton, *Training God's Army*, 84–5.

Hubmaier, Balthasar. "A Form of Christ's Supper." In *Balthasar Hubmaier: Theologian of Anabaptism*, edited and translated by H. Wayne Pipkin and John H. Yoder, 393–408. Classics of the Radical Reformation. Vol. 5. Scottdale, PA: Herald, 1989.

———. "On the Christian Baptism of Believers." In *Balthasar Hubmaier: Theologian of Anabaptism*, edited and translated by H. Wayne Pipkin and John H. Yoder, 95–149. Classics of the Radical Reformation. Vol. 5. Scottdale, PA: Herald, 1989.

———. "Theses Against Eck." In *Balthasar Hubmaier: Theologian of Anabaptism*, 49–57. Classics of the Radical Reformation. Vol. 5. Scottdale, PA: Herald, 1989.

Lindberg, Carter. *The European Reformations*. Oxford: Blackwell, 1996.

Lohse, Bernhard. *Martin Luther. An Introduction to His Life and Work*. Translated by Robert C. Schultz. Edinburgh: T&T Clark, 1987.

Luther, Martin. "Instructions for the Visitors of Parish Pastors in Electoral Saxony 1528." In *Luther's Works*, edited and translated by Conrad Bergendorf, 263–320. Vol. 40. Philadelphia: Fortress, 1958. Third reprint, 1975.

———. "Luther's Small Catechism (1529)." In *Confessions and Catechisms of the Reformation*, edited by Mark Noll, 59–80. Leicester UK: Apollos, 1991.

———. "Sermon on the Duty of Sending Children to School (1530)." In *Luther on Education*, edited by F. V. N. Painter, 210–71. Concordia, 1928.

———. "To the Councilors of All Cities in Germany That They Establish and Maintain Christian Schools. 1524." In *Luther's Works*, edited and translated by Albert T. W. Steinhaeuser and Walter I. Brandt, 341–78. Vol. 45. Philadelphia: Fortress, 1962.

Maag, Karin. *Seminary or University? The Genevan Academy and Reformed Higher Education, 1560–1620*. St Andrews Studies in Reformation History. Aldershot, UK: Scholar, 1995.

McGrath, Alister. *The Intellectual Origins of the European Reformation*. Grand Rapids, MI: Baker, 1993.

Potter, George R. *Zwingli*. London: Cambridge University Press, 1984.

Stephens, W. Peter. "Huldrych Zwingli: The Swiss Reformer." *Scottish Journal of Theology* 41:1 (1988) 27–47.

Zwingli, Ulrich. "On the Education of Youth." In *Zwingli and Bullinger*, edited and translated by G. W. Bromiley, 96–118. Library of Christian Classics. Vol. 24. Philadelphia: Westminster, 1953.

6

American Theological Education at the Beginning of the Nineteenth Century

The Edwardsean Legacy

RHYS S. BEZZANT

Abstract

At the turn of the nineteenth century, the United States of America was a newly-independent nation, in which new patterns were beginning to emerge in relation to training for ministry and mission. This chapter explores the emergence of Andover Theological Seminary, representing the first example of a new approach to theological education at the time. The deep roots underlying its formation, stretching back to the ministry of Jonathan Edwards, are examined, followed by a discussion of the factors which led Andover's founders to choose the model of formation which they did at the time. In so doing, the significance of context and established patterns are highlighted in relation to theological education today.

Introduction

EDUCATING BELIEVERS IS A never-ending process, for each generation must plan for their children's children to hear the gospel. A significant strategy to reach this weighty goal is to prosper the development of leaders, for which institutions that sustain the vision are critical. It will come then as no surprise that launching a seminary or theological college that achieves the mission will require extensive resources and energy. The historical moment in which a seminary is established will itself profoundly shape the institution's reason for being, even if sometimes the contextual pressures remain opaque to its champions. Under Western Enlightenment conditions, for example, the modern seminary can appear to be a neutral institution devoted to the pursuit of knowledge and higher learning, whereas in actuality it is value-laden, both in terms of the society in which it is located, and in terms of the education which it seeks to impart. It repays our effort to investigate not just individual institutions and their story (as difficult as they may be to tell), but also to relate the larger narrative of how seminaries came to take their place alongside university faculties of divinity in the early national period in the United States, for in doing so we are better positioned to reflect on Australia's own nineteenth-century roots and the needs of theological education in Australia today.

Indeed, the foundation of Andover Theological Seminary in Massachusetts in 1808 (later named Andover Newton Theological Seminary), the first ever graduate school for ministry and missionary aspirants, will be recounted here, but its beginnings belong to the larger narrative of eighteenth-century religion, in which Jonathan Edwards (1703–1758) played a central role. Known in some circles as a revivalist and in others as a philosopher-theologian, Edwards must also be understood as an educator, who had profound impact on the development and practice of theological education in North America and beyond.[1] His pedagogical importance is seen for instance in his sermonizing and publishing, which lent its weight to serious reflection on Calvinism in the American and Puritan context. His work as tutor and acting Rector at Yale, and at the end of his ministry as President of the College of New Jersey (later Princeton) might also be adduced as a contribution to theological education, which of course is true. However, more significant still was his ministry of mentoring, which was replicated in those who followed him (both theologically and chronologically), which in time led to Andover's foundation. Here we will track this fascinating story and analyze the shape of the resulting institution, first of

---

1. Minkema, "Jonathan Edwards on Education and His Educational Legacy."

all by describing Edwards's legacy, then investigating the American context, before highlighting particular lessons to be drawn from the founding of this significant institution.

The Pattern: A Theological Family Called the New Divinity

Before Andover, there was already momentum for applying new resources to theological education. Epistemological authority in the period surrounding the American Revolution was being contested as deist scepticism and political aspirations muted traditional respect for the Christian Scriptures.[2] The engagement of Edwards's heirs with these debates was so profound that they established America's first indigenous theological movement, known subsequently as the New Divinity, though in its day more often described as Consistent Calvinism. During the revivals of the 1730s and 1740s, Edwards himself had labored to steer a course between the rival interests of extreme separatism and moderate Calvinism which upheld the established order. This environment reflected a deeper theological concern for Edwards, namely to avoid on the one side rising Arminianism which, often motivated by deistic assumptions, promoted a kind of works righteousness, and on the other hand the persistent threat of Antinomianism, which downgraded the function of the law in the Scriptural witness and moral attainment in Christian experience. Illumination by the Spirit without due recognition of biblically authorized teachers had been the Achilles heel of New England church life since the earliest days.[3] To reconcile these poles, Edwards preached and wrote about the human will, the nature of conversion, the doctrine of providence and the place of regeneration in the life of the individual and of the church, though how successfully he did this has been the task of theologians ever since to adjudicate. This theological challenge he passed on to those whom he trained.

The heart of his project was to position the heart, or the will, at the center of the human person, and thereby adopt first of all a voluntarist understanding of human psychology, over against the faculty psychology of Puritan forebears, who created an anthropological hierarchy with intellect at the top of the tree. Edwards's decentering of rationality, though of course not its elimination, further enabled him to reconcile divine sovereignty with human freedom by distinguishing between two types of will, our natural will and our moral will, the first of which was free to pursue its own highest

---

2. See the excellent analysis of this process in Noll, *America's God*.
3. See Bozeman, *The Precisianist Strain*.

good. However the second most decidedly was not free, but always subject to our sinful or self-centered desires. God, in recreating the world continuously at every moment, made our own sin contingent upon our own desires, rather than drawing down on Adam's sin as the sole explanatory category. God's will established our will. Edwards could proclaim God's glory to save, preach for revival and defend the value of the ordered life of the church, all at the same time.[4] His ministry priorities needed substantial theological support to sustain.

This theological pattern was attractive to many of the New Lights, the pastoral leadership of New England who distanced themselves from the Old Calvinism which bordered on rationalism. They yearned for both truth and light. Many young men wanted to learn from Edwards, and indeed several of them took up residence in the Edwards manse to understand his doctrine as well as to learn and practice his ministry skills. There were perhaps around twelve aspirants who came to live with the Edwards family in Northampton, but it was Joseph Bellamy (1719–1790) and Samuel Hopkins (1721–1803) who most powerfully adopted (and adapted) Edwards's theological framework and imitated his ministry priorities. Indeed the next generation of Edwardseans was occasionally known as Hopkinsians, for Hopkins was an excellent proponent of these insights. Edwards mentored these men intensively, or using the language of Edwards himself "singly, particularly, closely."[5] In a world where mimesis was a leading philosophical category, through which knowledge and wisdom were passed on by means of impression or example, Edwards mentored the next generation of leadership by asking questions, stimulating debate and conversation, offering a model, and empowering through relationships of trust.[6] Edwards picked up the venerable tradition of forming a "school of the prophets," which Puritans had practiced as a method of catechizing and training when the English universities of the seventeenth century were resistant to their beliefs and aspirations.[7]

As much by accident as by design, those whom Edwards mentored created a powerful school of thought.[8] Spread throughout New England but concentrated in the rural counties of Connecticut (Lichfield and Hartford) and Massachusetts (Berkshire and Hampshire), the New Divinity men pur-

4. See further Bezzant, *Jonathan Edwards*.

5. See the letter from Edwards to a ministry patron: Edwards, "To Sir William Pepperrell, November 28, 1751," in *Letters and Personal Writings*, 406–14.

6. Bezzant, "Singly, Particularly, Closely: Edwards as Mentor."

7. See Haller, *The Rise of Puritanism*; Warch, *School of the Prophets: Yale College, 1701-40*.

8. Endy, "Theology and Learning in Early America."

sued a revivalist ministry which echoed the achievements of the colonial awakenings of the 1730s and 1740s.[9] They, like Edwards, tried to nudge the churches for which they had responsibility towards a model where an experience of regeneration rather than moral lifestyle was the defining criterion of membership. Formed in the crucible of opposition, and in an era when voluntary societies and independent structures were increasingly acceptable, the New Divinity became a tight-knit network agitating for theological and moral reform in the Congregationalist "denomination" which prized autonomous churches and covenant membership, with the hope that their own priorities might be effectively passed on to the next generation of leadership in New England, and beyond. Networks in the modern world are one of the most effective means to gather resources and impact society, as the New Divinity attests.[10]

The Protest: Education in the Early American Republic

It might be assumed that the Calvinist credentials of New Divinity were unexceptional in a region of America where Reformed faith had taken deep root from the earliest European contact, and which had generated such extraordinary new life through revival of the churches in the 1730s and 1740s. However, after the American Revolution, Reformed faith in its New Divinity guise came under pressure from the new social, political and geographic realities of the New World. It had become clear that new kinds of leaders were needed for the churches, though exactly what kind of leaders were needed led to debate between those prioritizing formal educational achievements (like the Presbyterians and Congregationalists) and those promoting the charismatic gifting of preachers and populist revivalists (like the Methodists and the Baptists). The value of vocational and specialist credentials was increasingly discussed as part of the broader discussion between centralizing Federalists and small-government Republicans as to how education would advance the goal of political stability and social improvement.[11]

Furthermore, debates in the early republic concerning the value of education were set against the religious sentiments of the leading thinkers of the American Revolution, who were often nominal Christians at best, deist

---

9. See Conforti, *Samuel Hopkins and the New Divinity Movement*; Kling, *A Field of Divine Wonders*; Valeri, *Law and Providence in Joseph Bellamy's New England.*

10. See Hunter, *To Change the World.*

11. Porterfield, *Conceived in Doubt*, 76, 128, 161.

in their theology at worst.[12] The extraordinary claim in the new American Constitution that this political union would have the pursuit of happiness as one of its leading missions was not only the first such occurrence in the world but also a clear indication of the Enlightenment principles of one of its chief drafters, Thomas Jefferson. He himself had created a Bible with all the miracles cut out, literally. Late eighteenth-century thinkers also repurposed more traditional Calvinist language. For example, the term "sovereignty" had been a commonplace in Reformed thinking, but now was cannibalized to justify how the American colonies might break with the English monarch and Parliament to establish the sovereignty of the people in a new independent America. The term was used to rebel against monarchical and arbitrary government, which England was increasingly seen to be, even though it had traditionally been a term applied to Christ the King!

However, after the American Revolution, the New Divinity men spoke and wrote in a context, where the notion of sovereignty was again attractive, for partisan spirit, mass democracy, and the testing of new institutions of government created distrust and disorganization.[13] Early nation building from the 1790s to the 1820s was responsive to a heightened sense of a spiritual vacuum. This was particularly evident after the election of 1800, with the victory of Jefferson and his Democratic-Republicans ousting John Adam's Federalists, despite it being a peaceful transition not just of power but of political faction too. Fears of instability were also exacerbated as a result of the godlessness of the French Revolution of 1789, and the concomitant growth of skepticism in relation to biblical authority. Appeal to a virtuous and Christian citizenry to offset the need for growth of intrusive government appeared desirable, so the use by the New Divinity of language oriented around law and government to defend atonement or provide stability was as much responsive to the cultural context as protective of a great tradition. As Mark Noll summarizes:

> The restatement of divine sovereignty from an older language of deferential hierarchy to a newer language of egalitarian contractualism represented a significant new emphasis . . .[14]

This was the age, often called the Benevolent Empire, in which commitment to causes of reform, local evangelism and global mission merged to reflect America's tumultuous beginnings and almost unlimited prospects. While these conditions were not limited to New England alone, and

---

12. See ibid., 18, 30.
13. Ibid., *Conceived in Doubt*, 76-77, 114.
14. Noll, *America's God*, 135.

non-Reformed Christians had a part to play in their development, this project nonetheless caught up the New Divinity leaders, and played into their millennial expectations, organizational competencies, pedagogical aspirations and commitment to civilization based on the assumptions of new birth and regeneration. The great fear of ecclesiastical sectarianism after the chaos of the Revolution reminded Congregational leaders of their responsibilities for empowering the church in the life of the new nation, and promoting God's kingdom abroad.[15]

One further challenge in the early republic was how to manage the constitution of the churches in a nation where no religion was to be established according to law by the federal government. Those churches in Massachusetts and Connecticut which already were established in their state's constitution continued for the time being, but within just a few years both states had surrendered this Christendom model, which then provoked serious questions about the role those churches could play without government support in a world of increasing spiritual competition and voluntarism. Disestablishment engendered an enormous emotional threat to the Congregationalist churches of these states. Indeed, they were known to be fractious in polity and in temperament even when they drew upon the unifying force of establishment. In the northern states, there was also increasing economic competiton, for manufacturing and trade were a more significant part of the economy here than in the southern states, with the concomitant fear of the loss of virtue and discipline as cities grew and accountability structures declined. It appeared that the successes of industry were driven by successes emerging from the hegemony of theistic Enlightenment sciences, which further marginalized commitment to supernaturalism and revivalism, for a "new social setting demanded a new form of ethical reasoning."[16]

On a deeper level, the threats of the religious and political environment of the early national period prompted the New Divinity leaders to start interpreting the revivals of the 1730s and 1740s in ways that highlighted the ongoing power of revivals to shape and stabilize the new republic. There was a new willingness to describe the earlier revivals cumulatively as a "great" awakening, rather than as geographically isolated ones, and that sense of unified activity and agency was transmitted into their own later revival and institutional work. As Conforti explains:

> At the outset of the Second Great Awakening, New Divinity men launched a process of historical interpretation and cultural containment that would be continued by other

15. Kling, "The New Divinity," 791-819.
16. Noll, *America's God*, 104.

evangelicals—invoking the social memory, cultural authority, and sacred texts of the past to respond to the democratizing changes and revivalistic conflicts of the present ... The memory of the behavioral excesses of the colonial awakening encouraged New Divinity ministers to channel and institutionalize the religious fervor stimulated by the revivals into socially constructive activities ... Edwards's disciples "New Englandized" the colonial revivals, defining their essence in terms of a tradition of temperate, locally based, institutionally mediated revivalism that was compatible with the socioreligious culture of the emergent white Federal villages of post-Revolutionary New England.[17]

The expansive frontier and new possibilities for the life of the nation, continuing military encounters with Britain, a communications revolution to match the political and economic ones, alongside theological threats, made of this period one in which freedom was not all good.[18] The time had arrived to protest more institutionally through the establishment of a new kind of ministerial training.

The Profession: The Invention of a Theological Seminary

The beginnings of theological education in nineteenth-century America cannot be understood without reference to this long story of eighteenth-century religion and politics, which overshadowed and underwrote new initiatives. Indeed, the theological and social pressures which flowed together in the early nineteenth century provide a compelling example of the nature of theological education in the modern world, both its strengths and weaknesses. Both Harvard and Yale had defected from the conservative Protestant cause, and Princeton, while not a defector, had nonetheless hitched its wagon to a different brand of Reformed thought, one ultimately less revivalistic in shape and more devoted to the Westminster formularies in content, drawing on common sense realism as philosophical underpinnings.[19] While the apostasy of the New England colleges had been developing for some years, Harvard in particular had more and more morphed into a center for Unitarian thought, building on some features of Reformed thinking which highlighted the atemporal character of the divine decrees

17. Conforti, *Jonathan Edwards*, 12, 14, 17.

18. See Stout, "Religion, Communications, and the Ideological Origins of the American Revolution," 519-41.

19. Porterfield, *Conceived in Doubt*, 32.

and channeling the deistic atmosphere of eighteenth-century metropolitan elites. A new day required a new approach to theological education.

New inspiration for clerical training was at hand in a new kind of education birthed in Germany.[20] The great traditions of German Protestantism, the rationalist and the pietistic strands, had found a new home at the University of Berlin, where Friedrich Schleiermacher led a pedagogical revolution. He was himself of Pietist parentage that colored his individualistic approach to Christian tradition and discipleship, but it was his sponsorship of non-sectarian, professional, and intellectual formation that flagged a new approach to the training of church leaders. In seminars, with reading, discussion, and Enlightenment assumptions about knowledge, order, system and anthropology, the Berlin model became renowned as an apprenticeship in doctrinal comprehension, mediated through the expectations of the Prussian Kulturstaat, which itself had sided with the Pietists over the Orthodox Lutherans in the eighteenth century chiefly for geopolitical reasons. Modern models from Germany were powerful in the early United States.

There had been some attempts at reforming secondary education in Massachusetts to encourage conservative Protestantism. Phillips Academy in Andover was established in 1778 with the intent of cultivating piety and promoting vocations. The Congregationalists soon realized however that more was needed than this nursery of piety. Now, a divinity school was to be added to the site and to the vision, drawing on two groups of distressed Calvinists (Old Calvinists from Andover and New Divinity men from Newburyport) to lay a non-sectarian foundation.[21] Building on the momentum, money and teachers were recruited to create a seminary after the German model in the same town. The energy and relationships of the New Divinity were of course significant factors in its early success, but this was joined with anti-Unitarian sentiment amongst the Old Calvinists. As Margaret Bendroth has said, the great birth sin of Andover Theological School was its imprecision,[22] because its constitution was first created by the Old Calvinists, to which the New Divinity then appended their own doctrinal statement which added a series of careful systematic qualifications, though these were to be subscribed not by students but only by faculty members.

Most importantly, this was to be a school, where only those with a previous degree could matriculate, and where three years of graduate study were to be undertaken with emphasis on systematics and homiletics. If Princeton was to specialize in biblical studies and engagement with

---

20. Miller, *Piety and Intellect*, 52-53.
21. Bendroth, *A School of the Church*, 10-14.
22. Ibid., 69.

higher criticism, then Andover was to be known not for its biblical syllabi but its consistent Calvinist theology and preaching. While Endy probably overstretches in his attempts to portray the New Divinity as rationalist and essentially a movement to reconcile divine providence with human sin and evil, the movement's apologetic function nevertheless does stand out:

> To the Consistent Calvinists, theology was not so much the interpreter of the dialogue between Scripture and historical and personal experience as it was a self-contained system of thought that captures the human understanding by its self-evident appeal and its logical coherence . . . Conceiving of religion as preeminently an affair of the understanding, and conceiving of theology as a deductive system, they appear to have given theology no intrinsic connection to the non-apologetic functions of the ministry.[23]

There was of course an appreciation of doctrine and words amongst the New Divinity men, and their challenging context in the early republic did motivate them to find law-based solutions to theological and moral dilemmas, but Endy's reading of the movement makes it seem that they were hermetically sealed against any external developments. In fact, leaders of the Second Great Awakening who had been trained at Andover were more in tune with the fluidity of the frontier and the need of "an audience oriented, mobile profession"[24] than Endy gives them credit for. They certainly wanted to Christianize the nation as was assumed by Congregationalists in the New England establishment, but this could and did take different forms.[25] The power of the preacher and the priority placed on homiletics at Andover were themselves signs that power had shifted in the United States from clergy to laity, for now the preacher had to win it back![26] The Second Great Awakening has often been seen as a nationalizing force, which picks up both the character of establishment in New England's mid-eighteenth-century revivals, and the need for social and religious cohesion given frontier conditions in the early to mid-nineteenth century, exemplified in Andover.

The lingering influence of Edwards can be identified at Andover with interest there in the example and philosophical legacy of David Brainerd (1718–1747). Though Edwards might espouse a kind of disinterested benevolence, which suggested that true religion can be located where the good

23. Endy, "Theology and Learning in Early America," 134, 146.
24. Kling, *Field of Divine Wonders*, 12.
25. Ibid., 230.
26. See the thesis of Hatch, *The Democratization of American Christianity*.

of the other is regarded highly, this ethical framework takes on new texture in the nineteenth century, where under New Divinity guidance it becomes less a trope in personal spirituality or assurance and more an ethic for social and ecclesiastical renewal. Andover's role in spotting and empowering missionaries for the expanding frontier within the United States and the expanding possibilities abroad drew heavily on the power of Brainerd's model of costly service for the sake of those who had not heard of the lordship of Christ. Amongst graduates of Andover, "Brainerd stood first in missionary hagiography. They spoke of him as continuing to inspire the missionary movement from heaven and as escorting the souls of deceased missionaries into the Divine presence."[27] What is more, the revered Edwardsean Timothy Dwight preached the opening oration and outlined the ideals of the seminary, and it was expected, in Edwardsean fashion, that "Andover professors were to be friends and spiritual guides . . . to be available for private instruction on sermon preparation."[28]

Andover was established to provide a new kind of theological education for a new kind of spiritual and political context. Its founding represented an unstable but nonetheless synthetic aspiration towards civilizing, evangelizing and systematizing priorities. In institutional guise, it was an expression of the voluntaristic impulse of the new nation and the revivalist spirit of the outgoing century, and espoused a longevity intended to sustain the movement of New Divinity. Indeed, its pure church mindset and its methodistic inclinations made it both an example of, and an encouragement to, the professionalization and specialization of ministry in the nineteenth century.

Protest and Pattern in Professionalized Formation

The dynamics which propelled Andover into being, and shaped its early life, can be experienced in the institutional story of many seminaries, theological colleges, or divinity schools. First of all, there is the story of protest against other theological currents, ecclesiastical declension or social mores. To harness the resources required to start such a costly project, meaning of course resources otherwise intended for local outreach or pastoral care, need to be diverted. This is particularly onerous for denominations that comprise independent churches where resources are less likely to be pooled in the first place. Protest can engender contingencies which do not exist in a subsequent generation, or can leave the institution reactionary, or espousing a

27. Conforti, *Jonathan Edwards*, 75.
28. Bendroth, *School of the Church*, 20.

mind-set which is not useful for positive pastoral ministry formation. Andover represents just such a protest, which was endemic to revivalism more generally and to the New Divinity in particular. The demographic status of many New Divinity ministers, often not originally members of urban elites, suggests a movement comprising outsiders who taught a remnant theology focused on the doctrine of regeneration. Many Australian colleges too have to beware this ever-present temptation to define themselves in opposition to a cultural moment, another college, or a particular theological heresy or trend. In a small market, we try to find a difference for marketing purposes, which can be unhealthy in the short term and disempowering in the long term.

More positively, Andover was a pattern for a new way of pedagogy in a new world of ministry opportunities. It prized orality in training preachers, which was itself a reflection of the cultural move against traditional authority which needed to be addressed with new kinds of clerical authorization in the field. It prized a pattern of deductivist theological reflection, which had as its aim securing Reformed thinking against acidic modernist attacks. It appropriated for the American context a new pattern of education from Germany, which also was meant to promote the best methods known in graduate study. The pattern of mentoring of early New Divinity morphed into a network model, which has powerful advantages in the modern world,[29] but through systematizing and defensiveness can lose the power of the personal. Its theoretical reach gave sound support to a movement, though it was in the end a step away from the more practical shape of the schools of the prophets, or home seminaries, and the mimetic model of ministry formation of the eighteenth century. Its pattern was strong, but not secure enough to ride the waves of the Romantic movement, known in America as transcendentalism, which denied the mimetic value of impression and example, and highlighted instead expression, the local over the universal, and therapeutic models of pastoral ministry.[30]

We too in Australia must recognize that a pattern is contextually related. We rightly want to teach not merely loosely connected ideas but to form students in a pattern of faith and doctrine which coheres and which will prove robust in the life of the churches. The Australian College of Theology is itself a body of oversight, which structures and nurtures a pattern of understanding through course progression and fields of study. However, we must also recognize that the pattern of faith and ministry might vary from

---

29. Ibid., 8.

30. See Endy, "Theology and Learning in Early America," 147, and Bebbington, "Evangelical Christianity and Romanticism," 9-15.

city to city, from denomination to denomination, and those needs should continue to be honored in our consortium. We can fall into the trap of seeing Australia's regions as sociologically similar, when in reality each region has significant and diverse theological challenges. The very real formational needs of each individual student must remain our case-by-case agenda.

Bibliography

Bebbington, David W. "Evangelical Christianity and Romanticism." *Crux* 26, no. 1 (1990) 9-15.

Bendroth, Margaret Lamberts. *A School of the Church: Andover Newton Across Two Centuries*. Grand Rapids: Eerdmans, 2008.

Bezzant, Rhys S. *Jonathan Edwards and the Church*. New York: Oxford University Press, 2014.

———. "Singly, Particularly, Closely: Edwards as Mentor." In *Jonathan Edwards, Theologica Wratislaviensia 7*, edited by Joel Burnell, 201-25. Wroclaw: Evangelical School of Theology, 2012.

Bozeman, Theodore Dwight. *Jonathan Edwards, Religious Tradition, and American Culture*. Chapel Hill: University of North Carolina Press, 1995.

———. *The Precisianist Strain: Disciplinary Religion and Antinomian Backlash in Puritanism to 1638*. Omohundro Institute of Early American History and Culture. Chapel Hill and London: University of North Carolina Press, 2004.

Conforti, Joseph. *Samuel Hopkins and the New Divinity Movement: Calvinism, the Congregational Ministry, and Reform in New England between the Great Awakenings*. Grand Rapids: Christian University Press, 1981.

Edwards, Jonathan. "135. To Sir William Pepperrell, November 28, 1751." In *Letters and Personal Writings*. The Works of Jonathan Edwards 16, edited by George S. Claghorn, 406-14. New Haven: Yale University Press, 1998.

Endy, Melvin B., Jr. "Theology and Learning in Early America." In *Schools of Thought in the Christian Tradition*, edited by Patrick Henry, 125-51. Philadelphia: Fortress, 1984.

Haller, William. *The Rise of Puritanism: Or, The Way to the New Jerusalem as Set Forth in Pulpit and Press from Thomas Cartwright to John Lilburne and John Milton, 1570–1643*. New York: Harper Torchbooks, 1957.

Hatch, Nathan O. *The Democratization of American Christianity*. New Haven: Yale University Press, 1989.

Hunter, James Davison. *To Change the World: The Irony, Tragedy, and Possibility of Christianity in the Late Modern World*. New York: Oxford University Press, 2010.

Kling, David W. *A Field of Divine Wonders: The New Divinity and Village Revivals in Northwestern Connecticut 1792–1822*. University Park: The Pennsylvania State University Press, 1993.

———. "The New Divinity and the Origins of the American Board of Commissioners for Foreign Missions." *Church History* 72, no. 4 (2003) 791-819.

Miller, Glenn T. *Piety and Intellect: The Aims and Purposes of Ante-Bellum Theological Education*. Scholars Press Studies in Theological Education. Saarbrücken: Scholars, 1990.

Minkema, Kenneth P. "Jonathan Edwards on Education and His Educational Legacy." In *After Edwards: The Courses of the New England Theology*, edited by Douglas A. Sweeney and Oliver D. Crisp, 31–50. New York: Oxford University Press, 2012.

Noll, Mark A. *America's God: From Jonathan Edwards to Abraham Lincoln*. Oxford: University Press, 2002.

Porterfield, Amanda. *Conceived in Doubt: Religion and Politics in the New American Nation*. American Beginnings, 1500-1900. Chicago: University of Chicago Press, 2012.

Stout, Harry S. "Religion, Communications, and the Ideological Origins of the American Revolution." *William and Mary Quarterly* 34, no. 4 (1977) 519–41.

Valeri, Mark. *Law and Providence in Joseph Bellamy's New England: The Origins of the New Divinity in Revolutionary America*. Religion in America Series. New York and Oxford: Oxford University Press, 1994.

Warch, Richard. *School of the Prophets: Yale College, 1701-40*. New Haven and London: Yale University Press, 1973.

7

A Thematic History of Theological Education in Australia

Les Ball

Abstract

This chapter offers an outline and interpretation of the history of Australian theological education through a thematic approach, giving an overview of the key institutions, students, staff, pedagogical approaches, and wider connections as they have evolved over time. It concludes with a discussion of the features and current trajectory of theological education in Australia.

Institutional Snapshot

CHARLES SHERLOCK HAS ANALYZED the institutional development of Australian theological education from its nineteenth century origins to 2010.[1] The Council of Deans of Theology undertook further qualitative work in 2010 to 2012.[2] Other case studies appear in this volume. Accordingly, a brief

---

1. Sherlock, *Uncovering Theology*, 21–38; Ibid., "Australian Theological Education," 458–65.

2. See Ball, *Transforming Theology*.

summary of the institutional development will serve here as a background for the following thematic analysis.

Early Australian theological agencies were denominationally-based in-house training centers, established to provide the classical theological study required for denominationally ordained ministry. First was a Catholic seminary (1834); then came a Church of England institution (1853, later taken up into Moore College in 1856); by the early 1900s, there followed Presbyterian, Baptist, Lutheran, and Salvation Army colleges in capital cities. The creation of the Australian College of Theology (1891) and the Melbourne College of Divinity (MCD, 1910) introduced the consortium concept. With divinity excluded from universities, such consortia developed to meet the growing needs of churches with sparse resources but a widespread constituency to service. Yet even in the consortia, the member colleges generally operated independently, with small enrollments and small faculties. Independent trans-denominational Bible colleges emerged in the first half of the century, emphasizing lay and missions training. This was the picture of Australian theological education until the latter half of the twentieth century.

Following the 1965 Martin Report, non-universities began to offer degrees, which commenced an era of significant expansion. From 1975, the ACT offered its Bachelor of Theology degree. There was a rapid development of consortial institutions: Adelaide College of Divinity (1979), Sydney College of Divinity (SCD), and Brisbane College of Theology (1983). Pentecostal institutions commenced: Tabor College (1979), Harvest Bible College (1985), and Christian Heritage College (1986). The general picture was a move towards more colleges and greater recognition of degree programs. This brought a new challenge, as the theological institutions had to balance the controlling needs of their ecclesiastical masters with the equally strong regulatory demands of government accreditors. This tension increased with the extension of government financial assistance to theological students and the additional strain on church resources demanded by higher levels of official recognition.

By the early 2000s, several consortia and individual colleges had attained Higher Education Provider status, which recognized their functioning on an academic level equivalent to universities. Some (e.g. ACT, SCD) have the enhanced standing of limited self-accreditation status. In 2011, MCD was the first theological body to become a specialist university (now University of Divinity). Contemporaneously, theology was being incorporated into universities, with the University of Newcastle Theology School (2006, lapsed 2014), the Australian Catholic University's Faculty of Theology (2009), Charles Sturt University's absorption of several theological colleges since 2009, the Theology Schools of Murdoch and Flinders Universities, and the University of Notre Dame Australia. Such moves elevated the overall academic standards of theological education to a genuinely tertiary level. However, this simultaneously generated fresh concerns regarding the personal spirituality and "work-readiness" of graduates for Christian life and ministry. The quest for the integration of deep theology, skillful ministry and spiritual personality is a pressing challenge currently facing Australian theological educators.

The Students

Theological students are "different." The composition of the student body, reasons for entering and anticipated outcomes of theological study, attitude to study and expectations on students throughout their study are all distinctive of the sector. While the general student profile has remained conservatively consistent, some noticeable nuances, if not radical changes, have emerged in the past thirty years.

Theological students are typically older than other tertiary students. Rarely school leavers, many enter theology from other occupations, bringing significant and varied life experiences. Until the 1970s, students were predominantly in their twenties.[3] By 2010, while the twenties were still the main group (58 percent), some 40 percent were in the thirty to fifty range, with nearly as many retirees as under twenties.[4] Recent Pentecostal development has attracted more young students, particularly in school-leaver programs. Students' prior educational level has also changed. The earlier picture of limited post-secondary education has evolved along the lines of the broader Australian population, with a higher formal educational level more common. Gender imbalance has traditionally marked theological education. Historically, students were mainly single males. By the early 2000s, Sherlock notes that male and female numbers were roughly equal.[5] However, later studies show a consistent proportion of males to females of around 2:1, with only Pentecostals likely to have equal numbers.[6] The overall profile of young single male students with limited education and life experience expanded over the past thirty years to a more varied picture, featuring a greater age range, wider life experience, higher educational standards, and

---

3. Sherlock, *Uncovering Theology*, 44.
4. Ball, *Transforming Theology*, 51.
5. Sherlock, *Uncovering Theology*, 44.
6. Ball, *Transforming Theology*, 152.

with more (though still a minority of) women. The challenges of catering for this ever-widening panorama of students have also expanded.

What are theological students seeking? Originally, theological education had one defined goal: training students for church-based ordained ministry. Students entered with that goal, tended to live in residence, undertook set courses with limited but clearly defined expected outcomes. From the late 1900s, goals and outcomes changed. While equipping of clergy remains the most common feature, it is no longer students' sole goal. Currently, little more than half of students enroll with ordained ministry in mind and slightly fewer ultimately enter the clergy.[7] The main interest of enrolling students has become the quest for deeper theological and biblical knowledge and growth in personal spirituality. Surprisingly, little emphasis is placed on the acquisition of ministry skills. The utilitarian goal of vocational outcomes has been largely replaced with more personal developmental goals. This presents a challenge for institutions established and commonly staffed on a clergy-training platform.

Such developments have impacted student attitudes to study and the demands on students. Traditionally, students entered theological study with a sense of personal calling, either as a personal religious prompting or as a church recommendation. Such sense of call generally remains strong and, in denominational colleges, remains a general expectation. Until the 1970s, students accordingly entered their denominational system, studied under the strong direction of the faculty, commonly living in residence with the lecturing staff for at least one year. They shared in the everyday college maintenance and spiritual exercises with regular commitments in a designated church. Students were generally expected to be devoted and passive recipients of the teaching and discipline of the college. In Catholic and Anglican organizations, in particular, theological education occurred either within or alongside priest-forming seminaries. Evangelical denominations and Bible colleges preferred a full-time residential model well into the 1980s, although they were progressively accepting non-residential students. Today, apart from a small number of significant institutions, there remain few residential colleges: most students are part-time, evening and distance programs have expanded greatly, and students engage in a far more limited way in regular campus-based spiritual or maintenance activities. The attitude of a tertiary student has thus permeated the broader theological sector. The wider social, educational and aspirational profile of students has developed a consumer approach as distinct from an institutional commitment, manifest in the

---

7. Graduate surveys for the period 2005 to 2009, for example, show that 47 percent of graduates entered religious occupations. See ibid., 157.

more critical inquiring ethos of higher education rather than the more passive recipient mode of the trainee ordinand. This development is one more major challenge to the status quo in matters of pedagogy, curriculum and student engagement.

The Faculty

Theological teaching faculty have undergone great development and change. Faculty recruitment, required personal and professional qualities, employment terms, academic standing: all have evolved significantly. Much of this is attributable to the wider societal developments and expectations in Australian education as a whole, which has matured rapidly in the last generation.

Colonial theological education was largely *ad hoc*, dependent on the initiative of individual ministers and churches. Until the mid-1900s, theological faculty were typically imported, often parish ministers teaching part-time. The main recruitment source was Europe, especially Oxford, Cambridge or Rome. Following World War II, attention turned to the United States, especially in reaction to the rise of European liberal teaching. By the 1980s, however, a generation of locally born and educated teachers emerged. While many leading teachers of 1980 to 2000 studied abroad, since 2000, more locally educated teachers have attained the highest levels of theological leadership. A growing number of such personnel have assumed teaching positions abroad, a sign of the heightened international standing of Australian theological education.

The qualities required of a theological teacher have developed, though not radically changed: a sense of personal commitment and calling to the role, an ethical and pious character, and a pervasive expectation of suitable academic ability. Historically, successful ministry experience was commonly required. The rationale for such pastor-teachers is the capacity to connect academic programs with real ministry based on personal experience. Sometimes, that experience became quickly dated, with a subsequent move in many traditions to require continuing church service to accompany the teaching role. Such pastoral requirement compounds the faculty gender imbalance, with a current overall male-to-female ratio of 4:1 and 7:1 at the levels of principals and deans. A further consequence of the pastor-teacher model is a noted lack of educationist training among theological faculty. The last twenty years have witnessed an expansion of the pastoral base, with significant faculty positions filled by qualified educationists who are theologically qualified but lack formal clerical experience.

Staffing has generally been the province of the churches, even in denominationally sponsored university theological schools. Early staff were often available and committed clergymen, teaching part-time in their own premises or a central location. With more settled colleges, the general system was a small core of full-time on-campus faculty, typically generalists delivering various subjects. Only the largest Catholic and Anglican institutions had more specialists. From the 1980s, with broadening curricula and the need for more specialized teaching expertise, the burden of resourcing an ever-widening teaching pool became problematic, with a greater reliance on part-time faculty. While the disciplines of Bible and theology were well supplied with full-time faculty, the curriculum expansion to include ministry-oriented subjects brought more part-time teaching practitioners into the fold. One effect of this is the reduced availability of specialist teachers in biblical languages and history, with a corresponding diminution of their core curriculum value. There is also a reduced "critical mass" among faculty, with fewer full-time faculty in collaborative association and the virtual exclusion of part-time faculty from such activity.

An outstanding faculty development is that of academic qualifications. Nineteenth-century teachers had minimal formal qualifications, commonly basic ministerial training or a university bachelor degree. Early-twentieth-century principals often held no more than a Master of Arts degree. After the 1950s, a doctoral degree was more common for a principal, but far from universal for all faculty. With increasing awareness of the value of higher education and research-led teaching, the past twenty years have witnessed a burgeoning of higher research degrees among theological faculty. In the 1990s, a PhD was noteworthy and far from common; in 2016, a review of full-time theological faculty in Australia showed that 71 percent held doctoral degrees and over 20 percent held masters degrees. An associated characteristic is the surge in faculty research activity, with research and scholarly publication being an expectation, especially of the highest teaching levels. Many institutions have accordingly adopted the university system of ranked academic titles. As theological students have adopted the persona of "tertiary student," theological educators have increasingly adopted the persona of "tertiary lecturer." The pastor-teacher has evolved into a teacher-researcher.

The Curriculum

Curriculum is arguably the most conservative element in Australian theological education, having remained virtually static for a century. Based on the inherited traditions of the British or Roman academy, it emphasized the "classical" study of Bible and theology (and philosophy in the Catholic tradition). Not much has changed even today. However, there are some discernible developments, mainly emerging in recent decades.

The driving force in curriculum has been the need to service the churches' ordination requirements, based on a mandate of what constitutes the theological requisites for ministers. In traditions where priestly formation occurred in separate seminaries, ordination needs shaped the theological offerings in the academy. In other traditions, where the theological college was the base for all ministerial training, the college role was similar, since the skills of practical ministry were developed "on the job" rather than in the college, with but occasional and tangential structural interface between theology and practice. The following academic diet was typical up to the 1950s:

> Student pastors normally took eight subjects, and full-time students ten or eleven. . . . The central subjects of the curriculum remained the same as in previous decades: Theology, Old and New Testament Introduction, Exegesis, Greek, Church History, and Homiletics.[8]

The degree of curriculum rigidity depended on the institution's ecclesiastical sponsor. Where global or national hierarchies prevailed, institutional ordination rules set the limited course parameters, with priority in content and delivery given to ordination needs. In congregationally autonomous traditions, ordination requirements were accommodated but, after the 1960s, were not exclusive. Yet even here, subjects were offered on the presumption that the classical studies were what the "general" student body required. Public universities, though not regulated by the churches, were nevertheless strongly influenced by the participating churches' curriculum requirements. Church-prompted curriculum innovation was slow and limited. For a century, there was little need for degrees and no sense of postgraduate needs, with the non-accredited Licentiate in Theology being the most recognized externally available award. The MCD Bachelor of Divinity remained for many years the sole Australian accredited degree course: anything more needed overseas affiliation.

The post-Martin Report 1980s ushered in an era of development, including curriculum advances. This coincided with the growing ecclesiastical and educational influence of the United States on Australia. Theological students started looking to American institutions for higher studies. In particular, the previously excluded "ministry" subjects were finding a home

---

8. Nickerson and Ball, *For His Glory*, 31.

in accredited awards, with expansion into pastoral and practical theology and missions, particularly in the increasingly popular Bachelor of Ministry and Master of Divinity as ordination-directed awards. Field Education developed in partnership with church and cross-cultural placements; however, such units tended to remain academically suspect, as lacking the more traditionally rigorous forms of accountability. There was a residual divide between the perceived academic and scholarly "theological" and the practical "ministry" disciplines, a divide that still persists today in many quarters.

A greater variety of American-inspired awards developed, most significantly with specialist postgraduate coursework awards and a Doctor of Ministry. With the Doctor of Ministry, academic reputability was afforded to the role of ministry education, which has flourished over the past twenty years. Simultaneously, there has been a growth of postgraduate degrees, such as the PhD in Practical Theology (The University of Queensland), Master of Islamic Studies (Charles Sturt University), Master of Missional Leadership (Morling Theological College), Master of Leadership (Alphacrucis College), Master of Transformational Development and Master of Practical Theology (Eastern College), and Master of Arts (Pastoral Care) and Master of Arts (Spirituality) at the University of Divinity. The earlier British system of an omnibus undergraduate degree in Theology with optional postgraduate degrees for high achievers has been largely replaced with an American style of basic undergraduate bachelor degree (in Theology or another discipline) followed by specialist coursework degrees, with higher level research a more remote step for the few. Yet still the perceived academic-practical dichotomy is pervasive and recent challenges revolve around the quest to achieve integration as a needed graduate outcome.[9] This quest has been a driving element in much pedagogic development in the current period.

Pedagogy

One area marked by recent innovation is pedagogy. Traditional pedagogy was essentially "stand and deliver" lecturing featuring an expert master delivering important theological content to a small group of absorptive students preparing for ordained ministry within a particular tradition. Content communication was generally one way, with little if any in-class interaction. Even in the 1970s, a request for clarification was met with: "These questions are unacceptable. I spent much time preparing my lecture

---

9. Curriculum was a major focus of the Council of Deans research project in 2010 to 2012. The need for integration of theology, vocational ministry, and the person of the graduate was a significant finding of the research. See Ball, *Transforming Theology*.

and your questions are preventing me from getting through my carefully prepared material. No more questions!" Direct instruction, occasionally supplemented by printed handouts, was the standard pedagogical method of the theological classroom. Personal spirituality and involvement in practical church-based ministry was encouraged, but as extra-mural activities, not the focus of the classroom. While theological education was primarily aimed at ordained ministry, the students' personal and vocational development was left to separate seminary or on-the-job experiential learning. The theological college focus was the transmission of sound theological knowledge.

The post-1960s saw theology taken beyond the classroom walls, first tentatively, later more radically. Field trips to historical sites, churches, missions enterprise, and places of worship of other traditions became popular. Visitors from various traditions, agencies, and religions featured in classrooms. Such moves had significant pedagogical ramifications, as students began to inquire and even criticize more openly as they encountered theology in the context of variable lived practice. The pervasive societal ethos of inquiry and critical engagement thus became incorporated into theological education: not always comfortably for conservative faculty (or for some students). However, gradually, an atmosphere developed of facilitated inquiry and guidance in matters of doctrine and practice. In the 1960s to 1980s, the traditional lecture, while remaining dominant, broadened to encompass various inquiry activities: problem-based learning for ministry, supervised field education and workplace learning, cross-cultural field experience, individual and group projects, internships, appreciative inquiry building on personal successes, and students' participation in designing learning activities to address items pertinent to their individual situations. Direct instruction was increasingly augmented by inquiry and experiential learning, while the vocational skills development of ministry preparation came increasingly into focus as an adjunct to the impartation of theological knowledge.

Despite this growing nexus of knowledge and skills, there remained that pervasive element of non-integration of the various aspects of learning, a disparity between learned theology and lived practice. Employing bodies noted during the 1990s and later that graduates were unable to marry their theoretical knowledge and their vocational practice. The default response to problems was often one of short-term pragmatics rather than a theologically-framed response, often leading to deeper unforeseen issues. The pedagogical response has been an intentional quest to promote integration in the person of the theological graduate: an integration of knowledge, skills and personhood. This has seen a shift in emphasis that moves "from competence to capability," from "producing competent map readers to producing capable map makers."[10] The classroom has become more than a place for knowledge impartation, with a growing awareness of the class meeting as an opportunity to process, apply, and personalize rather than simply receive information.

Such innovations have been facilitated by the rapid advances and increasing utilization of digital technology. Techniques such as the "flipped classroom," whereby students receive content prior to the class meeting and process that information when the class convenes, are used with various digital platforms and web-based communications systems. Students in "smart classrooms" engage with an infinite range of resources during the class meeting. Even the term "class meeting" (not "classroom") is significant, since physical classrooms are not universal, with different permutations of virtual meetings (synchronous or asynchronous) becoming increasingly operational. Early distance education based on printed lecture notes or video of classes has developed into alternative mixed modes of delivery via digital platforms such as Moodle or Blackboard, with specialized and individualized learning management systems, in association with group meetings, local facilitations, and local opportunities for processing, applying and personalizing learning. No longer are limited regional bases the extent of reach of theological institutions; a global clientele now marks the Australian theological scene. Consequently, the current era features dedicated efforts in instructional design development and innovation to manage more effectively the increasingly diverse and dispersed student world: a work still in progress.

Wider Engagement

Institutions have progressively learned to engage collaboratively across the national spectrum. Pre-1970s, most theological education occurred in separatist isolation from other bodies. Despite occasional social or sporting interaction, the educational programs remained very much in-house, with a somewhat defensive attitude to any sharing of educational enterprise. Since theology was primarily taught by denominational agencies, what little cooperative endeavor that occurred was safeguarded within protective denominational walls. Even in colleges with such a similar ethos as Bible colleges and evangelical Protestant colleges, the relationships were typically more competitive than collaborative.

---

10. Smith and O'Flynn, "Responding to Complexity: Moving from Competence to Capability," 119–28.

In 1970 to 2000, such exclusivity gradually eased. This was a period of burgeoning consortial involvement, fostered largely by increasing levels of government recognition and accreditation, bringing a corresponding increase in regulatory and financial imposts and the demand for heavier resourcing levels than a small college could provide. This "strength in numbers" pragmatism coincided with a general societal broadening of intellectual outlook concurrently permeating the churches. Such philosophical and pragmatic developments combined to encourage more meaningful engagement across both denominational lines and the church and universities divide. Yet even in the emerging consortia, such contact was generally at the level of regulatory and organizational needs of common interest with little if any actual sharing of on-the-ground delivery of tuition. Each member institution typically taught on its own campus the entire degree program that was accredited and regulated through the consortium. While relationships among member colleges and faculties were increasingly cordial and cooperative, and operations and academic standards were centrally monitored and regulated, the actual educational delivery remained strongly localized.

Though delivery remained the province of individual colleges, the centralizing regulatory trend had ramifications for the quality of such delivery. Increasingly, government regulations imposed a high degree of uniformity on curriculum design, faculty conditions, and resourcing based on sectoral norms as benchmarks. Standardization was prominent, local distinctives were minimized, and the language of theological courses was molded into more secular terminology to satisfy accreditation bodies. Collaborative engagement developed a somewhat defensive attitude which aligned theological bodies not against one another, but against what was often seen as oppressive accreditation regimes.

In 1968, the Australian and New Zealand Association of Theological Schools (ANZATS) formed to encourage communication among theological schools across Christian traditions. While it has focused mainly on conferences and publications, it has occasionally represented theological education to governments. A more vigorous lobby association emerged with the Council of Deans of Theology (CDT) in 2008, which has become the peak body representing the Australian theological education sector, with the aim of developing and maintaining standards in theological education, and promoting best practice in learning, teaching, research, and research training. Increasingly, the CDT has evolved from its original lobbying ethos into a proactive sponsor of research and standards, while maintaining a respected voice in government policy. Many CDT members (and other senior theological faculty) are recognized in the Register of Experts of the Tertiary Education Quality and Standards Agency (TEQSA), the national regulatory body of Australian tertiary education. There has also been further development in the theological publication world, with high standard journals such as *Colloquium, Pacifica*, and *eTheology*, and publishing houses such as Australian Theological Forum, Morning Star, and various college presses. What began as a defensive reaction against external forces has become a strongly self-confident and highly respected expression of theological education within the Australian educational world.

Contemporary Snapshot

Where does Australian theological education stand now? Current institutions, students and faculties are in an evolving situation arising from several decades of rapid development. But the question remains: is it now grown up or still growing up? A long tradition of conservative defensiveness confronting perceived opposition held it aloof from mainstream Australian education. Recently, a greater openness to progressive ideas and ideals in content, pedagogy, and delivery has expanded the scope of educational possibilities. Small, local campuses with limited resources and appeal have become institutions with a global reach and both physical and virtual presence, standards of academics and scholarship matching those of wider higher education, significant (though still limited) innovation in curriculum, and a growing focus on the quality of learning and teaching. These elements are as encouraging in their prospects as they are commendable in their achievements. Australian theological education has grown markedly in performance, self-confidence, reputation, and recognition. To that degree, it has grown up.

Yet for all this, the sector constantly faces pressures and challenges. The lack of wide public support and public funding, a heavy reliance for resourcing on voluntarist churches, and the limited observable vocational outcomes in the eyes of the general populace constitute distinctive risks for the viability of theological institutions. Increasingly burdensome operational costs and regulatory imposts have caused the closure or absorption of numerous smaller independent organizations, a trend which is likely to continue. Consequently, the move to consortium arrangements has provided needed organizational stability. Organizationally independent theological institutions will probably go the way of residential theological schools, in an overall move towards fewer and larger bodies involving numbers of collaborative partners.

If this trend continues, how will a denominational or other distinctive body maintain its distinctiveness and competitive edge while coexisting within a collaborative environment born of necessity rather than doctrinal or traditional like-mindedness? Despite the organizational viability facilitated by consortial arrangements, the vexed issue of independence within collaboration remains. The historical tendency has been a choice between absorption into a large body (such as a public university) or ecumenical cooperation with small bodies (such as a consortium). In both cases, the tension between freedoms and restrictions remains largely unresolved. The challenge is to create a genuine coalescing of forces with no diminution of distinctive strengths, to address not only the need for organizational viability, but also the emerging essential need for contemporary theological education to be typified by engagement in genuine dialogue. Such dialogue is perhaps the most fundamental need in the coming phase of Australian theological education: a need for today and tomorrow's world; a need for today and tomorrow's great issues; a need for a holistic theological worldview.

The achievements of Australian theological education are noteworthy and ongoing. Its challenges are large and complex. Its history suggests a capacity to meet such challenges and its recent development suggests it is well-placed to continue to do so. The future may be described as rosy, provided we note that roses have both blossoms and thorns.

Bibliography

Ball, Les. *Transforming Theology: Student Experience and Transformative Learning in Undergraduate Theological Education.* Preston, VIC: Mosaic, 2012.

Nickerson, Stan, and Les Ball. *For His Glory: 100 Years of the Queensland Baptist College of Ministries.* Brisbane: QBCM, 2004.

Sherlock, Charles. "Australian Theological Education: An Historical and Thematic Overview." In *Handbook of Theological Education in World Christianity*, edited by Dietrich Werner et al., 458–65. Dorpspruit, SA: Cluster, 2010.

———. *Uncovering Theology: The Depth, Reach and Utility of Australian Theological Education.* Adelaide: ATF, 2009.

Smith, Stephen, and Leon O'Flynn. "Responding to Complexity: Moving from Competence to Capability." In *Learning and Teaching Theology: Some Ways Ahead*, edited by Les Ball and James R. Harrison, 119–28. Northcote, VIC: Morning Star, 2014.

8

The Three (or Four) Identities of the Australian College of Theology, 1891–2016[1]

Geoffrey R. Treloar

Abstract

As an enduring feature of the landscape of Australian theological education, and incorporating a substantial percentage of the sector for virtually all of its existence, the history of the Australian College of Theology can tell us much about the shape of Australian theological education and its impact in Australia and beyond. This chapter outlines key developments in the history of the ACT, structured according to several primary "identities" which have defined its character and mission in different periods. In so doing, it tells a large part of the story of Anglican and later evangelical theological education in Australia in particular.

---

1. This chapter is based on the records of the ACT currently held in its office in Sydney. It anticipates a book-length treatment of the subject. I have benefited from the comments on an earlier draft by Richard Cardew, Brian Dickey, Charles Sherlock, and especially Mark Harding. Although the chapter is written from "head office," the views I express are my own and are not to be construed as in any way "authorized."

Introduction

THE AUSTRALIAN COLLEGE OF Theology (ACT) is the second oldest provider of Protestant theological education in Australia with a continuous existence from its late-nineteenth-century origins down to the present.[2] For much of its history the ACT has also been the largest provider nationally, measured by the numbers of students undertaking its courses, a standing due largely to its nature as a collective, bringing together into a single entity the students in theological and Bible colleges all around the country and, to an extent, New Zealand. Because of its longevity, national reach, and relative numerical strength the ACT has been a leader of Australian theological education which warrants consideration in a volume devoted to imagining what it means to be theologically educated in Australia through an examination of its foundations and current practices.[3]

However, the ACT has not been the same entity throughout the century and a quarter of its existence. Its evolution over this period evinces three major phases in each of which it assumed a distinct identity.[4] For identity, understood as the sense of meaning and function shared by the ACT's leaders and operatives, has been the expression of various interrelated organizational attributes which have changed over time. The organizational attributes that framed the decisions and practices of the ACT have included its relation to Australian society at large, especially the state; its relation to the church; its internal arrangements and power structure; prevailing views of the purpose of theological training; its theological complexion; its curriculum and pedagogy; and the place assigned to research. Such organizational attributes remain primary factors in how theological education is conceived. Tracing how they have changed illuminates not only the history of the ACT but also the pathway into the future for theological educators in contemporary Australia.

---

2. The fullest coverage of Protestant theological education is achieved by the essays collected in Treloar, *The "Furtherance of Religious Beliefs."* The oldest such provider is Moore College, founded in 1856. "Provider" in this context does not carry the technical sense it acquired in the regulatory environment after ca. 1980.

3. For a similar approach in the North American context, see Cannell, *Theological Education Matters*.

4. In differentiating the phases, the discussion draws on the suggestive typology proposed by Edgar, "The Theology of Theological Education," 208–17, while endorsing its caveats and qualifications.

Beginnings and Phase 1, 1891–ca. 1970: Identity 1

The ACT was established by a determination (or resolution) of the General Synod of the Church of England in Australia and Tasmania in 1891.[5] Determination III, as it came to be known, was the outcome of a debate of some twenty-five years' duration which had run at two levels.

The first level was fundamental and concerned the place of the Church of England in late colonial Australia. Against the background of an expanding and increasingly prosperous society following the gold rushes of the 1850s, generally it was held that the role of the church was to provide moral and spiritual leadership to communities still in the process of forming their identities.[6] Behind this conviction was the widely-held presumption that the patterns of British society were being replicated in a colonial setting. Although far from uncontested, with this view went the corollary that Christianity would provide the spiritual and moral foundation of life in Australia.[7] Evincing the establishment thinking sustained by the close connection with the home church in England, Anglicans felt that it was both their prerogative and responsibility to be in the forefront of providing this leadership.[8] To this end they created the institutions—parishes and dioceses, synods and provinces, home missions and schools, church congresses and newspapers—that were the standard means of carrying out their mission and ministry. The ACT was among the institutions established as the apparatus of the church's mission to colonial society.

The second level of the debate was the need for provision of a sufficiently numerous and qualified ministry for this mission.[9] At first, like everything else European in conception, the clergy had to be imported. Churchmen realized very early that this arrangement could not continue indefinitely; a local ministry would have to emerge.[10] Local theological colleges such as Moore College in Sydney (1856), Trinity College in Melbourne (1878), St Barnabas' College in Adelaide (1881) and Perry Hall in Bendigo (1895) were

---

5. "Determination III, Session 1891," *Report of the Proceedings of the General Synod of the Dioceses in Australia and Tasmania*, 1891, 96–99 and 126–8. The only narrative account of the origins of the ACT is Pritchard, *A Memoir of Bishop Chalmers*, 75–82.

6. Dickey, "Secular Advance and Diocesan Response 1861–1900."

7. Shaw, "Judeo-Christianity and the Mid-Nineteenth Century Colonial Civil Order," 29–39.

8. E.g. Barry, "Presidential Address," esp. 15–16 and 19–23.

9. Highlighted in W. Hey Sharp, "Supply and Training of the Clergy," 202–7.

10. E.g. "Need of Fresh Agency for the Work of God in the Colony." In *Church of England Record* [for Victoria] (May 1856), 88; "Our Clergy Supply." In *Church of England Messenger* (24 March 1870), 2–3. For the background and context, see Gladwin, *Anglican Clergy in Australia 1788–1850*.

established in the course of the nineteenth century.[11] These colleges were small and struggled to survive with few students, limited resources, and variable and generally low educational standards. These shortcomings were accentuated by the contemporaneous professionalization of the ministry in Britain which raised expectations of the educational and spiritual attainments of the clergy.[12] Accepting a causal relationship between theological training and preparation for the ministry, Australian church leaders set up the ACT as a means of meeting these expectations locally.

The specific task set for the ACT in order to serve these ends was "to foster the study of Divinity, chiefly among the clergy." What this meant in the minds of late-nineteenth-century Anglicans had been deeply affected by events in Britain from about 1860. In that year pioneering developments in theology stemming ultimately from the German Enlightenment were impressed on the Church of England by the *Essays and Reviews* controversy which raged through the entire decade.[13] A new "scientific" approach to biblical studies was commended by the New Testament commentaries of J. B. Lightfoot which set a standard others—most notably William Sanday for the Gospels and S. R. Driver for the Old Testament —sought to emulate.[14] Simultaneously with the emergence of this new biblical scholarship was the establishment of theological triposes at Oxford (1870) and Cambridge (1872).[15] The presumption of these new degree courses was the need for clergy to be trained in the theological disciplines up to the knowledge of the age. Around 1890, as the publication of the landmark volume *Lux Mundi* in 1889 highlighted, Anglican Divinity needed also to take account of developments in science, history and philosophy. Discussions at the Australian Church Congresses indicate that, however unrealistically, similar knowledge and understanding were becoming expected of the Australian clergy as a condition of their effectiveness.[16]

Developments in Britain presupposed that such studies would take place in a university where theology could easily interact with other fields

---

11. Cameron, "Aspects of Anglican Theological Education in Australia: 1900–1940." Chapter 1 is the fullest available account of nineteenth-century theological education in Australia.

12. Heeney, *A Different Kind of Gentleman*; Haig, *The Victorian Clergy*.

13. Altholz, *Anatomy of a Controversy: The Debate over "Essays and Reviews."*

14. Treloar, *Lightfoot the Historian*, ch. 10. The developing tradition of biblical scholarship in Britain is reflected in A. S. Peake, *Recollections and Appreciations*.

15. Treloar, *Lightfoot the Historian*, ch. 7.

16. E.g. Smith, "Biblical Criticism," 24–26; and addresses on "Old Testament Difficulties," 23–29 and "The Present State of Historical Enquiry into New Testament Writings," 147–155.

of knowledge. But this option was not available in the Australian colonies. When the higher education system was established in the 1850s, the study of Divinity was excluded from the curriculum of the nascent universities because of its divisiveness.[17] Fortunately, an alternative model lay ready to hand in the "redbrick" theological colleges recently established in England for men unable to attend Oxford or Cambridge.[18] For a time these institutions were not able to offer recognized credentials or claim to operate at publicly defensible standards, but these defects were overcome by the Universities Preliminary Examination (first held in 1874), an externally set examination used by the English bishops to ascertain the academic quality of the students of the theological colleges. Out of these elements the General Synod fashioned the ACT to provide a properly educated and authorized ministry for its mission to the Australian colonies. It would be an examining but not a teaching body, administering standard university practices of written examinations on a prescribed syllabus and course of reading mainly for the students of the diocesan theological colleges but also private students. By such means the church hoped to achieve the necessary credibility and comparability of the training received in Anglican institutions.[19]

Following the decision of the General Synod the next step was to establish the structures that would give effect to Determination III. Before the next meeting in 1896, the college itself was set up to consist of the bishops and other clergymen with suitable qualifications in Divinity with a Board of Delegates to function as the executive and W. Hey Sharp, Warden of St Paul's College, University of Sydney, as Registrar.[20] The college in turn created a system of what would now be called distance education. At three levels the ACT provided an award, prescribed a syllabus, specified a reading list and set an examination. For those seeking ordination, the Licentiate of Theology (ThL) was conceived as the course which the bishops might accept as the basic qualification for ordination. For the further education and professional development of those already ordained, the college established the Scholar in Theology (ThSchol), reckoned by some at the time as the equivalent of a

---

17. Treloar, "Towards a Master Narrative," 31–51; Sherlock, "The Foundation of the Melbourne College of Divinity," 204–24.

18. Dowland, *Nineteenth Century Anglican Theological Training*.

19. Cf. the emphasis on "credibility" and "comparability" in Sands, "A Framework for Theological Education and its Relation to Higher Education Reforms in Australasia Since 1980," 79–81.

20. Minutes of the Meeting of the College of Theology . . . 7 October 1896, Australian College of Theology Register 1898–1911. "(Appendix—No. XX.) College of Theology," *Proceedings of the General Synod of the Dioceses in Australia and Tasmania. Session 1896. Official Report*, xxxv–vi.

Bachelor of Divinity. For the laity—non-Anglicans as well as Anglicans—the ACT set up the Associate in Theology (ThA).[21] The characteristically Anglican curriculum consisted of the same elements required for theological degrees in northern-hemisphere institutions—biblical studies, doctrine, patristics, church history, Christian evidences, prayer book and homiletics, and other aspects of pastoral theology. In providing a body of required knowledge with a view to application in pastoral settings, the orientation was vocational and reinforced teaching by authority through lecturing as the prevalent pedagogy. While the inability to confer degrees reflected in the unusual nomenclature remained a sore spot, the new system of awards provided for the first time the means of organizing and certifying the theological knowledge of Australian Anglicans, and of assuring the professional capacity of the clergy.

With the basic structures in place, the college became operational towards the end of the decade. The availability of the awards was announced in a promotional leaflet distributed through Australia and New Zealand and the church press in 1897. The first exams for the ThA and ThL were conducted in 1898. Seven candidates sat for the ThA, and sixteen for the ThL. In relation to the ThL the examiners commented: "the Candidates should have made *a more careful study of the prescribed text books.*"[22] It was not until 1901 that the first ThSchol exams were held. Three candidates were successful, one with a first class. The earliest available examiners' reports include comments like: "The papers were very disappointing, none rising above mediocrity."[23] Evidently the teaching colleges and the students experienced difficulty in meeting the standard required for sound Divinity.

If these were small and unpromising beginnings, they nevertheless marked the advent around the time of the inauguration of the Commonwealth of Australia on 1 January 1901 of a new instrument of theological teaching and learning. As the creation of the Church of England in Australia and Tasmania the ACT reflected the separation of church and state in the new constitution as a provider of higher theological education outside the public system. In the broad setting of fostering the study of Divinity, its primary purpose was to train the clergy to a standard at which they might be expected to provide moral and spiritual leadership to a community in the process of creating a nation. While receiving little acclaim in Australia, the

---

21. The system also provided for a ThSoc or "Fellow of the College of Theology" which was open to all clergymen holding the ThSchol with first class honours of at least five years standing, and was able to be conferred *honoris causa*. The first recipient of the award was J. Stephen Hart, subsequently Bishop of Wangaratta from 1927 to 1952.

22. *Manual of the College of Theology for the Year 1899*, 11. Emphasis in the original.

23. *Manual of the College of Theology for the Year 1906*, 19.

ACT was showcased at the 1897 and 1908 Lambeth Conferences and hailed as an innovation that might well be imitated by the Church of England in other settler societies.[24]

For the next seventy years of the twentieth century the college operated with this view of its character and purpose. The adequacy of its arrangements was continually reviewed and the curriculum was reformed from time to time to take account of developments in theology and the perceived requirements of ministry to the host society. At the same time progress and effectiveness were hindered by chronic difficulties which included lack of resources, limited finances, long distances and slow communications. As Australian society changed the aspiration of fostering Divinity for the Christianization of the nation also became less realistic. Yet the ACT was relatively successful. Apart from the effects of the national disruptions of the two world wars and the Great Depression which inevitably reduced the number of students and the finances, in every course it produced a steady flow of graduates which effectively ensured a local supply of clergy and competent lay people. It also provided a start for men—such as J. Stephen Hart, A.V. Green, Marcus Loane, Leon Morris, Robert Banks and Bruce Kaye—who went on to significant careers in the church and theological teaching and scholarship. To a large extent in this phase of its history, the ACT achieved the objectives for which it was established.

The Second Phase, ca. 1970–ca. 2000: Identity 2

In 1962 Rev. Dr. Colin Duncan, at the time the Vicar of St Michael's, North Carlton, was appointed as the first full-time Registrar.[25] Duncan's appointment entailed a shift of the center of operations from Sydney to Melbourne as the ACT was run from the home of the new Registrar in Mont Albert. This shift was emblematic of the beginning of an era of change in the history of the ACT. In both the church and society major shifts occurred at this time which impacted the operation and ends of the college.[26] Also in 1962, after half a century of internal wrangling, the church adopted a constitution and twenty years later altered its name to the Anglican Church of Australia. These were changes which secured full independence from the English

---

24. *Manual of the College of Theology for the Year 1899*, 17–18. "Extracts from the Encyclical Letter and Resolutions of the Lambeth Conference of 1908," *Manual of the College for the Year 1909*, 7–8.

25. Duncan's appointment was initially part-time (1961) but was made full-time under the pressure of business the following year.

26. Hilliard, "Pluralism and New Alignments," 124–48.

Church and asserted identification with the post-British society that had emerged from recent demographic change and policies of multiculturalism. Simultaneously secularization subverted not only Anglican pretensions to be the national church but also the claims of Australia to be a Christian nation. In the later decades of the twentieth century the operating environment of the ACT became much less favorable.[27]

But not every change ran against the interests of the ACT. In 1964, a committee of the Australian Universities Commission handed down its report on the future of tertiary education in Australia.[28] One of the recommendations of the Martin Report was that universities and other tertiary institutions should consider introducing courses of a non-dogmatic character relevant to theological studies. Individuals training for the ministry were also encouraged to include degree courses in their preparation, and financial incentives were foreshadowed to persuade denominations to permit it. These recommendations took theological educators by surprise.[29] Suddenly the century-old exclusion of theology from the higher education system seemed to have been lifted. Colin Duncan and several members of the Board of Delegates joined other representatives of the sector at Morpeth early in 1966 to consider how their circumstances had changed.[30] For the ACT the Martin Report heralded a decade or more of change which transformed the character if not the purpose of the organization.

Almost immediately the long-cherished hope of being able to grant degrees in theology was stirred to fresh life. Of the various ways of achieving this objective, the most favored was for the ACT to obtain an act or charter from either the Victorian or NSW state parliaments, and negotiations with the Victorian Minister for Education reached the point at which he was prepared to bring a bill to a second reading in his parliament.[31] When opinion in Victoria suddenly swung against the idea, it was decided that the ACT already had the authority to grant theological degrees on the basis of accreditation by the General Synod.[32] But even with degrees already estab-

27. Jackson, *Australians and the Christian God: An Historical Study*, ch. 13.

28. *Tertiary Education in Australia: Report of the Committee on the Future of Tertiary Education in Australia to the Australian Universities Commission (Martin Report).* 3 vols., 1964–5, esp.143–55.

29. See Roberts-Thomson, "Theological Education in Australia—The Martin Report," 104–10 for one reaction.

30. Davis, *The Morpeth Papers*.

31. See the account of the negotiations and the consequences in Babbage, *Memoirs of a Loose Canon*, 188–90.

32. "No. 9 of 1973. A Canon to Repeal the Australian College of Theology Canon 1966 and to Provide a New Canon for the Good Order and Government of the Australian College of Theology," 5–9, includes the Bachelor in Theology (BTh) and Master in

lished, the ACT, anxious as ever about the credibility of its awards and now relocated to Sydney, sought the approval of the Government of NSW under the provisions of the Higher Education Act (1975). After extended negotiations which resulted in the adoption of more rigorous and defensible quality assurance procedures, the BTh was approved by the Higher Education Board in 1981, the DTh in 1982 and the MTh in 1983.[33] With these approvals the ACT became a degree granting body under the authority of the state.

While approved by the NSW Board of Studies, the new degrees had already been designed and introduced under the direction of the ACT's own Board of Studies established in 1972. The Bachelor of Theology was intended to "provide a programme of theological training at the tertiary level" with "a strong Biblical emphasis."[34] The new course did not significantly change the curriculum, with the eleven subjects required for the degree to be drawn from Old Testament, New Testament, Theology, Church History, Liturgiology, Missiology, and Philosophy and Ethics. For graduates the Master of Theology was introduced for "advanced theological study and systematic research."[35] Encouraging research had been envisaged as a possibility from the outset, but the results were meagre. The ACT itself lacked the resources to train and encourage postgraduate students. The men who came forward as candidates tended to lack the necessary academic preparation and the time to work successfully at this level. Very few surmounted the obstacles to success in the first seventy-five years of the ACT's operations. By its support for first stage research the MTh was the beginning of the reversal of this situation. While doctorates remained unusual, over the next quarter of a century a rising tide of masters awards heralded the beginnings of a genuine research culture.

Degree-granting authority ought to have strengthened the ACT, but it was not enough to preserve it from de-Anglicanization. A further effect of the Martin Report was to encourage the development of capital city-based colleges of Divinity in imitation of the Melbourne College of Divinity.[36] Between 1979 and 1985 Colleges of Divinity emerged in Adelaide, Sydney, Brisbane and Perth. The result was a hemorrhage of colleges as they—ever

---

Theology (MTh) in "Part V The Certificates of the College" for the first time. *Manual for the Year 1974*, 7–8.

33. Minutes of the Council of the ACT, 26 October 1981 and 27 October 1982, *Minutes of the Council of the Australian College of Theology—1978—*; and Stuart Barton Babbage, "Memorandum on the Relationship Between General Synod and the ACT" (1983).

34. *Manual for the Year 1975*, 66–82.

35. *Ibid*, 83.

36. Sherlock, *Uncovering Theology*, 29–32. Nobbs, "From Nowhere to Know How. Sydney College of Divinity: The First Twenty Years," 121–36.

keen to expand their own autonomy, and perceiving the ACT as unresponsive to their needs and dominated increasingly by Moore College and its idiosyncratic Principal, Broughton Knox—realigned themselves with the new organizations.[37] During this period St Barnabas, Adelaide, went to the Adelaide College of Divinity; St Francis, Brisbane, to the Brisbane College of Divinity; and St Mark's, Canberra, to the SCD.

Universities too recognized that theology could now become part of their operations. Earlier the University of Sydney and the University of Queensland had swum against the tide by instituting a Bachelor of Divinity degree in 1937 and 1953 respectively, but now Flinders University forged a connection with the Adelaide College of Divinity, and Charles Sturt and Murdoch Universities created theology departments which seemed to provide Anglican theological colleges with a better alternative than the ACT. By early 2002, Ridley College, Melbourne, was effectively the only remaining full-fledged Anglican college in the ACT.[38]

The effects of de-Anglicanization were offset by a limited ecumenism which persuaded the ACT to accept the use of its degree-granting facility by non-Anglican theological and Bible colleges. These colleges were attracted by the possibility of being able through the ACT to achieve degrees for their graduates. They were further attracted by the *de facto* evangelicalization of the ACT resulting from the departure of liberal Catholic Anglican institutions and the rising dominance of Ridley and Moore College. At the same time, they were deterred from entering the colleges of Divinity by a lingering sectarianism that would not countenance cooperation with Roman Catholic institutions.[39] Similarly alignment with universities jeopardized control over student selection and management of staff, and also portended an overly academic approach at the expense of spiritual formation. For these colleges, unable to achieve degree-granting authority on their own, the ACT was the best available option. When in 1981, after almost a decade of deliberation, it fully opened its courses to other denominations, the ACT took on "a useful ecumenical role" and added Protestant inclusiveness to its defining characteristics.

De-Anglicanization and the entry of non-Anglican institutions changed the relationship of the ACT with the teaching colleges that utilized its resources. Up until this point the relationship had been slight.

---

37. Babbage, *Memoirs of a Loose Canon*, 193. For Knox's views on theological education, see Cameron, *An Enigmatic Life*, chapters 8 and 9.

38. See below for the withdrawal of Moore College. Mary Andrews College and Youthworks College, both arms of the Anglican Diocese of Sydney, were specialist colleges.

39. E.g. Eldridge, *For the Highest: A History of Morling College*, 250–63.

Historically the ACT had seen itself as serving the dioceses of the Church of England in Australia. While it barely recognized the college connection of graduates, it faithfully listed the number of graduates from the various dioceses. However, the need for approval to teach the new degrees required a different kind of relationship. In 1974, Ridley College, Moore College, the Bible College of Victoria (BCV) and the Bible College of New Zealand applied to teach the new BTh. This approval was formalized in the first of the affiliation agreements which became the standard arrangement between the teaching institutions and the ACT. These agreements brought with them a center-periphery tension characteristic of federations as the affiliated colleges used the Board (later Boards) of Studies and representation on the Board of Delegates to maximize their self-determination vis-à-vis the central administrative body. These tensions became a perennial feature of a new kind of organization in which authority was distributed.[40] They came to a head when BCV withdrew its affiliation for undergraduate degrees at the end of 1998 and Moore College followed in 2001, each to pursue its own preferred line of development.[41] For the time being, however, while still under the authority of the General Synod, the ACT had evolved into an always somewhat fragile consortium of Protestant theological colleges.

A further consequence of de-Anglicanization was the diversification of the undergraduate degree courses. For the Anglicans, and especially Moore College, the BTh was sufficient for the purposes of theological training. Indeed, it became a cherished object—"the flagship degree"—to be defended almost at all costs. However, for other colleges it was overly academic. They preferred a closer integration of theory and practice and greater attention to the vocational skills of ministry. They also sought the presence of specific spiritual formation in the students' courses.[42] Their lobbying led to the introduction of the Bachelor of Ministries degree in 1992 as an alternative primary degree to the BTh. Of the underlying impulse Stuart Barton Babbage, the Registrar, observed: "In a day of ever-growing religious pluralism, the College finds itself called to serve an increasingly diverse constituency,

---

40. Minimization of the administrative center from the standpoint of the teaching periphery is evident in recent college histories which treat the ACT as a presumption of their operations. See Brammall, *Out of Darkness: 100 Years of Sydney Missionary and Bible College*, 207, 213–15, 230–1, 254, 299 and 302; Adam and Denholm, *Proclaiming Christ: Ridley College Melbourne 1910–2010*, 39, 51 and 69.

41. BCV (now Melbourne School of Theology, MST) retained affiliation for the research degrees, while Moore retained affiliation for the MTh until 2004. The Queensland Baptist College of Ministry (QBCM, now Malyon College) disaffiliated for the BMin in 1999. Both BCV and QBCM returned to full affiliation in 2004.

42. E.g. "Bachelor of Ministries Degree," Minutes of the Board of Delegates . . . December 14, 1990.

both denominational and interdenominational."[43] At the same time the BMin, while no less vocational in orientation than the BTh, represented a shift to the more "classical" approach with its greater emphasis on students' personal development and spiritual formation.[44] Responding to the different outlooks inherent in the age-old tension between theological training and ministry preparation had broadened the ACT's approach to theological education.

Inevitably this sequence of changes altered the theological complexion of the ACT. The departure of most of the Anglican colleges and the hegemony of Ridley College and especially Moore College created an evangelical, not to say Reformed, ethos which was consolidated by the adherence of many theologically conservative non-Anglican denominational and Bible colleges. By preserving a critical mass of teachers, students and resources, however, this development actually favored achievement of the ACT's objects during this second phase of its history which lasted until the late 1990s. Now a partnership of the Anglican Church of Australia with other Protestant organizations, the ACT's purpose of fostering the study of Divinity was pursued by means of state-accredited and quality assured degree level study and the emergence of a substantial research culture. The number and (seemingly) the quality of students continued to increase. At the same time, there remained serious limitations which meant that on-the-ground-realities in the teaching colleges did not always match the educational rhetoric while the centrifugal pressures inherent in the structure restricted the degree of cooperation achievable in such an organization.[45]

The Third Phase, ca. 2000–2016: Identity 3

Towards the end of the twentieth century a new wave of change washed over the ACT. The primary impulse was again external. Change in the regulatory environment resulting from initiatives of successive Commonwealth governments required reform for compliance reasons and also to take advantage of new conditions as they arose. Intervention by the government of NSW also suggested the need for further internal rearrangement.

The first instalment resulted from the West Review of Higher Education commissioned by the new government of John Howard in 1997 which

---

43. Stuart Barton Babbage, "Preface," *The Australian College of Theology Manual 1990*, 2.

44. Edgar, "Theology of Theological Education," 209–11.

45. See Treloar, "Running the ACT: An Interview with Dr John Pryor," In Treloar, *The Furtherance of Religious Beliefs*, 180–202.

reported in the following year.⁴⁶ Very important for the ACT was the insistence of the Chairman Rod West that the private sector be regarded as integral to the higher education system.⁴⁷ This brought the ACT within the scope of the Higher Education Support Act (2003). Among the benefits was the formal approval of the ACT as a Higher Education Provider (HEP) and inclusion in the FEE-HELP system. As a HEP the ACT became subject to five-yearly quality audits at the hands of Australian Universities Quality Agency (AUQA), an exercise in external quality assurance which it negotiated successfully in 2006 and 2011. Provision of income contingent loans for tuition by the government enabled more students to undertake ACT courses, including many who did not intend to pursue careers in professional ministry. As the "provider" and "owner" of its suite of courses, the ACT became a distributor of the revenue delivered by the then Department of Education, Science and Technology (DEST) rather than as hitherto a collector of administrative fees, a change which fundamentally altered the relationship between the ACT and the affiliated colleges.

Oversight by government also required the reform of governance structures that led to the ACT becoming a company limited by guarantee. In 2006, the NSW Department of Education and Training (DET) recommended that corporate and academic governance—both of which were at the time the responsibility of the Board of Delegates—be separated on pain of deregistration at the next institutional assessment in 2011. The delegates responded by registering the ACT under the Commonwealth Corporations Act in 2007. This change did not sever the connection with the Anglican Church of Australia. The ACT remained "an associated organization" of the General Synod to whose triennial meetings it still had to report. However, the strategic and financial management of the ACT was explicitly vested in a Board of Directors which acted quickly to bring academic governance into line with standard university practices, a move which led to the establishment of an Academic Board and its committees from late 2008. As their vision for the organization matured, the Directors replaced the ACT's self-description (in use from 2007 to 2014) as "a cooperative partnership of the Anglican Church of Australia and Christian theological colleges" with: "The ACT is an Australian government approved higher education provider, leading and fostering a robust consortium of independent affiliated colleges

---

46. *Learning for Life: Review of Higher Education Financing and Policy: Final Report (West Report)*. http://hdl.voced.edu.au/10707/57886.

47. This paragraph is based on Mark Harding, "The State of the Union: The ACT 1996–2005." Unpublished paper read to The Heretics Club, 9 February 2006 and held with the papers of the club; and "A Brief History of the College," dated September 2015.

. . ."[48] They declared "the mission" arising from this identity to be the provision of "quality assured curriculum and specialist administrative support to enable affiliates to achieve efficient, cost effective theological education."[49] Academic leadership of this kind combined with credibility in the higher education sector, economies of scale, sharing of resources and a collective voice in negotiations with government had emerged as the leading benefits available to members of the consortium.

The next step logically was for the ACT to acquire self-accrediting status, a landmark achieved by a decision of NSW DET in 2010 on the basis of a record with government authorities of successful registration, accreditation and quality assurance. The effect was to make the ACT a full participant in the Australian higher education sector, effectively self-determining but largely funded (albeit indirectly) by and accountable to the Commonwealth.[50] Inclusion in the unified national system inaugurated by the Commonwealth in 2011 by the institution of the Tertiary Education Quality and Standards Authority (TEQSA) entailed compliance with the new Higher Education Standards, an obligation which engendered two main benefits. Generally, it brought the approach to learning and teaching in the ACT (and in all other providers) under the direction of the state and led to increasing sophistication of its educational culture. The standards also led to the adoption of emphatically Christian "graduate attributes" with generic academic skills enshrined in course learning outcomes. This reform enabled ACT students to emerge from their courses with the same broad skills as their counterparts in other disciplines within the framework of a Christian understanding and commitment to ministry and community service. Together with the need to supply student course experience data, the impact of these changes was to instigate a move away from the traditional teacher-dominated teaching methods to a student-centered learning environment, a change facilitated by technologically enabled "blended learning."

It was during this phase that the ACT emerged as a largely successful and fully modern institution in the higher education marketplace. The AUQA audits returned encouraging commendations and affirmations along with various recommendations but set no conditions. Reaccreditation was achieved in 2011 and 2016. Student numbers steadily increased. New courses and units were developed alongside traditional priorities in a perennial negotiation between continuity and innovation. The curriculum was

48. *Undergraduate Handbook 2007*, 8; *Undergraduate Handbook 2015*, 5.

49. Ibid.

50. The ACT itself receives no funding from the Commonwealth, but from 2010 75 to 80 percent of students have paid for their courses through the FEE-HELP tuition loans scheme.

restructured in the interests of greater coherence and stronger leadership from the heads of the teaching departments, and new awards in Christian Studies and Missional Leadership were introduced to cater for the rising "missional" interest in relating Christian believing to all dimensions of life.[51] A similar capacity to move with the times pedagogically was evinced when the Board of Directors overruled the concerns of several teaching colleges and withdrew all limits on off-campus delivery and supported technologically driven innovation in the consortium. The board similarly led a deeper commitment to the development of a research-oriented culture among both students and faculty, a change symbolized by the accreditation of the PhD degree in 2011 and the funding of its own scholarships for higher degree research. Educational challenges and tensions within the consortium remained, but they too were signs of life and the desire for effectiveness. Like the other features of this era they were also tacit recognition at the level of the higher education system of an underlying need for the churches to engage boldly with a post-Christian society, pluralistic and radically present-minded in character and little interested in its cultural and ethical foundations.[52]

Conclusion: A Fourth Identity?

Through its 125-year history the ACT has maintained a strong fidelity to its original purpose of fostering the study of Divinity. It has done so through three main phases determined by the changing nature of the institution as defined by its organizational characteristics. The resultant identities are encapsulated in the following table:

Organizational Characteristics	Phase/Identity 1: 1891–ca. 1970	Phase/Identity 2: ca. 1970–ca. 2000	Phase/Identity 3: ca. 2000–2016
Australian society	Nominally Christian (Anglican)	Secularizing	Post-Christian
Relation to the public higher education system	Non-degree outside	Degree granting accredited by the state	Degree granting, self-accrediting, directed by the state

---

51. Edgar, "Theology of Theological Education," 212. The Doctor of Ministry degree introduced in 2000 was a further expression of this commitment to on-the-ground effectiveness.

52. Jackson, *Australians and the Christian God*, esp. ch. 13.

Organizational Characteristics	Phase/Identity 1: 1891–ca. 1970	Phase/Identity 2: ca. 1970–ca. 2000	Phase/Identity 3: ca. 2000–2016
Relation to the church	Anglican	Anglican but inclusive	Independent and non-denominational
Nature of authority	Centralized	Distributed	Distributed
Purpose of theological education	Vocational (training for ministry)	Vocational and "classical" (training for ministry)	Missional (Christian education, including training for ministry)
Pedagogy	Teacher dominated	Teacher dominated	Student centered
Theological complexion	Anglican	Evangelical and reformed	Evangelical
Curriculum	Theology	Theology and ministry	Theology, ministry, Christian studies, missional leadership
Research	Occasional	Supportive	Oriented

At present the ACT is providing Christian education at every level of the higher education system for a variety of purposes in a post-Christian setting as an independent, non-denominational company servicing the needs of affiliated theological and Bible colleges by means of an increasingly diverse range of courses largely under the educational direction of the state which makes funding available to students in the form of FEE-HELP. The contrast with earlier identities reveals a gradual broadening of function and increasing educational sophistication enabled largely by government policy which gradually expanded the structural possibilities and resources available to the ACT and its affiliated colleges for the pursuit of their aims in theological education.

Against this historical background yet another identity for the ACT may well be in gestation. In March 2016, the Dean lodged with TEQSA an application for registration as an Australian University of Specialisation (AUS). At the time of writing, this application is under active consideration. If successful it will raise the standing, and make more intelligible the place, of the ACT in the higher education system. That such an application is taken seriously by the higher education regulator enforces the two main lessons to emerge from this account, the benefits to small institutions of collective action and the value of participation in the higher education sector at large. As its supporters contemplate the future of theological education, continued cooperation between the ACT and its affiliated colleges, and careful and constructive engagement with the state emerge as the best means of continuing to foster the study of Divinity, still for the benefit of the clergy, but also for the benefit of the men and women who seek an informed approach to Christian living in contemporary Australia and beyond.

Bibliography

Adam, Peter and Gina Denholm, eds. *Proclaiming Christ: Ridley College Melbourne 1910–2010*. Parkville: Ridley College, 2010.

Altholz, Josef L. *Anatomy of a Controversy: The Debate over "Essays and Reviews."* Aldershot: Scholar, 1994.

Barry, Alfred. "Presidential Address." In *The Church of England in Australia and Tasmania. Proceedings of the General Synod, 1886*, 8–24. Sydney: Joseph Cook & Co., 1886.

Babbage, Stuart B. *Memoirs of a Loose Canon*. Brunswick East: Acorn, 2004.

Brammall, Anthony C. *Out of Darkness: 100 Years of Sydney Missionary and Bible College*. Croydon: SMBC, 2016.

Cameron, Marcia H. "Aspects of Anglican Theological Education in Australia: 1900–1940." PhD diss., Macquarie University, 1999.

———. *An Enigmatic Life: David Broughton Knox: Father of Contemporary Sydney Anglicanism*. Brunswick East: Acorn, 2006.

Cannell, Linda. *Theological Education Matters: Leadership Education for the Church*. Newburgh, IN: Edcot, 2006.

Church of England in Australia and Tasmania. *Report of the Proceedings of the General Synod of the Dioceses in Australia and Tasmania, 1891*. Sydney: Joseph Cook & Co., 1891.

Church of England in Australia and Tasmania. *Report of the Proceedings of the General Synod of the Dioceses in Australia and Tasmania, 1896*. Sydney: Joseph Cook & Co., 1896.

Committee on the Future of Tertiary Education in Australia. "Tertiary Education in Australia" (Martin Report). Report of the Committee on the Future of Tertiary Education in Australia to the Australian Universities Commission. 3 vols. Canberra: Australian Universities Commission, 1965.

Davis, Rex, ed. *The Morpeth Papers: A Collection of Papers Read at the Bishop of Newcastle's Conference on Theological Education Held at St John's College, Morpeth, NSW, February 14–17, 1966*. Morpeth: Anglican Diocese of Newcastle, 1966.

Dickey, Brian. "Secular Advance and Diocesan Response 1861–1900." In *Anglicanism in Australia: A History*, edited by Bruce Kaye et al., 52–75. Carlton: Melbourne University Press, 2002.

Dowland, D. *Nineteenth Century Anglican Theological Training: The Redbrick Challenge*. Oxford: Oxford University Press, 1997.

Edgar, Brian. "The Theology of Theological Education." *Evangelical Review of Theology* 29, no. 3 (2005) 208–17.

Eldridge, V. J. *For the Highest: A History of Morling College*. Macquarie Park: Greenwood, 2015.

Gladwin, Michael. *Anglican Clergy in Australia 1788–1850: Building a British World*. Woodbridge: Boydell, 2015.

Haig, A. *The Victorian Clergy*. Beckenham and Sydney: Croom Helm, 1984.

Harding, Mark. "The State of the Union: The ACT 1996–2005." Unpublished paper read to The Heretics Club, 9 February 2006.

Heeney, B. *A Different Kind of Gentleman: Parish Clergy as Professional Men in Early and Mid-Victorian England*. Hamden, Connecticut: Archon, 1976.

Hilliard, David. "Pluralism and New Alignments in Society and Church 1967 to the Present." In *Anglicanism in Australia*, edited by Bruce Kaye et al., 124–48. Carlton: Melbourne University Press, 2002.

Jackson, H. *Australians and the Christian God: An Historical Study*. Northcote: Morningstar, 2013.

Kaye, Bruce et al., eds. *Anglicanism in Australia: A History*. Carlton: Melbourne University Press, 2002.

Nobbs, Raymond. "From Nowhere to Know How. Sydney College of Divinity: The First Twenty Years." *Pacifica* 17 (2004) 121–36.

Peake, A. S. *Recollections and Appreciations*. London: Epworth, 1938.

Pritchard, W. Charles. *A Memoir of Bishop Chalmers*. Melbourne: Melville and Mullen, 1904.

Roberts-Thomson, E. "Theological Education in Australia—The Martin Report." *Journal of Christian Education* 8 (1965) 104–110.

Sands, Edward W. "A Framework for Theological Education and Its Relation to Higher Education Reforms in Australasia Since 1980." PhD diss., Griffith University, 1997.

Sharp, William Hey. "Supply and Training of the Clergy." *Papers Read at the Church Congress Held at Sydney*. Sydney: Joseph Cook & Co., 1889.

Shaw, George. "Judeo-Christianity and the Mid-Nineteenth Century Colonial Civil Order." In *Re-Visioning Colonial Christianity: New Essays in the Australian Christian Experience 1788–1900*, edited by Mark Hutchinson and Edmund Campion, 29–39. Sydney: Centre for the Study of Australian Christianity, 1994.

Sherlock, Charles. *Uncovering Theology: The Depth, Reach and Utility of Australian Theological Education*. Hindmarsh: ATF, 2009.

Sherlock, Peter. "The Foundation of the Melbourne College of Divinity." *Journal of Religious History* 40, no. 2 (2016) 204–24.

Smith, William Saumarez. "Biblical Criticism." In *Official Report of the Church Congress Held at Hobart on January 23rd, 24th, 25th and 26th, 1894*, 24–6.

———. "Old Testament Difficulties." In *Report of the Church Congress Held at Melbourne 19th to 24th November, 1906*, 23–29.

———. "The Present State of Historical Enquiry into New Testament Writings." In *Report of the Church Congress Held at Melbourne 19th to 24th November, 1906*, 147–55.

Treloar, Geoffrey R., ed. *The "Furtherance of Religious Beliefs": Essays on the History of Theological Education in Australia*. Sydney: Centre for the Study of Christianity in Australia for the Evangelical History Association, 1997.

———. *Lightfoot the Historian*. Tübingen: Mohr-Siebeck, 1998.

———. "Towards a Master Narrative: Theological Learning and Teaching in Australia Since 1901." *St Mark's Review* 210 (2009) 31–51.

West, Roderick. *Learning for Life: Review of Higher Education Financing and Policy: Final Report (West Report)*. http://hdl.voced.edu.au/10707/57886.

9

Sydney Missionary and Bible College
A Case Study in Australian Theological Education

Anthony Brammall

Abstract

The history of Australian theological education can be explored by way of case study and example as well as through broader narratives. This chapter gives an overview of the history of Sydney Missionary and Bible College, now more than a century old, and both an important contributor over many decades to Australian theological education in its own right as well as illustrative of trends within the evangelical sector as a whole. The aims and context of the college's founders are discussed as well as key developments since, with a number of those that have had enduring significance throughout the college's life being identified.

Introduction

CALLED TO BE IN the world but not of it, theological educational institutions are a peculiar hybrid. They are products of their time which reflect prevailing cultural patterns, but they simultaneously exert countercultural influences on society: in many ways anachronistically traditional, yet in other respects avant-garde.

Sydney Missionary and Bible College (SMBC), recently celebrating its centenary, exemplifies long-term development, growth and adaptation in an Australian theological training institution. Its history demonstrates initiatives and changes in theological education provision in response to changing historical, socio-cultural, theological, missiological and pedagogical contexts. Especially, it highlights interdenominational colleges' unique approaches to preparing students for diverse avenues of Christian service.

SMBC was founded in 1916 in Croydon, an inner-western suburb of Sydney. It has continued in that location for a century. In a darkly tumultuous year, undeterred (and galvanized to action) by the disruption and slaughter of the Great War, Australian evangelical Christians were surprisingly active. The NSW Baptist Theological College (now Morling College), the Australian council of the Africa Inland Mission, and the reorganized Deaconess House (now Mary Andrews College) were established that same year. Within about a decade, other interdenominational institutions would follow: Melbourne Bible Institute (1920, MBI, now MST), the Adelaide Bible Institute (1924, now Bible College of South Australia) and Perth Bible College (1928).

The rationale of SMBC's founding principal, Charles Benson Barnett, was bold and straightforward. His reply to detractors who questioned the timing of his initiative was simply:

> Was not the war draining the country of men and means? In a time like this ought not such a work as this to wait? God's work wait! It seemed like blasphemy. God's work wait! While the Devil's went on unabated with the most diabolical fury, and while Christians supply fuel for the fire he has started. No! No! Never! if we could help it. We were caused to remember that such great institutions as the British and Foreign Bible Society, the work begun by Carey, The Church Missionary Society, The London Missionary Society, and others, were begun when Europe was convulsed by the wars of Napoleon, when England was in almost hourly dread of invasion; and we thanked God and took courage in Himself.[1]

Barnett, a Congregational minister from Tasmania, had served with Hudson Taylor's interdenominational China Inland Mission from 1894 until he and his wife were forced to return to Australia in 1907 with health problems. Fresh from the field, Barnett was captivated by the need

---

1. SMBC, *The Story of the Missionary and Bible College*.

for cross-cultural gospel workers, and astonished by the remarkably scant resources to train them. Apart from Angas College in Adelaide, the only specific missionary training institutions were several small evangelical missionary "training homes," most of which had closed or amalgamated by the early war years.[2]

Aside from the earlier-established denominational theological colleges, which served to train clergy, the only general theological training colleges in Australasia open to laypeople were Angas College and the Chapman-Alexander Bible Institute, both in Adelaide. The CABI had begun in 1914, to nurture converts and sustain the evangelistic impetus of the recent Chapman-Alexander evangelistic missions in several Australian cities. Both these institutions had closed by the mid-1920s. Otherwise, there were no generalist Bible colleges in any of the Australian states or in New Zealand, and little alternative to the theological colleges, which tended to perpetuate their denominational loyalties, and were hardly attuned to practical evangelistic strategies. Amid the growing worldwide movement of evangelistic revival and interdenominational faith missions, there was, quite simply, nowhere in eastern Australia for lay evangelical Christians to appropriately equip themselves.[3]

Foundational Objectives of the College

Hence Benson Barnett's vision and intention to establish a college which focused on knowing God through knowing the Bible, and on preparation for Christian service, whether evangelism amongst the growing urban masses at home, or in missionary work abroad. The college's aim from the beginning was to produce deeply biblically literate, practically capable, cross-culturally adept, evangelistically competent, missionary-minded Christians, through teaching and nurture in a devotional environment. Knowing God, not simply knowing biblical content, was emphasized.

> The Missionary and Bible College, Sydney, is an attempt here in Australia, to meet a very definite and deep need by providing the opportunity for any young man of consecrated life and character, to fit himself by definite study, and training in the

---

2. Mainly in Melbourne, these had included Dr. and Mrs. Warren's missionary home, in Kew; James and Emily Griffiths' "Hiawatha," in Fitzroy; the Rev. John Southey's training home for young men in Grey Street, East Melbourne; "Rehoboth" Wesleyan Methodist mission training home, also in East Melbourne; and Eliza Hassall's "Marsden House" for lady missionary candidates, in Ashfield, NSW.

3. Parker, "Theological and Bible College Education in Australia," 10–12.

knowledge of the things of God, for any Christian service he may wish to undertake . . . to provide a place where they may find a congenial spiritual atmosphere, where they may gain such experiential [sic] knowledge of God, that they shall truly "know Him," and go out and be strong and do exploits, as a result of that knowledge.

. . . In the training, the one thing stressed is the Word of God itself. We aim to drill into those who come here, a knowledge of what the Book says . . . If men knew what the Bible said, and were prepared to accept it, as it is, the Word of God, then it would be better for all. We therefore aim to give our Students the Word itself, not so much opinions or thoughts about it, which may or may not be after His mind, but the Word itself. We believe in the Holy Ghost "in a practical way," and that if we teach and preach the Word, then He will give enlightenment to those who will listen to Him.

The Word is with us the ultimate and infallible authority for guidance in all conduct and belief. We hold to the whole Word of God . . . We stand for a "definite experience" of the love of God as revealed in Christ Jesus. We teach that men must know God, if they are to preach or teach about Him.

. . . But not only are we a Bible College, but we are a Missionary College, and believe that the Church has lagged in her duty in sending forth the message of salvation to all the ends of the earth . . . The result is this home, open to anyone who wishes to go out and preach the gospel, and be a labourer in the harvest field.[4]

Early Patterns of Theological Education at the College

From the start, college life and its strongly devotional, community emphasis was modeled by Barnett on his experiences of Angas College in Adelaide and the China Inland Mission. In many ways, too, it reflected the convictions and personality of its principal. The evangelical, interdenominational Bible college movement—spawned in Britain and the United States in the 1880s—was based around the concept of the principal (and other theological staff) as mentors who intentionally modeled piety, prayer and Christian life to their students. Pietistic influences from the Keswick holiness movement were also formative. "Only by living with people do we learn to know

4. Barnett, *Annual Report*.

them," Barnett wrote. "Ours is not a casual acquaintance, but a close contact all through the day in the same house, generally for two years, but sometimes more, sometimes less. When we are asked to report on a student, we do not hide the faults that we know to exist, but when knowing a man fully, and recognising the sterling qualities he possesses, we recommend him to any society . . . and we do it unto God."[5]

Barnett felt that Christian character formation through mentoring, and acquisition of practical evangelistic skills, were most effectively achieved by students studying in a residential community. Residence was never mandatory, but was considered desirable for those whose obligations permitted it. Nonetheless, the urgent need to train lay Christians as gospel workers, and the recognition of competing life responsibilities, meant that some studied as day students. It also stimulated the early inception of correspondence studies: by the end of the college's second year, 1917, eight subjects were already available by correspondence.[6] By 1920, the college had established a city Bible class on Thursday evenings, for working men and women wanting to study the Bible seriously and acquire practical skills. The principal taught subjects including *Romans* and *Soul Winning* at the Cathedral Chapter House and later at the Bathurst Street Baptist Theological Hall.

Without the backing of a denomination, SMBC (like many Bible colleges and "faith" missions) depended on God's provision through donations from sympathetic supporters. Without the direction of a denomination, the college depended heavily on the principal's leadership, spirituality and theological outlook as a Christian. There was always a need for the principal to "hold the theological line" with meticulous care, as well as maintaining the loyalty and trust of supporting stakeholders. Wide denominational diversity amongst the founding members of the Board of Reference was echoed in the student body, which in 1916 and 1917 alone included Methodists, Baptists, Brethren, Presbyterians, Lutherans, Anglicans, Church of Christ, Gospel Crusaders and members of independent churches. The college was avowedly *interdenominational*, although not *non-denominational*: individual students' denominational membership and loyalties were respected and strongly encouraged, and as far as practicable, students continued participating in their existing denominations.

The college's standard two-year, full-time course comprised Bible, doctrine, mission, and practical skills-based evangelism and ministry

---

5. Ibid. For this and further observations on Angas College and other later Australian Bible colleges, see also Paproth, "Faith, Personality and Leadership," 64–89.

6. The initial eight correspondence subjects were: *Truths Which Every Christian Should Know*; *Bible Content*; *The Four Gospels*; *Foundation Facts of the Faith*; *Genesis*; *The Lord's Return*; *Dispensational Truths*; and *The Holy Spirit*.

subjects. Initially called the "Diploma" and later the "Diploma of Divinity and Mission," this would remain the mainstay of the college program for over seventy years. Lectures took place in the mornings only. And as with Bible colleges in general, preparation for practical aspects of ministry was, from the outset, an integral element in the college's theological training. Although sometimes fairly rudimentary by modern standards, practical skills were taught and practiced with enthusiasm. Early students, for example, were required to stand at opposite ends of the tennis lawn and shout memorized biblical texts to each other, which enhanced Scripture memorization and voice projection simultaneously.

In the lecture-free afternoons, besides personal study and manual chores, students frequently attended and spoke at open-air evangelistic meetings, distributed tracts door-to-door, and assisted the Sydney City Mission with slum ministry. Supervised Sunday preaching engagements at churches around Sydney were arranged by the principal or the students themselves. Within months of commencement, the college's students—under supervision—had initiated public evangelistic meetings at Bankstown Railway Works. It was wartime, however, and unfortunately, the chief engineer called a halt to the meetings, by military order. An anti-conscription meeting had been held at the Works by others, and the engineer felt he could not forbid one meeting without forbidding all.[7]

By 1918 the college was already beginning to prove its worth to missionary agencies seeking training for recruits: graduates had by now been accepted by China Inland Mission, NSW Bush Missionary Society, Australian Aborigines Mission, Aborigines Inland Mission and the South Sea Evangelical Mission, as well as various home mission societies recruiting junior pastor-evangelists. Other graduates seeking ordained pastoral ministry roles were being accepted by denominational colleges to do supplementary study in denominational distinctives. It seemed the new college was producing exactly the blend of Christian character formation, prayerful holy living, Bible knowledge, practical skills and cross-cultural training that organizations considered appropriate and essential for the work of the gospel. The hard work of teaching, mentoring and preparation by the principal and his wife and several part-time lecturers, along with the students' supervised practical ministry engagements, were proving effective.

---

7. Australian Christians were divided in their attitude to the war, and conscription was a delicate issue. Prime Minister Billy Hughes had attempted to introduce compulsory military service, but this was defeated in a referendum in October 1916.

The Inclusion of Women Students

Having started with only male students, moves to admit women were considered almost immediately by the principal. Largely excluded from leadership in Australian churches, faithful and motivated women were increasingly being accepted and sent by missionary societies. A string of dynamic, long-serving women were already making enormous contributions to gospel growth amongst indigenous Australians and in China, India, East Africa, and the Solomon Islands. As more women applied for overseas service, the demand for theological training became pressing. The small mission training "homes" of the early twentieth century which had trained numbers of women for cross-cultural service were now mostly defunct. There were few training options, if any, for women.

Miss Beer, an adventurous and outspoken Sydney missionary on furlough from China, strongly urged the new college to consider systematic, practical preparation of women for the mission field. The Board of Reference agreed the idea was worthy, but postponed action, due to the significant extra accommodation arrangements and expense required. It was simply not viable given the college's precarious financial circumstances. As soon as correspondence courses were instituted by SMBC, women enrolled in them.

Finally, in 1927 the decision was made—a bold step of faith, especially in the deteriorating pre-Depression economy. The first female students were admitted in 1928, initially accommodated in a local rented cottage. Several sacrificial gifts and a bequest in 1929, along with rapidly falling real estate prices as the Depression struck Australia, enabled the purchase of an adjoining property which became the women's accommodation building: Carlyon House. The subsequent influx of both male and female students partly compensated for an acute shortage of funds through the lean Depression years. Later, during World War II years, women were to become the overwhelming majority of the college's student body. Since then, on average, numbers of male and female students attending the college have been roughly equal.

Threats and Responses in the Inter-War Period

In the absence of church support, financial viability was a constant challenge for interdenominational Bible colleges, especially during the austere 1920s and early 1930s. The resource-poor college continually faced the threat of closure as its rented campus was gradually subdivided and sold off. Many students and prospective students facing insolvency were compelled to withdraw. Others replaced campus attendance with postal correspondence studies. Donations largely kept the institution from closing—more often in the form of equipment, furniture, food and animals than money. The principal drew no salary, providing for family necessities through a stipend paid by Leichhardt Congregational Church which he pastored part-time. Other lecturers—mostly clergy—gave their services unremunerated. Nonetheless, the principal took student mission groups on long evangelistic preaching tours throughout rural NSW. Camping out and cooking their own meals, they preached and distributed tracts at country shows, football matches and town centers.

More perilous by far, however, was the theological milieu. Churches and denominational theological colleges were displaying a decreasing respect for biblical authority and a growing movement towards theological liberalism. This Barnett called the "dethroning" of the word of God from its rightful preeminence. Having arisen in late-nineteenth-century Europe, it had made large inroads into Protestant churches by the time of World War I. Now, in the post-war years, it began insidiously infiltrating Australian Christian life and thought. Most mainline Protestant denominations succumbed, to varying degrees.

Liberalism undermined and attacked the foundations of orthodox Christian belief. Scripture's authority and truth was challenged by higher criticism: new, naturalistic interpretations which attempted to demythologize its content—especially the New Testament. Those standing against liberalism, who came to be identified as "fundamentalists," generally asserted five or six essential doctrines which they regarded as being under attack: biblical inerrancy, Christ's substitutionary atonement, his virgin birth, bodily resurrection, the historical reality of miracles and the second coming of Christ. Warfield and Hodge in North America published evangelical defenses of biblical inerrancy against the enemy tide of liberalism and modernism.

Like other evangelicals, Barnett was greatly concerned. He urged supporters to pray for the college's witness to the Bible's inspiration, inerrancy, sufficiency and authority. He responded to the onslaught in two particular ways. First, by bolstering and promoting events like the Katoomba Christian Convention and the Upwey Convention in Victoria, which aimed to refute unbiblical ideas gaining currency in many churches. His second response was the publication of a booklet he wrote to put the case for the Bible's inspiration and inerrancy: *Authority or Anarchy—Which?* It was not adversarial or exclusivist in style, but an impassioned plea for Christians, and clergy in particular, to hold the line on the orthodox, biblical tenets of the faith which were being eroded by modernism. Barnett, no stranger himself to academic rigor, argued that his stance was not anti-intellectual or anti-scholarship, but anti-unbelief:

> Take for instance the fact of Christ's birth. Certain men reject the New Testament account of this, and pose as scholars in doing so. It is simple dishonesty. The Virgin birth of Christ has absolutely nothing to do with Scholarship. Scholarship will never settle that question, only faith will do so . . . The only thing that Scholarship will do in this case is to make it harder for the scholar to reject the plain statement of the word . . . He can only get over the obstacle of admitting that Scripture states it, by autocratically rejecting those passages in which it occurs; not because there is anything in the "documents" which causes this rejection, there is absolutely nothing, but because the statements made do not meet with his approval; in other words, he descends from being a scholar and becomes a literary dilettante, and cuts out a part because it offends his fastidious taste. No, no, this is not a matter of scholarship, it is a matter of rejecting what the wisdom of man deems foolishness and impossible.[8]

The principal typified evangelically orthodox conservatives who responded to their wayward liberal brothers by speaking the truth fearlessly. Australian Presbyterians, Congregationalists and Methodists were severely affected by liberalism in the inter-war years, which rotted the gospel heart of their theological colleges. The Baptist and Anglican theological colleges were often dealing with their own internal theological vagueness or disagreements, and still struggling to come to terms with questions raised by the slaughter of the war.

Stuart Piggin notes that at a time when many Australian denominational colleges were doctrinally weak, and intimidated by surging liberalism, the interdenominational Bible colleges were, and still are, "remarkable for the continuity they have achieved in evangelical doctrine, Keswick piety, and interdenominational comity."[9] Australian evangelicalism in the 1920s and 1930s was in many ways safeguarded by the Bible colleges; and the long tenure of some of their principals—Barnett (SMBC) and Nash (MBI) each served for over twenty years—ensured consistent protection against anti-evangelical trends. The young college at Croydon became something of a rallying point and meeting place for conservative evangelicals, or

---

8. Barnett, *Authority or Anarchy*, 12–13.
9. Piggin, *Spirit, Word and World*, 92.

"fundamentalists," given a relative vacuum of leadership from the denominational colleges.[10]

Arguably, the local epitome of the forces inimical to the gospel was Dr. Samuel Angus, Professor of New Testament at the Presbyterian St. Andrew's College, Sydney University from 1914 to 1943. Angus also taught students for Presbyterian, Congregational and Methodist ordination in the Joint Theological Faculty. The modernist, "scientific" liberalism Angus propagated so persuasively would emasculate all three denominations. By 1934, he was refuting such orthodox, biblical beliefs as Christ's deity; his penal substitutionary atonement of sin by his sacrificial propitiatory death; God as Trinity; Jesus' physical resurrection; his sinlessness; and especially the authority and accuracy of the Gospels.

SMBC played an integral part in the response. Two of Angus's most strident evangelical opponents were the principal, Benson Barnett, and Rev. Robert McGowan. McGowan was the minister at Ashfield Presbyterian, a founding member of the Board and a popular part-time lecturer whose "magic lantern" glass plate visuals added great technological appeal to his lectures. The interdenominational SMBC became a focus for evangelical activity, filling the void left by several now-suspect theological colleges. McGowan led the charge against Angus within the Presbyterian Church, attempting to have him convicted of heresy.

McGowan was assisted by an SMBC graduate, J. T. H. Kerr—his student minister at Ashfield. By then a Presbyterian theological student, Kerr took fluent shorthand, and kept verbatim transcript notes of Angus's lectures, which McGowan utilized in his heresy case. Although Presbytery decided in 1936 to proceed no further, the damage wrought by Angus lasted for generations. Kerr later became a long-serving principal of SMBC (1946–1964).

Upheaval, War and the Post-War Christian Landscape

Benson Barnett's chronic illness and demise in the late 1930s necessitated the appointment of a replacement principal. Eventually, with a measure of hesitation, the Board appointed as "Dean" Dr. C. J. Rolls, a scholarly New Zealander with missions experience and an international convention speaking ministry. Although appreciated by many, Rolls was a determined, private and idiosyncratic man who, although visionary, proved an awkward fit as leader. After considerable upheaval stemming from a combination of personal, theological, stylistic and administrative differences of opinion, he

---

10. Emilsen, *A Whiff of Heresy*, 120, 133.

resigned, took with him many students and much equipment, and immediately set up a new college two suburbs away: Sydney Bible Training Institute. This ran successfully for about twenty years before closing down. Largely stripped of students and resources by Rolls's departure, SMBC regained strength during World War II under the wise honorary principalship of Wilfred Porter, an esteemed high school principal and Katoomba Convention stalwart.

The 1940s and 1950s were exciting times of new initiatives and ardent evangelistic activity. After the war, large numbers of demobilized Christian servicemen took up studies at the college, fired with gospel urgency for unreached world regions. Evangelistic tent missions, lantern lectures, second advent conferences, itinerant rural missions and powerful street preaching by Open Air Campaigners and the Sydney Evangelistic Crusade all flourished in Sydney and Australia. Post-war global instability and the reestablishment of Israel galvanized interest in biblical prophecy, with the return of Christ becoming a powerful motivator of evangelistic preaching.

In the early post-war period, the established churches, by and large, did not exercise strategic leadership in public evangelism. More often, the interdenominational "young laymen with fire in their bellies" developed strategies, took evangelistic initiatives, planned large rallies, founded organizations, ran Bible conventions, and set agendas outside of clergy directives.[11] Much of this in Sydney was spearheaded by SMBC: local evangelists like William "Cairo" Bradley, Lionel Fletcher, Alec Gilchrist and R. H. (Roy) Gordon had strong connections with the college, and taught students evangelistic skills. Although some evangelical denominational leaders heartily supported evangelistic initiatives, most serious evangelism—in Sydney and Melbourne at least—was still led by the strong interdenominational movement and its supporting organizations and colleges. This became less pronounced in the later twentieth century as denominations took a greater lead in evangelism, the 1959 Billy Graham Crusade being a watershed event for widespread denominational involvement.

The Changing Tertiary Education Culture

Like many other Bible and missionary colleges, SMBC had until the 1970s embraced a diploma program comprising direct, uncritical Bible teaching along with practical ministry and communication skills, in the pietistic or devotional tradition. Calls for change began in the 1960s: partly fueled by Australia's post-war movement towards more, and more diverse, tertiary

11. Piggin, *Spirit, Word and World*, 144.

education; and partly by denominations and mission agencies becoming more aware of the value, even necessity, of higher education. Arthur Deane (SMBC principal 1965–1974) experimented with teaching Licentiate in Theology subjects to a few select students at the college. Howard Green (principal 1974–1983), cognizant of rapid cultural change, realized that degree qualifications were increasingly required for mission personnel to enter and work in many nations, and in 1975 began discussions with the Australian College of Theology (ACT). The ACT assessed the college, and determined that both the library and the lecturing staff's qualifications would need substantial upgrading.

From some quarters, there was considerable suspicion and reluctance to change. The transition to degree courses would prove slow, and at times uneasy. Some staff, Board members and other stakeholders were convinced that the theological and devotional uses of the Bible were incompatible, and that liberalism lurked incognito in academic approaches.[12] Several attempts to introduce a degree course in the late 1970s and early 1980s were only partially successful. Eventually a new, purpose-built library, the recruitment of full-time lecture staff with research degree qualifications, and eventually the introduction of the Bachelor of Theology (BTh) in 1990, served to raise academic standards as well as diversifying students' course options. In addition to overseeing a less regimented, more relaxed college than his predecessors, David Cook (principal 1986–2011) argued that spiritual devotion and the academic approach are not enemies. The college's longstanding Diploma of Bible and Missions course was finally replaced in 2002 by the ACT's Diploma of Theology, and the Master of Divinity graduate degree was adopted soon after, complementing the BTh undergraduate course. Affiliation with the ACT consortium has opened to students greater portability of courses between SMBC and other theological colleges.

These developments continued with the addition of the postgraduate Master of Arts (Theology) coursework degree from 1997. Again, recognition of the necessity of postgraduate research degree qualifications—for various avenues, and locations, of missionary service and for theological lecturing—led to the adoption of the ACT's Master of Theology in 2007 and, not long afterwards, doctoral programs followed. Already a center of excellence in cross-cultural studies and preaching, and with so many graduates serving the gospel across the world, SMBC undoubtedly has an important

12. Trevor Morling, the son of long-serving Baptist College principal George Morling, reports that when his father—who held a university BA—took up his first pastoral charge in a rural church, some of the deacons commented darkly that they had "never met a BA graduate who hadn't gone to hell!" (Trevor Morling, interview by author, Sydney, April 2012.)

contribution to make in missiological and biblical research. A challenge is to develop this in a way that enhances, and does not dilute, the community and spiritual health of students and teaching staff, as the college continues its priority task of preparing men and women for cross-cultural and local gospel ministry.

Growth in student enrollments post-war, and again in the early twenty-first century, has shifted the college from a small to a medium-sized educational institution. This necessitates increases in administrative, academic and ancillary staff, and associated needs for more formalized policies, governance, compliance, and employment arrangements. Gone are the days when it could be managed, taught and maintained by the principal and his wife, with voluntary student labor.

In the rapidly changing tertiary education environment, the ascendancy of part-time study has called for some reevaluation of the college's traditional demarcation between full-time and part-time study. While remaining strongly persuaded that optimal equipping for Christian ministry is done with at least some full-time study in the learning community of the college, SMBC recognizes the difficulty of that for many students, constrained by work, family, ministry responsibilities or location. Consequently, the part-time studies program—always healthily supported—has become more accessible and flexible, with the addition of intensive mode units at all levels. Changing digital and IT landscapes, along with pedagogical evolution, have also demanded increased integration of technology into all modes of study.

The Unchanging Heart of the College

SMBC's distinctive internal (non-award) subjects continue to be an integral part of student life: practical preaching and pastoral training, abundant missions exposure, community living and devotional life, field ministry experience, Christian formation, and biblical input beyond what is included in degree-level studies. Accommodation in or adjacent to the campus—single, married and family—remains a popular option, still taken up by some seventy students plus spouses and children.

Sydney Missionary and Bible College continues to make its distinctive contribution to Australian and global Christian theological education and ministry preparation. About 40 percent of graduates enter cross-cultural mission service; 40 percent work with Australian churches or para-church organizations; and 20 percent return to their professions, equipped by the word of God to serve and bear testimony to Christ. Many Australian theological education institutions have changed their names over the years.

SMBC has not, for its name describes the essence and intention of the college so eloquently. What Barnett intended and envisioned for his college in 1916 still defines its heartbeat: *missionary* and *Bible*, in an interdenominational, evangelical, devotional learning community.

Bibliography

Barnett, Charles Benson. *Authority or Anarchy: Which?* Sydney, NSW: The Missionary and Bible College, 1918.

———. *The Missionary and Bible College Annual Report*. Sydney, NSW: The Missionary and Bible College, 1916.

Brammall, Anthony C. *Out of Darkness: 100 Years of Sydney Missionary and Bible College*. Croydon, NSW: SMBC Press, 2016.

Emilsen, Susan. *A Whiff of Heresy*. Kensington, NSW: New South Wales University Press, 1991.

Morling, Trevor. Interview by Anthony Brammall. Sydney, NSW. April 2012.

Paproth, Darrell. "Faith, Personality and Leadership: William Lockhart Morton and Angas College." *Lucas: An Evangelical History Review* 27–8 (2000) 64–89.

Parker, David D. "Theological and Bible College Education in Australia: 1. Historical Development." *Journal of Christian Education*, Papers 86 (July 1986) 5–18.

Piggin, Stuart. *Spirit, Word and World: Evangelical Christianity in Australia*. Rev. ed. Brunswick East, Victoria: Acorn, 2012.

SMBC. *The Story of the Missionary and Bible College*. Sydney, NSW: The Missionary and Bible College, 1936.

Part III

Current Practices

10

Five Years On
The Long-Term Value of Theological Education

ANDREW M. BAIN AND IAN HUSSEY

Abstract

Amongst others, Christian educationalist Perry Shaw advocates that theological training institutions need to engage with the stakeholders who they serve in order to ensure the training they offer is relevant. One such stakeholder is the body of theological graduates. Little research has been done to investigate how well pastors/ministers believe their theological education has prepared them for their ministry. This research investigated the perceptions of ministry practitioners of how effectively their theological education has prepared them for their current vocation. The sample was composed of practitioners from two different religious traditions (Presbyterians and Baptists) who completed their theological education in the last three to eight years and are still in vocational ministry. The qualitative method of telephone interviews was used to collect the data. Findings are discussed and conclusions drawn.

Introduction

THE OVERSEAS COUNCIL INTERNATIONAL (OCI), was founded on the conviction that the development of the church is in direct proportion to the development of theological education.[1] For more than thirty years the OCI has been working with theological seminaries worldwide with the goal to help educational institutions prepare church leaders in the best way possible. In 2002, the OCI Board of Directors established a task force to answer two questions: 1) How effective in preparing new leaders for church ministry are the schools all over the world that cooperate with OCI? and 2) How effectively does OCI help them in carrying out that task? The first question is a bold and self-affronting question that this chapter seeks to address in the Australian context.

The effectiveness of theological education as a preparation for vocational ministry remains under question. In 2006, Cannell[2] identified that institutionalization, fragmentation of curriculum, curriculum overload, poor assessment methods, inadequacy of the schooling model, and problems emerging from prescribing courses for identified needs like spiritual formation, has resulted in a failure to produce skilled leaders in ministry. Scharen[3] asserts that many students experience their preparation for ministry as more about information than formation. Too often, such information is taught in discrete and seemingly disconnected disciplines and the knowledge is decontextualized from the ministry settings in which most students intend to use all that they learn.

There is a tendency in many theological institutions to attempt to deliver in three or four years everything that a student will need in order to be able to minister effectively.[4] Few would argue that the most a training institution can hope to achieve in three to four years is to provide students with a basic working knowledge of the area and a capacity to learn. Nevertheless, this does not abrogate the responsibility of the institution to seek to assess how well the education they have offered to the students has actually equipped them for their vocational ministry.

In his critique of theological education, Shaw advocates that theological training institutions need to engage with the stakeholders who they serve in order to ensure the training they offer is relevant. In asserting a widespread dissatisfaction with theological education, he argues that "curricular

---

1. Ferenczi, "The Effectiveness of Theological Education in Ukraine: A Research Project," 178.

2. Cannell, *Theological Education Matters*, 32–42.

3. Scharen and Campbell-Reed, "Learning Pastoral Imagination: A Five-Year Report on How New Ministers Learn in Practice," 18.

4. Shaw, *Transforming Theological Education: A Handbook for Integrative Learning*, 20.

reform is one of the most pressing needs facing theological education in the twenty-first century."[5]

The Australian College of Theology has generated a series of "Graduate Attributes" for each of the courses it offers. This profile of the ideal graduate should play a substantial role in shaping the educational offering. A survey of current or graduating students regarding the way their theological education has contributed to their ministry readiness should also shape the curriculum of theological training institutions.

Other stakeholders such as denominations, the churches in which the graduate serve, and the communities that those churches serve, all have a stake in the utility of theological education in preparing the church leader for ministry. Indeed, in the Australian context, the federal government regulators, who make available the student loans for theological education, are also a keen observer of the quality and utility of theological education.

However, alumni are likely the most significant voices for the assessment of curriculum. Indeed, they may be the best placed to make an assessment of the value of their theological education for their current ministry effectiveness. As Shaw points out,[6] it often takes several years after graduation to determine (a) what learning from the program has been most useful for ministry; (b) what learning has been largely irrelevant; and (c) what areas of knowledge and skill necessary for effective ministry were missing from the program.

There has been little research done to investigate how well pastors/ministers believe their theological education has prepared them for their ministry. Shaw cites just four.[7] Banks,[8] in a survey of theological schools discovered that fewer than 40 percent of theological students felt theological education helped them to grow spiritually. Dearborn,[9] expressing his conclusions in bluntly negative terms, found that graduating students felt "spiritually cold, theologically confused, biblically uncertain, relationally calloused and professionally unprepared." Burke[10] found that 45 percent of students felt that deficiencies in their theological education caused stress because it did not provide training in practical, interpersonal and counseling skills. However, these research projects focused on current and graduating

---

5. Ibid., 17.

6. Ibid., 56.

7. Ibid., 89.

8. Banks, *Reenvisioning Theological Education: Exploring a Missional Alternative to Current Models*, 200.

9. Dearborn, "Preparing New Leaders for the Church of the Future: Transforming Theological Education through Multi-Institutional Partnerships," 7.

10. Burke, "Time to Leave the Wilderness?: The Teaching of Pastoral Theology in Southeast Asia," 263–84.

students only, rather than those several years beyond their initial training and in the pastorate.

VerBerkmoes[11] and his colleagues did, however, research the experience of practicing pastors. Nearly 700 pastors based in the United States were surveyed to identify competencies and dispositions they believed were most essential to effective pastoral ministry and the experiences that were most influential in developing these qualities. The competencies and dispositions were further clarified through a series of six focus groups. Finally, an online questionnaire (n=453) was used to rank the importance of the competencies and which experiences fostered each competency.

The competencies, ranked in order of importance as identified by the participants, were defined as follows:

1. Integrity: Being honest, trustworthy, moral and genuine
2. *Bible*: Understands the themes and content of Scripture
3. Loving: Love for God and others, compassionate and forgiving
4. *Exegesis*: Knowledge and skills to interpret and apply Scripture
5. *Preaching*: Ability to proclaim Biblical truth in a manner that connects with your listeners to motivate transformation
6. Theology: Foundational beliefs of one's own and other Christian traditions
7. Humility: Teachable, servant's heart, accepts criticism
8. *Teaching*: Ability to communicate biblical information in a way that people understand
9. Interpersonal Skills: Ability to relate with people in an open, affirming and direct manner
10. Resilient: Persevering, committed, and faithful through complex relationships and circumstances
11. Leadership: Ability to influence others to live out the biblical values and to pursue a shared vision
12. Self-Aware: Understanding one's own giftedness, personality, and emotional health
13. Patient: Slow to anger, calm
14. Impartial: Fair-minded, not choosing favorites, not rushing to judgment

11. VerBerkmoes et al., *Research Report: Transformation Theological Education 1.0*.

15. Pastoral Theology and Care: Provides care for congregants from a theologically informed perspective
16. Positive: Joyful, optimistic, friendly
17. Cultural Awareness: Understands and responds to attitudes, beliefs and values of local community and broader context
18. Administration: Ability to organize and manage self, people, and resources
19. *Counseling*: Ability to listen to, encourage, and guide people to experience wholeness rooted in Christ
20. *Church History*: Understands historical development of the church including denominational history
21. *Languages*: Able to utilize Greek and Hebrew and related resources in the study of Scripture.

Participants identified that formal theological education was the most influential factor in fostering only those competencies that are listed in italics above. In other words, formal theological education was only an influential factor in developing about a third of competencies that practitioners identified as being essential for effective pastoral ministry. Although three of the five most important competencies were developed during their formal theological education, so were those regarded by participants as being the three least important.

Although emerging from a different context, VerBerkmoes' research informs the design of the research reported in this chapter. The idea of asking participants to first identify the key competencies for successful pastoral ministry and then asking them to identify the extent to which their theological education has equipped them for pastoral ministry will be adopted. The identified competencies are also a good starting point for this research.

Methodology

The research reported in this chapter aimed to learn from ministry practitioners the aspects of their theological education that have proved most helpful for ministry effectiveness. In order to answer this question, the researchers drew on a sample of ministry practitioners based in the same part of the same country (Queensland, Australia) but from within their two different Christian traditions: Queensland Baptists (graduates of Malyon College, Brisbane, Queensland) and Queensland Presbyterians (graduates of Queensland Theological College (QTC), Brisbane, Queensland). Although both are evangelical colleges, they represent the two ends of a spectrum of colleges in the Australian College of Theology consortium. QTC is self-described as a Reformed evangelical institution with a strong emphasis on the Bible as the fundamental basis of ministry. Hence, it tends to focus on the teaching of the Bible and theology and relatively less so on pastoral and practical ministry subjects/units. In contrast, Malyon has a greater emphasis on practical theology and so teaches a greater number of ministry and practical units as well as Bible and theology.

The Baptist researcher, Ian Hussey, conducted research amongst the Presbyterians, and the Presbyterian researcher, Andrew Bain, conducted the research amongst the Baptists. This was to assist participants to be more open and honest because the researcher they were speaking to did not come from within their own denomination nor the theological training college where they had studied.

Using the denominational databases, ministry practitioners who completed their theological education between three and eight years prior to the research were invited to participate in the research. The selection of this particular sample was purposeful. It was based on the assumption that this sample group would have been involved in pastoral ministry for a sufficient period of time to be able to make an informed judgment of what competencies were needed for effective ministry, but were also "close enough" to their theological education to be able to remember and identify what aspects of that theological education have proved to be valuable for ministry effectiveness.

The participants were invited to take part in the research via an email. If the ministry practitioner agreed to participate they were contacted by one of the researchers to arrange a telephone interview which lasted for about thirty minutes. A series of open-ended questions were asked and the responses recorded and analyzed. The questions were:

1. How long have you been in pastoral ministry?
2. How long since you finished your primary theological education?
3. What have you discovered, from experience, are the key competencies which enable vocational ministry effectiveness?
4. What adjectives would you use to describe your theological education?
5. How effective was your theological education in preparing you for vocational ministry?
    - Very effective, somewhat effective, ineffective or very ineffective?

6. What aspects of your theological education have proved most helpful for your ministry effectiveness? Why?
7. Can you tell a story of when some aspect of your theological education proved useful in pastoral ministry?
8. What aspects of your theological education have proved least useful for your ministry effectiveness?
9. What could be done to make theological education more useful for equipping people for vocational church ministry?
10. Counseling, languages and church history have been identified in one study as being least important for pastoral competency. What are your thoughts on these aspects of theological education?

A summary of the data emerging from these interviews is presented in the next section.

Findings

Sixteen participants, eight from Queensland Theological College (Presbyterians) and eight from Malyon College (Baptists) participated in the research. Their period in vocational ministry varied between three and seven years, and the period since they had graduated from their primary theological education also varied between three and seven years.

When asked what they had discovered through their own experience of ministry to be the key competencies to enable ministry effectiveness, the two strongest responses were "people skills" and preaching/teaching. More than one of the participants also identified pastoral care and counseling, administration, spiritual vibrancy, the ability to think theologically, listening/communication, self-awareness, and a good grounding in the Scriptures.

When asked to nominate adjectives to describe their theological education the most common response was "stretching/pressured." Other common responses included "interesting/stimulating" and "helpful."

All sixteen participants indicated that their theological education was either "very effective" (4) or "somewhat effective" (12) in preparing them for vocational ministry. Given that the participants were given the option of also nominating "ineffective" and "very ineffective" this finding suggests that ministry practitioners are at least generally satisfied with the effectiveness of their theological education, although the fact that only four nominated "very effective" suggests that there is still some scope for improvement.

When asked to identify what aspects of their theological education proved most helpful for ministry effectiveness, the most common responses were preaching, exegesis, and access to faculty. One student commented, "Skills in interpreting the Bible in a biblical theological system. If you can't do that it doesn't matter how good your website is." Study of church history and the benefits of the college community were also identified as helpful contributors. One student commented, "I was somebody who was passionately disinterested in church history when I started Bible college and I became interested in it. I was able to see that essentially there is no new thought happening in the world." With respect to community one student said, "Knowing lots of other people in pastoral ministry and being supported by them, and supporting them, bouncing ideas off them, knowing just the right things to pray for at just the right time, is really effective." The Malyon graduates also indicated that the field education program was valuable in developing general practical skills. (It should be noted that QTC does not offer the ACT's field education units as Malyon does. Student placements with churches are instead organized at a denominational level.)

When asked what aspects of their theological education had proved least useful for ministry effectiveness, most students indicated that it was "all helpful." As one student said, "I don't remember thinking, 'That was not useful.'" The least useful aspect of their college experience for more than one student was rote learning of languages. Although two students from Malyon also struggled to identify the relevance of exegesis units, three other students identified the exegesis units as the most helpful aspects of their theological experience.

When asked what could be done to make theological education more useful for equipping people for vocational church ministry a number of the QTC graduates suggested "lecturers with real-world experience in pastoral ministry." This appears to reflect their having studied at QTC during a period in which the principal at the time was a leading academic but with limited church leadership experience. Three of the Malyon graduates suggested that more on conflict resolution would be useful, and students from both colleges indicated that a closer connection between training in the local church and the college would have significantly improved their training experience for ministry.

When asked to respond to the findings of VerBerkmoes[12] and his colleagues which suggested that counseling, languages and church history were the areas of study least critical for effective pastoral ministry, generally the graduates disagreed. In each case the majority were able to give examples

12. Ibid.

where skills in counseling and languages and insights from church history units had proved helpful in their pastoral ministry. Graduates almost uniformly indicated that they were not seeking advanced counseling expertise, but the basic skills which would enable them to be able to make initial responses and referrals when necessary. However, several graduates suggested that the rote learning of languages had not proved helpful. For a number of students, Hebrew had proved less useful than Greek.

Discussion of Findings

Perhaps the most significant finding of the research is that all the graduates from both colleges identified their theological training as somewhat or very effective for pastoral ministry. This affirmation of their theological training was confirmed by their responses to the question about which aspects of their theological education proved least useful—over half the participants indicated that it was "all helpful" and the possible improvements were quite diverse reflecting the individual preferences of the students and no consistently common issues.

Rightly, students, colleges, the government that provides loans for student fees, and other stakeholders, are keen to see that the theological education offered by colleges is "fit for purpose." Although there is certainly scope for improvement, this research would indicate that, on the whole, their theological education has adequately equipped the students for their ministry practice.

A majority of the participants indicated that "people skills" are a key competency to enable ministry effectiveness. Students certainly appreciate the biblical and theological foundation they are receiving in the colleges, but they discover in pastoral ministry that they also need relational skills in order to be effective, and often come to the view that greater training and development in this area during their studies would have been helpful. This would confirm Burke's[13] (2010) finding that many students felt that deficiencies in their theological education caused stress because it did not provide training in practical, interpersonal and counseling skills. Even though QTC offers fewer formal church leadership and pastoral ministry units than Malyon does, graduates still reflected on the skills that they had informally learnt from their lecturers. For example, one QTC graduate, when asked about what aspect of theological education proved useful for ministry, recounted a lecturer who gave the saying, "Slowly, slowly catch the monkey."

13. Burke, "Time to Leave the Wilderness?: The Teaching of Pastoral Theology in Southeast Asia," 263–84.

He went on to say, "When you start ministry you can want to start lopping off heads. But you have to start slowly in ministry." This would appear to indicate that additional input from the colleges in this area may not necessarily need to take the form of requiring further formal units of study.

Coupled with the fact that when students were prompted they identified pastoral care and people skills as areas where their theological education could have been more helpful, equipping students with interpersonal and church leadership skills (whether formally or informally), is clearly an area that colleges need to take seriously, investigating how they might be able to help students develop more effectively. This can be done while still recognizing that some training in a practical area such as this might occur beyond the college and in the local church for students.

Although students at both colleges found their theological education was somewhat or very effective in preparing them for pastoral ministry, when asked to give an adjective to describe their theological training experience the most common response was that it had been a stretching and challenging experience. One of the notable points of difference between the colleges in relation to this research is that students at QTC tend to be full-time students with an undergraduate degree when they commence, while the students at Malyon tend to be part-time students without an undergraduate degree. Given the study considered two groups of graduates whose study experience was quite different in this regard, it is quite notable that the primary adjectives used across both groups to describe their experience was "stretching" or "challenging." In some senses this is not a negative thing. Education by its very nature should be stretching and challenging, and for some respondents these terms were clearly used to refer to both positive and negative elements of their training. However, colleges need to carefully consider student workloads to avoid placing undue pressure on students if possible, while still working to "stretch" students in a positive sense. As Cannell warns, curriculum overload can result in a failure to produce effectively skilled leaders in ministry.[14]

Reflecting the evangelical ethos of both colleges, graduates identified the training they received in preaching and exegesis as being the most helpful aspects of their theological education now that they are ministry practitioners. Both colleges are clearly "getting it right" when they emphasize these more "traditional" aspects of theological education, even though two of the Malyon graduates struggled to see the relevance of the exegesis units. There are doubtless dozens of different units that could be integrated into theological degrees in ACT consortium colleges, but this research confirms

---

14. Cannell, *Theological Education Matters*, 32–42.

the assumption of evangelical training colleges that the students who study at their college need to be able to exercise well developed exegesis and preaching skills when they move into pastoral ministry.

That being said, one of the interesting aspects that emerged from the research was the high value that the Malyon graduates put on their field education experience. Certainly, they valued their Bible and theology units, but the sheer strength and consistency with which they spoke of the positive benefits of a formal and structured field education experience invites colleges which do not offer field education to consider whether they could better equip their students for vocational ministry if they were to also offer the students a supervised field education experience as a unit.

The research also confirmed the utility of counseling, languages and church history for ministry practice. The divergence from the finding of VerBerkmoes[15] and his colleagues is probably explained by the different contexts. Certainly, within the Australian evangelical context of the colleges in this research the theological education they offer, the basic practical counseling skills provided for students, and the insights gleaned from the biblical languages and church history, are highly valued. Another factor in this diversion from VerBerkmoes' findings may be that church history at both QTC and Malyon is taught by specialist church historians who are full-time faculty members. It is reasonable to conclude, though, that student satisfaction with any unit is dependent to a large extent on the quality of the teacher of that unit.

However, this research does suggest, based on the feedback of graduates of both colleges, that the rote learning of original languages has not always proved useful for graduates, even while some have found substantial language study to be quite useful for ministry. Driven by denominational requirements, students at QTC must study substantial Greek plus some Hebrew. In contrast, at Malyon all students are required to do a basic unit of Greek which does not require extensive memorization. Students can, and many do, elect to study Greek in more depth and undertake Greek exegesis units. A similar option is being developed for Hebrew. Colleges obviously need to respond to the expectations of their stakeholders, but the option of offering original languages for those who want to pursue them as valuable for their ministry training, while also offering the option of a more basic engagement with original languages, especially with use of the technological tools now available, would seem a favored option for a number of graduates. The responses of the graduates considered in this exercise would also indicate that the current pedagogical assumption built into the ACT's

---

15. VerBerkmoes et al., *Research Report: Transformation Theological Education 1.0*.

requirements (and those of some other institutions) for language learning and assessment, that memorization is central to the exercise, could be reconsidered.

Conclusions and Recommendations

1. The research reported in this chapter is largely affirming of the colleges' current approach to theological education of students for pastoral ministry. Although there is still scope for improvement the research indicates that the training provided by these two colleges, and by implication potentially other colleges within the ACT consortium, is "fit for purpose."

2. The foundations laid by biblical units (especially exegesis), systematic theology, church history, preaching and languages, form a basis which meets the expectations of not just the students but other stakeholders such as local churches.

3. However, ministry practitioners also highlight the critical importance of training in people skills and pastoral leadership. Whether colleges pursue this goal informally or through offering practical ministry units or field education, they need to be intentional about developing these skills because otherwise the biblical foundation that is laid may not be effectively applied in real relationships and ministry situations. Related to this is the importance of colleges, together with denominations and pastors, working to develop creative and effective ways of better integrating the learning that occurs at college with that which occurs simultaneously in their churches.

4. Colleges should consider whether they are philosophically committed to the ideal that all students study the original languages (or do so to a substantial degree), and learn these in a manner which relies heavily on memorization. Whilst it is doubtless of great benefit to some students, for others it was the least helpful aspect of their theological education and detracted from their capacity to learn and develop in other areas. Certainly, pedagogical choices should be driven by philosophy, not just the preferences of students, but clearly a valid contributor to any well-formed pedagogical philosophy is the incorporation of the preferences of stakeholders, including the students themselves.

Bibliography

Banks, Robert. *Reenvisioning Theological Education: Exploring a Missional Alternative to Current Models*. Grand Rapids: Eerdmans, 1999.

Burke, David. "Time to Leave the Wilderness?: The Teaching of Pastoral Theology in Southeast Asia." In *Tending the Seed Beds: Educational Perspectives on Theological Education in Asia*, edited by A. Harkness, 263–84. Quezon City: Asia Theological Association, 2010.

Cannell, Linda. *Theological Education Matters: Leadership Education for the Church*. Newburgh: EDCOT, 2006.

Dearborn, Tim. "Preparing New Leaders for the Church of the Future: Transforming Theological Education through Multi-Institutional Partnerships." *Transformation* 12, no. 4 (1995) 7–12.

Ferenczi, Jason. "The Effectiveness of Theological Education in Ukraine: A Research Project." *Theological Reflections*, no. 7 (2006) 178–205.

Scharen, Christian A.B., and Eileen R. Campbell-Reed. "Learning Pastoral Imagination: A Five-Year Report on How New Ministers Learn in Practice." *Auburn Studies* 21 (2016).

Shaw, Perry. *Transforming Theological Education: A Handbook for Integrative Learning*. Carlisle: Langham Global Library, 2014.

VerBerkmoes, John F, et al. *Research Report: Transformation Theological Education 1.0*. Grand Rapids: Grand Rapids Theological Seminary, Cornerstone University, 2011.

11

A Chinese Perspective on Theological Education

Wally Wang

Abstract

The research reported in this chapter investigated the interplay between Chinese culture and theological education through the eyes of six lecturers teaching in the three Chinese programs within the Australian College of Theology consortium. It looked at how Chinese culture would influence the teacher-student relationship, classroom delivery method, choices of lecture materials and assessment instruments. The research found that the Chinese cultural background of these lecturers was a valuable asset in their teaching, especially in their choices of lecture materials and assessment instruments. However, their cultural background, as well as their students', did affect their interaction with their students as well as the classroom delivery method.

Introduction

According to cultural anthropology, culture is a comprehensive system of meanings and instructions, which is developed by a group of people over a long period. This system helps this group to organize their lives by guiding their interactions with one other and providing meanings to their actions and goals so that they can survive as a coherent group within this world. Just as human beings living on earth are not conscious of the air they are breathing, those living within a particular culture will not be aware of their own culture.[1] Only when people encounter a different culture will they start to recognize their own culture. Furthermore, culture is learned and not innate.[2] As the circumstance facing a group changes, its culture will also change in order to adapt to the new situation.[3] Therefore, culture is never a static phenomenon and it will evolve over time. In addition, we know that no human being can comprehend an event with total unbiased objectivity. Not only do people understand things through their own cultural lens but they also express thoughts in their own peculiar cultural way. When people from different cultures come to the Bible, they are seeking answers to their concerns arising from that particular cultural setting. They also express their findings through their own cultural conventions. Consequently, different cultures will construct theology differently.[4] There is no single Christian theology, but Christian theologies. So, if the influence of culture upon theology cannot be denied, it will also be apparent in theological education.

Within the Australian College of Theology (ACT) consortium, three colleges have Chinese programs. Faculties in these programs mainly consist of first-generation migrants from Asian countries, as do the student bodies. Even though the courses and subjects (units) offered are set up and regulated under the ACT guidelines, the subjects are taught in Mandarin. In this chapter, we will look at the interplay between Chinese culture and theological education through the eyes of lecturers teaching in these three programs. We will first discuss briefly the Chinese culture, especially with respect to the teacher and student relationship. The methodology of the investigation and data collected will be described next. Then the interpretation of the collected data will be discussed.

Chinese Culture: The Teacher-Student Relationship

Not every Chinese is a follower of Confucianism but its ideas are deeply embedded into Chinese culture.[5] Understanding Chinese culture and under-

1. Schumacher, "Theology for Culture," 214.
2. Ibid., 215.
3. Ibid., 216; Schreiter, *Constructing Local Theologies*, 44–45.
4. Bevans, *Models of Contextual Theology*, 11.
5. Huang and Gove, "Confucianism and Chinese Families," 10; King, *Chinese Society and Culture*, 45.

standing Confucianism are inseparable. It is impossible to give a thorough introduction to Confucianism in such a limited space. Rather, we shall focus on the teacher-student relationship. According to Confucian teaching, the purpose of education is to teach people how to act properly within a society. If people can behave according to their given roles, the society will be harmonious and stable. All social relationships in the Chinese society can be classified into five classes: "Between father and son, there should be affection; between sovereign and minister, righteousness; between husband and wife, attention to their separate functions; between old and young [brothers], a proper order; and between friends, fidelity."[6] One should notice two things: First, family relationships occupy the primary position—three out of five relationships are dealing with family, the other two relationships are modeled after those three family relationships. For example, the proper relationship between ruler and his subjects is modeled after the father-son relationship. Second, these relationships are hierarchical. For example, the affection between a father and son is expressed through filial piety (*xiao*). The father has to care for his son but his son needs to submit to every demand of his father. Even relationships between friends are not strictly egalitarian. Certainly, one can choose anyone to be a friend but pragmatically one will choose those whom will be beneficial to oneself. In popular culture, friend-to-friend fidelity is expressed in terms of favor (*renqing*), as well as face and shame.[7] Thus, the benefiter and the beneficiary have a hierarchical relationship. The latter is expected to show loyalty to the former.

How does the teacher-student relationship fit into this system? The teacher-student relationship is defined in terms of the father-son relationship.[8] Therefore, teachers are required to care for their students and students are required to obey and respect their teachers. However, the teacher-student relationship also belongs to the category of friend-friend relationships.[9] The learners choose those who are able to teach what they intend to learn, and the teacher chooses those who are teachable. In this instance, the teacher-student relationship is still cast in a hierarchical order: the teacher has something to offer and the student is always indebted to the teacher. We expect this particular Chinese tradition will influence the

---

6. Mencius, "English Translation of *Mencius: Teng Wen Gong I*," 10.8.

7. See King, *Chinese Culture and Society*, 21–47, for a detailed discussion on the relationships between "xiao" and "renqing."

8. Kee, "Adult Learning from a Confucian Way of Thinking," 167; King, *Chinese Culture and Society*, 3.

9. The main reason for this is that the teacher can choose who is to become his student and the student can choose who is to be his teacher.

teacher-student relationship among the first-generation Chinese migrants as well as the delivery method in the classroom.[10]

As mentioned before, the ACT course guidelines follow the Western tradition with a bias towards the Australian context. Although it intends to reflect local culture, this pedagogical approach is biased toward Anglo-Saxon culture. If these three Chinese programs are training ministers to work in Chinese churches, we anticipate that the Chinese culture will have some influence on the teaching materials as well as on assessment instruments.

Methodology

In order to investigate how Chinese cultural background will influence the teaching of theology, we sent out questionnaires to different lecturers who are teaching in the Chinese programs within the ACT consortium. The questionnaire was divided into three parts. The first section collected personal details of the lecturers, who all happened to be male. This consisted of information about his birthplace, his high school education, and the seminary where he received his theological training. The second section obtained information about the institution where the lecturer is now teaching, including the demographics of its student body, as well as the teacher-student relationship. The third section was divided into three parts. Each part dealt with a specific area of teaching, including the selection of materials within a given syllabus, the choice of delivery method within a classroom, and the choice of assessment instruments.

Findings

Questionnaires were sent to ten lecturers. From this number, six people responded. To simplify the presentation, these responders were labeled as lecturers one to six, respectively. Their personal details and information about the college in which they were teaching were summarized in the following table.

---

10. Traditional Chinese delivery mode is content-driven and teacher-centered while the Western delivery mode is student-centered and experience-driven learning. For an overview of the differences between Eastern and Western modes of delivery from the perspective of cultural anthropology, please see: Greenlee and Stuck, "Individualist Educators in a Collectivist Society," 491–503.

College	Average Age of Student Body	Student Body	Lecturer	Birthplace	High School Education	Subjects They Are Teaching Now
A	>40	Chinese migrants from China, Taiwan, Hong Kong, and other East Asian countries.	One	Australia	Australia	Biblical
			Three	Hong Kong	Hong Kong	Theological, practical
B	>40		Two	China	China	Practical
			Five	Hong Kong	Hong Kong	Biblical
C	~38		Four	Malaysia	Malaysia and Australia	Biblical, theological, practical
			Six	China	Hong Kong	Biblical

Two things can be observed from this table. First, according to the average age of the student bodies, students of these three colleges can be described as mature students. One expects that Chinese culture may have significant influence on their behaviors. Second, Australia is a highly westernized society. While both Hong Kong and Malaysia are quite open to Western influence, China is a traditional and hierarchical society. One anticipates that Chinese culture will affect lecturer two more deeply than the rest.

High School Experiences

Lecturer one received high school education in Australia. His high school classroom experience was a typical westernized classroom experience, combining lectures, interaction, and creative group projects. Teacher-student relationships were not strictly hierarchical. Lecturer two received his high school education in China. He believes that the purpose of his high school education was to reinforce the traditional Chinese culture. The teacher-student relationship was strictly hierarchical. Classroom experience was strictly uni-directional: teachers taught and students were expected to listen quietly and respectfully. Lecturers three, five and six received their high school education in Hong Kong. Although one of them was taught in English, all considered their high school education was intended to reinforce traditional Chinese values. Their classroom experiences were similar. There were no interactions among students or group projects. Teaching was always content-driven and the delivery mode was uni-directional. The teacher-student relationship was hierarchical. Lecturer four received his high school education in Malaysia as well as in Australia. As a result, his classroom experience was both traditional and westernized; his experience of the student and teacher relationship was both hierarchical and egalitarian.

Seminary Experiences

Lecturers one, five, and six received their theological training in Western theological seminaries. Two of them studied in the United States and the other one studied in Australia. The curriculums of these seminaries were set up according to Western tradition. Certain subjects taught reflected particular aspects of the local culture. For example, lecturer one mentioned that the modern church history subject focused more on American denominational history. Regarding the question of whether local culture would influence the choice of materials, their answers were quite different. Lecturer one pointed out that in his seminary, the content of most subjects, especially biblical subjects, were considered to be free of cultural bias. On the other hand, lecturer five thought that teaching and classroom discussions in his seminary were highly contextualized to the local culture. Their classroom experiences were also not similar. In lecturer one's experience, all biblical subjects were taught via lecturing. Only in the practical subjects were group work and class discussions encouraged. However, for lecturers five and six, classroom delivery was a blend of traditional lectures and open discussions. Classroom interaction was strongly encouraged. They all perceived that the teacher-student relationship in their seminaries was egalitarian.

Lecturers two, three, and four received their theological training in the same Hong Kong seminary though in different periods. The curriculum of this seminary conformed to the Western tradition. For lecturer two, he considered that the local culture did not influence the materials being taught in the seminary. Lecturer three thought that some subjects were added into the curriculum in order to respond to the local culture. For example, it added "Chinese Church History" and "Chinese Culture and Christianity." For lecturer four, he considered that the teaching and discussions were highly contextualized. Because of this, some materials were modified in order to better engage local culture. Their classroom experiences were also different. For lecturers two and three, the delivery mode in the classroom was uni-directional. Rarely would a lecturer encourage group projects or group discussion. For lecturer four, he remembered that most lecturers encouraged open discussions in the classroom. Overall, they described the teacher-student relationship in this seminary as between hierarchical and egalitarian.

Present Teaching Experience

All lecturers described their relationships with their students as somewhat egalitarian. Lecturer three believes that the boundary between teacher and students should be strictly observed, and lecturer five considers that mutual respect between teacher and students is the key.

Choice of Materials

In preparing lecture materials, lecturers one and six follow the syllabus prescribed by the ACT. They do not introduce any additional materials in their teaching. Lecturer two brings additional materials in when teaching certain units and makes a special emphasis on particular aspects of its syllabus. The motivation for doing this is to prepare students well to serve in Chinese churches. For example, the syllabus requires the lecturer to discuss the Baptist tradition so lecturer two includes discussion specifically on the Chinese Baptist tradition within Australia. Similar to lecturer two's motivation and practice, even though lecturer five follows the prescribed syllabus, he does adjust it to maximize the benefits for his students. For lecturer three, when he teaches theological subjects, he follows the prescribed syllabus closely. However, when he teaches practical subjects, he brings in additional materials to accommodate Chinese culture. For lecturer four, because of his own research interest, he also emphasizes certain aspects of a given syllabus as well as bringing in additional materials. For all six lecturers, whether they make adjustments to the given syllabus or not, they believe that their choices are free from their own cultural background.

Classroom Delivery

Lecturers three and six prefer lecturing. Yet both encourage students to ask questions, because by asking questions they will know whether students truly understand the material. In addition, meaningful questions can lead to further discussions on some practical issues in ministry. Lecturers four and five prefer a blend of traditional lecturing and open discussions. The latter strongly believes participation in class discussions will enhance his students' learning experience. Lecturer one is aware that his students prefer a traditional style of lecturing but he encourages students to participate in group work as well as in classroom discussions. Similarly, lecturer two believes the best way for an adult to learn is to encourage them to ask questions and express their opinions freely. Both lecturers view their roles as a facilitator of learning. Both believe the learning experience is as important as the goal of learning.

Assessment Instruments

When lecturer one sets up essay questions and examination questions, the main purpose is to evaluate whether his students understand the content of the unit. His students do not need to reflect upon their own cultural background. The other five lecturers, to a greater or lesser degree, have set up questions requiring students to reflect upon their cultural background. On the one hand, they have to recognize their own cultural bias so that they will be able to understand the word of God better. On the other hand, they can think ahead to possible cultural issues raised in their future ministry so that they will be better equipped to serve in Chinese churches.

Discussion of Findings

In this section, the data will be analyzed in terms of four categories: teacher-student relationship, classroom delivery, choices of materials, and assessment instruments.

Teacher-Student Relationship

All lecturers describe their present relationship with students as somewhat egalitarian. Considering lecturer one's cultural background, it is not surprising that he responds this way. However, for the remaining five lecturers, their responses merit closer scrutiny. These five lecturers grew up and received high school education in Asian countries. They identified that their high school education was intended to reinforce traditional Chinese culture, that is, to strengthen the hierarchical relationships within the Chinese society. Thus, their relationships to their high school teachers were strictly hierarchical. However, their seminary experiences were quite different. Two of them studied in a Western seminary. They described their relationships with their teachers as egalitarian. Even though the other three were studying in a Hong Kong seminary, they also described that their relationships to their lecturers were somewhat egalitarian.[11] It indicates that their seminary experiences allowed them to realize that the teacher-student relationship can be managed in some other way other than in a hierarchical order as prescribed by traditional Chinese culture. In other words, new experiences allowed them to unlearn and relearn.

Nevertheless, one can still observe traces of traditional Chinese culture in their dealings with their students. Lecturer three indicates that a strict boundary between teacher and students should be kept within the college. Lecturer five asserts that mutual respect between him and his students is the key to their relationship. This suggests that the teacher and students have to keep some distance from each other. They have to treat each other in an appropriate way. They cannot be just friends standing on the same ground. Certainly here, one can sense the subtle influence of Chinese culture. Furthermore, lecturer two also mentioned that his relationships with students should ultimately be viewed as teacher and friend. This can be interpreted in an egalitarian sense: he and his students will eventually become friends. However, this can also be interpreted according to a Chinese aphorism: the teacher-student relationship lasts a lifetime. This means that the roles of teacher and students will never change and their way of dealing with each other will not change. This ambiguity signals the remnant of Chinese culture looming behind in their thinking.

Classroom Delivery

It is interesting to look at lecturer one first. He describes that the teaching styles of his teachers, in high school and in seminary, were mostly based on experience-driven and student-centered learning. Thus, classroom delivery consisted of lectures, group projects, and classroom interactions. It is not surprising that he uses similar methods to teach students now. However, he is deeply aware that his students long to have a content-driven lecturing style. This indicates clearly that those first-generation Chinese migrants expect their teacher to deliver the contents in a traditional way.

However, given lecturer two's background, it is quite surprising to see him choosing a student-centered approach by emphasizing the learning experience of his students. Instead of being a traditional lecturer who lectures only, he assumes the role of a facilitator in helping his students to learn on their own. Does this mean that he has left his Chinese culture behind? Perhaps. He has mentioned the reason that he chooses this delivery method is because he considers that open discussion is an effective method for adult

---

11. Lecturer two mentioned that even though the boundary between teacher and students was strictly observed, his seminary teachers were very humble and approachable.

learning. Perhaps he learned about this from his students' direct feedback.[12] Most likely, lecturer two decided that this method would be beneficial to help his students to learn the content. This may reflect the basic tenet of the teacher-student relationship in Chinese culture: the teacher is always seeking to care for his students like their fathers.

Lecturers three and six prefer a monological pedagogy. Given the background of lecturer three, it is not surprising to see that he prefers a teacher-centered approach. Even his encouragement to his students to ask questions in class is aiming to make sure that they understand the content correctly and can apply the newfound knowledge appropriately. However, it is unexpected to see lecturer six choosing this approach, especially as his seminary classroom experience was a typical Western classroom one. Therefore, this may indicate that the traditional understanding, that the teacher must have some valuable things to teach, is deeply ingrained in both lecturers' minds. Experiences of different approaches may not be able to change their mindset.

Lecturers four and five prefer a blend of monologue and open discussions. Through private communication, lecturer five indicates that he values a highly student-centered approach, but because of the Chinese cultural background of his students, he has to resort to a blended approach. One way or another, Chinese culture does exert its influences in classroom delivery.

Choice of Materials

Four lecturers have made adjustments to the prescribed syllabus, either by bringing in additional materials not required by the syllabus or by emphasizing particular topics within this syllabus. The motivations are twofold. First, this is done because of the lecturer's research interest. Second, this is done for the sake of equipping their students better so that they will be ready to serve in Chinese churches. All of them declare that what they have done has nothing to do with their own Chinese cultural background. This statement is certainly true in regarding biblical and theological subjects. However, when it comes to practical subjects, we need to make some qualifications. If one wants to serve effectively within a Chinese church, one needs to recognize how Chinese culture affects believers' behaviors. For example, the ways Chinese people communicate with each other are different from the ways Westerners interact among themselves. In preparing students to become an effective minister to serve in a Chinese church, the Chinese cultural background of these lecturers becomes very valuable. Their background will

---

12. This is quite unlikely. See discussion by Greenlee and Stuck, "Individualist Educators in a Collectivist Society," 499–500.

help them to choose, by emphasizing or by adding, appropriate materials that will helpful for their students. This explains why lecturer two needs to include discussions on the Chinese Baptist Church tradition, and lecturer three needs to bring additional materials in to his preaching class.

Assessment Instruments

All lecturers, except lecturer one, set examination and essay questions in such a way that students are forced to reflect upon their cultural background. On the one hand, this makes them aware of their possible cultural bias so that they can understand the messages of the Bible better. On the other hand, this prepares them to serve in Chinese churches. As indicated above, lecturers' awareness of their own cultural background is essential. Their Chinese cultural background indirectly affects the way they set up the assessment instruments.

Conclusion

In this study, we have explored the interplay between Chinese culture and theological education in the Australian College of Theology through the eyes of six lecturers coming from three different institutions. The following observations can be concluded from the collected data.

First, the Chinese cultural background of these lecturers is a valuable asset for them in helping their students to prepare for their future ministry. In biblical and theological subjects, the awareness of their own cultural background helps the lecturers to make adjustments in assessment instruments so that their students can learn to correct their Chinese cultural bias in interpreting Scripture. In practical subjects, this awareness allows these lecturers to bring in additional materials so as to equip their students to be a better minister within Chinese churches.

Second, the traditional understanding about the teacher-student relationship, to a greater or a lesser degree, is still exerting an influence on those lecturers who grew up in Asian countries. For them, there is always a clear boundary between teacher and student. Teacher and students are not standing on the same ground.

Third, the Chinese cultural background of these lecturers, as well as of their students, is affecting the classroom delivery method. The lecturer is *expected to lecture* in the class. In this regard, these lecturers will not be able to fully adopt the Western way of teaching.

In view of these observations, the following recommendations are made. First, the research demonstrates that the syllabus of most subjects in the ACT curriculum is flexible enough for the lecturers to make adjustments so that the subject can become relevant, sensitive and beneficial to Chinese students. However, for certain subjects, like apologetics, the main objective for Chinese students is to learn how to defend the Christian faith against Buddhism and Confucianism, and so the ACT should consider how to give Chinese lecturers more freedom in choosing the appropriate materials.

Second, because of the Chinese cultural background of lecturers and students, Chinese lecturers should not try to completely implement a Western way of teaching. They should develop their own unique style of classroom delivery so that they can gradually introduce their students to Western ways of teaching. This in turn will help students to become effective ministers to second-generation Chinese born in Australia.

Bibliography

Bevans, Stephen B. *Models of Contextual Theology*. Rev. ed. The Society of Divine Word: Sta. Cruz, 2002.

Carter, Charles, W. "Culture and Theological Education." *Wesleyan Theological Journal* 14, no. 2 (1979) 77–81.

Crowley, Eileen D. "Participatory Cultures and Implications for Theological Education." *Theological Librarianship* 6, no. 1 (2013) 60–68.

Greenlee, David and James Stuck. "Individualist Educators in a Collectivist Society: Insights from a Cross-Cultural Model Applied to China." *Missiology: An International Review* 32, no. 4 (2004) 491–503.

Huang, Grace Hui-Chen and Mary Gove. "Confucianism and Chinese Families: Values and Practices in Education." *International Journal of Humanities and Social Science* 2, no. 3 (2012) 10–14.

Kee, Yongwha. "Adult Learning from a Confucian Way of Thinking." In *Non-Western Perspectives on Learning and Knowing*, edited by Sharan B. Merriam, 162–73. Krieger: Malabar, 2007.

King, Ambrose Y. C. *Chinese Society and Culture*. Oxford: Hong Kong, 2013.

Mencius, "English Translation of *Mencius: Teng Wen Gong I*." http://worklish.com/show.asp?id=1613.

Schumacher, William W. "Theology for Culture: Confrontation, Context, and Creation." *Concordia* 43, no. 3 (2016) 211–22.

Schreiter, Robert J. *Constructing Local Theologies*. Orbis: Maryknoll, 1996.

Wang, Chaoran. "Why Are My Chinese Students So Quiet?: A Classroom Ethnographic Study of Chinese Students' Peer Review Activities in an American Multilingual Writing Class." *INTESOL Journal* 13, no. 1 (2016). https://journals.iupui.edu/index.php/intesol/article/view/21248/20646.

12

Women in Theological Education in the ACT in Twenty-First Century Australia

Kara Martin, Megan Powell du Toit, Jill Firth, and Moyra Dale

Abstract

In the last century or so, the halls of higher education, including theology, have opened to women. This chapter explores the place of women in the Australian College of Theology today. Looking at both faculty and students, it asks about their numerical presence, and their experiences, as teachers, and as learners, within the context of evangelical theology. What do women take from their involvement in theological colleges, and what do they bring? The chapter identifies issues of female representation, female role models, pathways for women, focused mentoring, flexible and non-linear pathways, recruitment of female students and opportunities for connection with peers, and concludes with possibilities for enriching and expanding women's involvement in theological education.

Introduction

> At college, I gained confidence in handling the Bible, and felt my heart expand as I located myself within Christian history. These things gave me permission to ask the questions I'd been quietly ignoring for many years because they weren't considered important by my church tradition, and to pursue my gifting more fully. Now several years down the track I've also discovered how the relationships I formed with other women at college have endured and been life-giving in our different ministry paths.[1]

WHAT DO WOMEN BRING to theological education as learners and teachers, and how can their experience of theological education be enriched? A statistical snapshot of women in the Australian College of Theology reveals the numbers of female students, lecturers, and academic supervisors. These statistics and the results of an anonymous survey of female ACT students and lecturers are discussed in the context of Australian and international trends in higher education and business with key findings relevant to theological education in the ACT in twenty-first-century Australia.

Women in the ACT: Proportions of Students and Faculty

Female Students in Coursework Degrees

Women have been studying through the ACT since its inception.[2] A century ago (1916), 15.7 percent of graduates were female (8 of 51). This grew to 24.8 percent (31 of 125) fifty years ago (1966), and to 27.8 percent (77 of 277) twenty-five years ago (1991). During the last decade (2005–2016), the proportion of women enrolled in ACT accredited coursework awards has been steady at about 36 percent EFT (Equivalent Full Time).[3] Women comprise 40 percent of the raw student numbers in the ACT. These figures show a gradual increase in the proportion of women studying. Over the last decade, an average of 2778.3 individual students enrolled each year. Of these, on average, 245.5 women and 508.9 men studied full-time, with

---

1. Female ACT graduate.

2. These figures from 1916–1991 are based on names, as gender information was not retained by the ACT until 2005.

3. All ACT figures were provided by the ACT, between June and December 2016. The University of Divinity provided their data to the authors. Other figures are referenced.

883.4 women and 1140.5 men part-time. If we put this in terms of study load, on average each year 477.6 (EFT) women and 834 (EFT) men were enrolled. While the percentage of women studying part-time (78 percent) is higher compared with 69 percent of male students, in raw numbers men predominate in part-time as well as full-time study in the ACT.

Between 2005 to 2016, on average 374.3 female ACT coursework students were enrolled in courses of under two years' full-time duration, while 429.7 were enrolled in three to four year duration courses. In comparison, on average 383.8 male coursework students were enrolled in courses of under two years, while on average 925.8 were enrolled in courses of three to four years' duration. Thus, 46.5 percent of female but only 29.3 percent of male coursework students were enrolled in courses of less than three years' duration. Women's enrollment in shorter courses reduces their options to pursue careers in ministry or theological academia.

The proportion of female students in the ACT does not reflect numbers of women in the general population or in secular higher education in Australia. According to the Australian Bureau of Statistics, 58 percent of domestic higher education students were female (2010).[4] Even in the traditionally male-oriented STEMM fields, half of higher education students were female (2014).[5] In the University of Divinity, a comparable Australian theological institution, 49 percent of students were female (2015).[6] The ACT enrollments over the last decade have been static, rather than growing the proportion of women who are being equipped for God's service.

Female Students in Higher Degree Research (HDR)

Female enrollments in HDR numbered twenty-three out of a total of 205 research enrollments (11 percent) for the period 2006 to 2013 in the ACT. There were no female graduates in any of the four research degrees offered by the ACT (MTh, DMin, ThD, PhD) in the years 2005 to 2007. Female research graduates have fluctuated between 0 to 20 percent of graduates in the years 2008 to 2015, averaging 13 percent per year. This indicates that women in ACT colleges do not progress to higher level research studies

---

4. Australian Bureau of Statistics, "1301.0—Year Book Australia, 2012, Higher Education."

5. STEMM stands for Science, Technology, Engineering, Mathematics and Medicine; data from SAGE: Science in Australia Gender Equity. "Gender Equity in STEMM," updated 16 August 2016."

6. Australian Government: Department of Education and Training, "Higher Education: 2015 All Students."

in the same numbers as male students, reducing the number of potential women qualified for careers in the theological academy. Comparatively, at the University of Divinity, from 2012 to 2015 female research enrollments (PhD, DTheol, MTheol, MPhil) have remained steady at 37 percent of overall candidates, while for the same time period female research graduates of the University of Divinity have fluctuated between 35 to 60 percent of overall graduates. These statistics should be feasible for female students in ACT research degrees.

Even when women excel in research degrees in the ACT, the path to employment in academia is not commensurate with male applicants. The David Garnsey Scholarship, awarded to a superior candidate enrolling in the ACT MTh, is one possible measure of suitability for an academic career. In the first nine years of the scholarship's availability (1977–1985), only one woman received the award. In the past thirty years since 1986, sixteen men have been recognized with the award, with twelve currently in permanent faculty roles (75 percent), eight of these male lecturers at ACT colleges. However, of the seven women who received the award since 1986, only two are now permanent faculty (28.6 percent), and only one at an ACT college. Academic excellence signified by the David Garnsey Scholarship commonly led to an academic career for men, but not for women.

Women in Teaching and Research in the ACT

In 2016, women comprised 13.2 percent (EFT) of permanent teaching and research academic staff in the ACT, with 24 women (17.2 EFT) among 164 (130.2 EFT) staff. This included 12 part-time women (5.2 EFT) out of 52 permanent part-timers (18.2 EFT), so women comprised 28.6 percent of part-time academic staff by EFT. In the general Australian university figures (2016), 44.7 percent of permanent academic staff are women.[7] At the University of Divinity, the percentage of women in permanent academic staff for the last five years has been 30 to 38 percent. The number of casual female academic staff in the ACT, who comprise 40.4 percent (EFT) with 46 women (7.4 EFT) out of a total of 135 casual staff (18.3 EFT) reveals a talent pool of women not reflected in the proportion of permanent appointments.

---

7. Australian Government: Department of Education and Training, "Selected Higher Education Statistics—2016 Staff Data."

Senior Roles

Women are also missing in HDR leadership in the ACT. No women are on the HDR examination panel, there is one woman on the research committee, and only one woman is a director of research at an ACT college. Of 103 currently approved supervisors, four are women, with only one listed as Principal Supervisor. If women are to be encouraged and supported towards academic careers, it would be useful to have women in teaching positions, and also in positions which directly support research.

In the ACT, numbers of female academics decrease as seniority increases. Using the college reported level classifications and including both permanent and casual teaching staff, 37.7 percent (EFT) of junior and adjunct academics are women, 16.5 percent (EFT) of middle-level academics are women, while just 13.5 percent (EFT) of senior-level academics are women. In Australian universities, 32.6 percent of academics above senior lecturer level are women.[8]

Beyond the ACT

Statistics regarding female participation for the University of Divinity and the Australian University sector have already been given as comparisons with the ACT data. These reveal that there is work to be done in increasing female participation in Australian higher education as a whole. In this, Australia reflects the global situation. A recent international report shows that female research output has increased since 1996, but it is still not at parity.[9] In the American Association of Theological Schools, only 18 percent of professors are women.[10] This figure may be lower in the evangelical academy, though there are no official numbers available for female faculty. The Evangelical Theological Society (ETS) has just 6 percent female members, but the Institute for Biblical Research (IBR) has 12 percent, an improvement of over 4 percent since 2013.[11]

---

8. Australian Government: Department of Education and Training. "Selected Higher Education Statistics—2016 Staff Data."

9. Baker, "Women in Research: Bibliometrics Show Progress Over 20 Years."

10. Zimbrick-Rogers, "'A Question Mark Over My Head': Experiences of Women ETS Members at the 2014 ETS Annual Meeting."

11. See Zimbrick-Rogers, "'A Question Mark Over My Head': Experiences of Women ETS Members at the 2014 ETS Annual Meeting" for the ETS statistic. The IBR statistic is from Beth M. Stovell, IBR Secretary and Chair of Membership, email to author Jill Firth, 21 March, 2017.

Summary of Statistics

The inclusion of women at all levels of the ACT lags behind that of Australian universities in general and also of a comparable consortium, the University of Divinity. The proportion of women in undergraduate courses in the ACT (36 percent EFT) has not changed in the past decade. Proportionally more women are enrolled in shorter courses than men. The small percentages of women in research degrees (11–13 percent) and at senior academic levels (13.5 percent) shows that women do not progress in the same proportion as men along an academic path. Issues in achieving equal female representation in the ACT reflect wider dynamics in higher education, and in the evangelical theological academy.

Survey Results: Issues and the Way Ahead

A survey was distributed among female students and lecturers of the ACT asking what women bring to their involvement in theological colleges, and how women's experience at college might be enriched.[12] Twenty lecturers responded (fourteen faculty and six adjunct, four of whom were also studying), and 201 students (42 full-time, 159 part-time). Some experiences were generally relevant, while others may relate only to particular colleges. When placed in the context of wider national and international research offering critical insights into best practice in higher education and business, the results can assist us in distinguishing which factors are peculiar to theological education or the ACT, and which factors are pervasive in our culture as a whole. Key themes emerging from the survey responses were the perceived needs of a female perspective, female role models, pathways to ministry and academia, mentoring, flexibility, targeted recruitment and peer connections.

The Need for a Female Perspective

Students desired a female perspective, particularly relating to biblical texts, ministry implications and enriching the church (40 percent).[13] Valued dimensions, often contributed by women, included the emotional/spiritual life of those around, empathy, pastoral care, pragmatism, complex view of relationships, compassion, counselling, emotional engagement with Scrip-

---

12. See appendix for details of the survey method and questions.

13. In this section, the percentages in brackets reflect the percentage of total respondents.

ture, pastoral implications of biblical exegesis, experiential approach to spiritual formation, humor, ability to multitask, nurturing ability, building community, dynamics of class interactions, serving God in the messiness of everyday life, and a holistic view (31 percent).

Some pointed to the unique life experiences of women as daughters, sisters, mothers, wives, widows, and women in paid ministry (24 percent). This was closely linked to women bringing an understanding of discrimination and injustice, and especially application to issues such as domestic violence or body image (7 percent). Some women wanted to contribute to an understanding of ministry to women and children (17 percent).

Students also mentioned that studying theology set an example for other women (13 percent) as well as challenging the assumptions of some men about women in academia or ministry (12 percent). Others noted that women provide mentoring, encouragement and support to other women on campus (6 percent). Four percent of respondents commented that they bring excellence to academic study, often receiving top marks.

Some students experienced college as "lonely" and/or "isolating" (6 percent) with a perceived lack of support for women within the college, as well as outside, in the church and the wider community (6 percent). Almost 20 percent of female students mentioned being spoken over, ignored or openly discouraged by lecturers or other students, or prohibited from enrolling in some subjects (usually preaching). Some experienced a lack of respect including gender-based commentary or joking (6 percent).

Twelve percent commented that they did not feel gender played any part in what they brought to study, and a further 38 percent did not comment on positives or negatives in relation to gender.

The most important distinctive that female lecturers felt they brought was as role models, and advocating for female students (60 percent). Valued characteristics included empathy, inclusiveness, integration, a holistic vision, and teaching with a practical emphasis. There were also comments about providing mentoring, pastoral care and building community (40 percent). Twenty percent mentioned the advantage of bringing a female perspective in teaching style and content. One-tenth of respondents emphasized personhood and general life experiences and/or giftedness, rather than gender distinctives.

While some lecturers reported only positive experiences, some felt the pressure of being the only woman in meetings, or having to change their relating style to be "heard." Some felt "invisible," or had received disrespectful comments or responses from students. Some women were limited in areas that they could teach due to the theological views of their colleges.

The Need for Role Models

The most common issue for ACT female students was the lack of female role models, whether in lecturing, writing, research, speaking at college, or even mentioned in biblical studies or church history. Suggestions for enriching the experience of women in college included increasing the number of role models, especially the number of female lecturers (17 percent), allied with increased numbers of women in leadership roles (5 percent), wider opportunities for ministry placement (6 percent), and promoting women's writing and resources via unit bibliographies (6 percent).

Among female lecturers there was a desire to include women in all aspects of college life, promoting female theologians, and proactively recruiting both women lecturers and scholars, creating more platforms for women to learn, teach, write and speak (65 percent). One college was developing a register of speakers and presenters.[14] Lecturers wanted to see the promotion within colleges and churches of the validity of women studying theology, and for teaching, pathways and ministry examples to include a range of foci besides becoming a lead pastor, and to include both genders (40 percent). For some, the struggle to represent female students was a concern, in particular, identifying suitable pathways for them. Coaching for employment interviews was suggested.

The Need for Pathways

Some students desired increased opportunities after studies, clarifying professional pathways for women (11 percent), and promoting how theological study is useful for all professions (2 percent). There was concern about the impact of unconscious gender bias (8 percent) in graduates finding jobs through ministry networks. Some students desired open discussion of gender issues including women's roles in general and in ministry (7 percent).

A number (13 percent) experienced limited support in exploring their calling or identifying future pathways for jobs, including finding ministry placements. Related concerns included a focus in some colleges on training for church leadership, and more limited opportunities for women in speaking, ministry roles or access to resources. One student suggested that the ACT considers developing further policy on gender equity.

Australian business research by Bain & Company has shown that women aspire to be senior leaders at almost the same rate as men, but

---

14. Some resources for bibliographies and speakers can be found at the websites *Women Biblical Scholars* and *Here She Is*.

this is not reflected in senior management statistics of around 10 percent women, unchanged in Australia the past decade. According to the Bain research, "only 15 percent of women believe they have equal opportunity to be promoted to senior executive positions on the same timeline as men." Targets of 40 percent were suggested as an "acid test" of objective selection criteria. Women (80 percent) saw "differences in style" as a key issue in promotion. Women's styles were undervalued or misunderstood, as when a woman who felt completely confident was told she needed to develop confidence, and other confident women were criticized as abrasive or aggressive. Some felt they had to prove themselves over and over.[15] Studies worldwide have demonstrated gender bias from the initial stage of receiving CVs and throughout the interview process.[16] An unequal load of service tasks in academia has been shown to impact women's promotion opportunities, as women typically carry a larger load of pastoral tasks compared with male colleagues, which decreases the time they can spend on research and so affects promotion.[17]

A target of at least 30 percent female leadership is commonly recommended in business and the professions. The Australian Institute of Company Directors set a target of 30 percent female representation on ASX 200 boards by the end of 2018, with the option of quotas for those who do not achieve their targets.[18] The Law Council of Australia set a target at 30 percent for the briefing of female barristers by 2020. Retired High Court Chief Justice Robert French commented that this does not mean briefing less capable women, but seeking gender diversity when starting with "a basket of people of roughly equal abilities."[19]

While the question of the place of women in leadership and teaching is the subject of debate in some evangelical circles, the lack of women in leadership in the wider Australian workplace suggests that other cultural factors may also be involved. Affiliated colleges can encourage women's participation in study and ministry to the full extent of their theology.

---

15. Sanders et al., *Bain Report 2013: Creating a Positive Cycle: Critical Steps to Achieving Gender Parity in Australia*.

16. Steinpreis et al., "The Impact of Gender on the Review of the Curricula Vitae of Job Applicants and Tenure Candidates: A National Empirical Study," 509–28.

17. Misra et al., "The Ivory Ceiling of Service Work," 22–26.

18. Khadem, "Still No Gender Balance in Boardroom," 6.

19. Whitbourn, "Top Judge Laments Slow March of Equality," 4.

The Need for Focused Mentoring

In a study amongst US theological colleges, mentoring was key in promoting well-being among female students and enabling female scholars and leaders.[20] Creegan and Pohl reported that female scholars in the US benefited from being mentored by male professors: "very few women or men survive in the academic world without some positive mentoring. This was true of the women we surveyed, and interestingly, their mentors were almost always male."[21] According to the Bain research in Australia, sponsorship includes proactively identifying and encouraging development and progression opportunities and offering entry level and management experiences to women.[22] Leadership development for women was a major proposal of the European Commission's study on women in research, *She Figures* (2015), for increasing the number of female leaders in academia.[23]

ACT female students suggested mentoring for women (11 percent), and sponsorship and encouragement for women doing research (5 percent). ACT female lecturers enjoyed providing mentoring and pastoral care for women students and suggested focused mentoring of female students as scholars and leaders (25 percent). If women are to receive a similar level of access to networks, conference presentation and other opportunities as male students, male faculty may need to develop a greater openness to building healthy mentoring relationships with female students. This is particularly true in the ACT since there are so few female lecturers or supervisors. Each of the authors of this chapter has valued sponsorship by male mentors.

Lois Zachary has developed the Learning-Centered Mentoring Paradigm, clustering mentoring around learning.[24] This opens up the possibility of group mentoring, virtual mentoring via email or social media, external mentoring of students by faculty in other colleges, and mixed mentoring of men and women with common goals. Zachary's model emphasizes relationship, collaboration, and a focus on development. Strong relationships motivate, inspire and support mentoring, so mutual respect and trust are essential. The mentor can act as a facilitator, collaborating with students to share knowledge, seek consensus, actively working together to shared goals. There is a need to clarify and articulate learning goals, and to focus

---

20. Creegan and Pohl, *Living on the Boundaries: Evangelical Women, Feminism and the Theological Academy*, 180–4.
21. Creegan and Pohl, *Living*, 79.
22. Sanders et al, *Bain Report 2013*.
23. European Commission, *She Figures 2015*, 5–6.
24. See definition in Art of Mentoring, "What is Virtual Mentoring?"

on promoting a mentee's development and growth.[25] Such mentoring can be focused on producing pastors, teachers, scholars and leaders who can in turn influence others.

Each of the authors mentor women who have the potential for leadership roles. One focuses on being a spiritual guide, coach, sponsor and model to empower such women to flourish, and seeks also to access networks of other women and men that will enable them to move beyond what she can offer. Another comments, "I myself have made a point of mentoring the women coming after me, often at the cost of precious time in the juggle of work, study, and motherhood. This is also despite the knowledge that with few positions open for women, I may well be mentoring my competition." A third author leads a small team of female academics and editors in offering dinners for female undergraduate students which include sessions on writing blogs, magazine articles, conference papers and journal articles.

The Need for Flexibility

While some women praised the flexibility of their colleges around caring responsibilities, an equal number of female students were frustrated by the lack of adaptability. They suggested that the learning experience could be enriched by greater flexibility for women and men juggling multiple roles (8 percent), and the recognition that women who study often carry a heavier load of caring and house management responsibilities.

Colleges could consider a non-linear pathway for female academics.[26] Provisions for women returning from a parenting-based career break were recommended by *She Figures*.[27] Significantly, while 79 percent of fathers of young children would prefer to choose their start and finish, work a compressed work week, or work part of regular hours at home,[28] most are reluctant to use flexible work hours for fear of career penalties.[29] A majority of men (60 percent) considered family responsibilities to be the main barrier to women's progress, but only a minority of women (20 percent) perceived competing needs of family and work as a reason for lack of promotion in business.[30]

   25. Zachary, *The Mentor's Guide: Facilitating Effective Learning Relationships*, 3–4.
   26. Sanders et al, *Bain Report 2013*.
   27. European Commission, *She Figures 2015*, 5–6.
   28. Diversity Council Australia, "Employers Take Note: Men Want Flexible Working Too!"
   29. See also Gilmore, "We Need to Start Talking about Working Dads."
   30. Sanders et al, *Bain Report 2013*.

The Need for Targeted Recruitment

Bain's recent Australian research indicates that recruitment of women is impacted by a lack of women leaders in business organizations. A track record of promotion of women and a critical mass of women at the top (minimum of 25 percent) is a key factor in women's satisfaction with the workplace, and the likelihood that they would recommend their workplace to others.[31] There is also international "robust evidence" that higher profitability is associated with growing the percentage of women in the C-level (Chief Executive Officer, Chief Financial Officer, Chief Operating Officer).[32] ACT students suggested specific recruitment for more female students, in marketing and promotion by colleges (8 percent), along with recruitment of women lecturers (17 percent), and senior staff (5 percent).

The Need to Build Connection with Peers

A significant student suggestion was to meet for mutual encouragement and support at a college or inter-collegial colloquium (12 percent), enabling women to promote their own research and to network. Female lecturers also wanted to build community across colleges (40 percent), via city-wide gatherings or online networking for mutual encouragement and to promote female scholarship.

Social media is increasingly becoming a place to connect with other women in theology. This provides crucial encouragement and opportunities and is becoming a movement within Australia of women connecting and developing a female voice in the Australian church.

For one author, the experience of working with a male co-supervisor, and also co-organizing an international conference for female academics, has given a deeper appreciation of the distinctives brought by both women and men to the academic experience, and the richness of allowing both voices to be heard. Some of the authors meet in an academic writing group for women which includes faculty members, adjuncts, and research students, with the goal of developing female academics and producing writing by women. The group has worked collaboratively to produce book reviews, conference papers, and journal articles.

---

31. Sanders et al, *Bain Report 2013*.

32. Peterson Institute for International Economics, "New Peterson Institute Research on over 21,000 Companies Globally Finds Women in Corporate Leadership Can Significantly Increase Profitability."

Key Findings for ACT Colleges

1. Encourage female representation in bibliographies, essay topics, and historical and biblical figures discussed in lectures, issues addressed, and practical examples in ministry classes and chapel sermons.
2. Increase the number of female role models at senior levels in colleges (including management and faculty) with initial targets of 30 percent, by implementing an appointment process which recognizes implicit bias and equity of service expectations.
3. Establish ministry pathways for women including appropriate opportunities, coaching, and training.
4. Provide focused mentoring for female researchers by male and female supervisors, providing advocacy, sponsorship, publishing, and teaching experience.
5. Consider flexible and non-linear career paths for academics and those in ministry who are parents of young children, and strategies to allow career continuance after a career break.
6. Target female students in recruitment to longer coursework awards and HDR.
7. Promote connections with peers: support opportunities for female students and faculty to build collegiality through colloquia and social media.

Conclusion

Statistical research reveals lower female student and faculty numbers as key issues in the ACT. Surveys of female students and lecturers in the ACT, and wider research in academia and business, have identified improvement factors: female representation, female role models, pathways for women, focused mentoring, flexible and non-linear pathways, recruitment of women students and opportunities for connection with peers. Many issues can be addressed immediately and will impact recruitment, well-being and gospel training for all.

Appendix

The chapter analyzed statistical data provided by the ACT, supplemented with experiences of women, as teachers, and as learners in ACT colleges. An email was sent to ACT colleges, asking for volunteers from female lecturers and students to answer the research question via an online survey. Where students also identified as lecturers, material was analyzed depending on the predominant viewpoint represented by the answers. The survey was completely anonymous, with no naming of participants or institutions. Participation in the survey was deemed to give permission to use the responses in the analysis section of the book chapter.

The survey was distributed directly to students using the email addresses available on the ACT database. Input from faculty and adjunct lecturers was coordinated via a direct appeal from the Dean of the ACT to College Principals. A follow-up email increased the response from female faculty. Unfortunately, few female adjunct faculty received the email.

1. Please identify your involvement in theological education. (You can tick more than one answer.)
2. Please comment on the positives and negatives of your experiences in theological education, as it relates to your gender.
3. As a woman, what is distinctive about what you bring to your involvement in theological education?
4. List any suggestions for how the experience of women in theological education could be enriched.

Bibliography

Art of Mentoring. "What is Virtual Mentoring?" http://artofmentoring.net/virtual-mentoring/.

Australian Bureau of Statistics. "1301.0—Year Book Australia, 2012, Higher Education." http://www.abs.gov.au/ausstats/abs@.nsf/Lookup/by%20Subject/1301.0~2012~Main%20Features~Higher%20education~107.

Australian Government: Department of Education and Training. "Higher Education: 2015 All Students." https://docs.education.gov.au/node/41696.

Australian Government: Department of Education and Training. "Selected Higher Education Statistics—2016 Staff Data." https://education.gov.au/selected-higher-education-statistics-2016-staff-data.

Baker, Simon. "Women in Research: Bibliometrics Show Progress Over 20 Years." *Times Higher Education*, 8 March 2017. https://www.timeshighereducation.com/news/women-in-research-bibliometrics-show-progress-over-20-years.

Creegan, Nicola Hoggard and Christine D. Pohl. *Living on the Boundaries: Evangelical Women, Feminism and the Theological Academy*. Downers Grove: IVP, 2005.

Diversity Council Australia. "Employers Take Note: Men Want Flexible Working Too!" https://www.dca.org.au/News/News/Employers-take-note%3A-men-want-flexible-working-too!/293.

European Commission. *She Figures 2015: Gender in Research and Innovation*, 5–6. https://ec.europa.eu/research/swafs/pdf/pub_gender_equality/she_figures_2015-final.pdf.

Gilmore, Jane. "We Need to Start Talking About Working Dads." *Sydney Morning Herald*, 9 December 2016. http://www.smh.com.au/lifestyle/life-and-relationships/parenting/we-need-to-start-talking-about-working-dads-20161208-gt7ewc.html.

Here She Is. http://heresheis.org.au/.

Khadem, Nassim. "Still No Gender Balance in Boardroom." *The Age*, Thursday 15 December 2016, 6.

Misra, Joya et al. "The Ivory Ceiling of Service Work," *Academe* 97, no. 1 (2011) 22–6.

Peterson Institute for International Economics. "New Peterson Institute Research on Over 21,000 Companies Globally Finds Women in Corporate Leadership Can Significantly Increase Profitability." 8 February 2016. https://piie.com/newsroom/press-releases/new-peterson-institute-research-over-21000-companies-globally-finds-women.

SAGE: Science in Australia Gender Equity. "Gender Equity in STEMM, updated 16 August 2016." https://www.sciencegenderequity.org.au/gender-equity-in-stem/.

Sanders, Melanie et al. *Bain Report 2013: Creating a Positive Cycle: Critical Steps to Achieving Gender Parity in Australia*. http://www.bain.com/publications/articles/creating-a-positive-cycle.aspx.

Steinpreis, Rhea E. et al. "The Impact of Gender on the Review of the Curricula Vitae of Job Applicants and Tenure Candidates: A National Empirical Study." *Sex Roles* 41, no. 7 (1999) 509–28.

Whitbourn, Michaela. "Top Judge Laments Slow March of Equality." *The Age*, 15 December 2016, 4.

Women Biblical Scholars. https://womenbiblicalscholars.wordpress.com/.

Zachary, Lois. *The Mentor's Guide: Facilitating Effective Learning Relationships*. San Francisco: Jossey-Bass, 2012.

Zimbrick-Rogers, Emily. "'A Question Mark over My Head': Experiences of Women ETS Members at the 2014 ETS Annual Meeting." *A Question Mark Over My Head: Special Edition Journal*. Minneapolis: Christians for Biblical Equality, 2015. http://www.cbeinternational.org/resources/article/question-mark-over-my-head.

13

Theological Education for Missional Leadership

KARINA KREMINSKI
AND
MICHAEL FROST

Abstract

Those scholars who have promoted a missional paradigm for the church have argued that such a paradigm requires a new kind of leader. This chapter will explore the distinguishing contours of a distinctly missional approach to leadership, including the need for such shifts as moving from an internal to an external focus; from program delivery to people development; from a spirituality of retreat to a spirituality of engagement; and from traditional church-based leadership to apostolic leadership. When these shifts are properly understood they have significant implications for the kind of theological education needed for developing missional leaders. This chapter will explore what is uniquely needed for the formation of missional leaders within the academic environment, using the rationale for and design of the Masters of Missional Leadership as a case study of such formation. This course, which commenced at Morling College in 2016, was specifically designed by the authors to provide a learning experience which would suit practitioners who needed to further their leadership skills within a missional framework. The chapter will also explore future opportunities for missional leadership studies, where we will look at what opportunities and challenges exist for further developments in the field of missional leadership within an academic context.

Mission as Alerting Others to the Reign of God

WE TAKE DAVID BOSCH's shorthand definition of mission as our starting point:

> Mission is more and different from recruitment to our brand of religion; it is alerting people to the universal reign of God through Christ.[1]

The mission of God's people must not be reduced to mere recruitment, something that the least reflective proponents of the Church Growth Movement could be accused of doing. Neither can mission only be seen as evangelism, as some evangelicals have viewed it. While mission includes the spoken ministry of evangelism, it is a broader endeavor, linked to a belief in the inaugurated reign of God and anticipating its full consummation. Mission and kingdom are irrevocably linked. Mission is both the announcement and the demonstration of the reign of God through Christ. Mission is not primarily concerned with church growth, but with the reign and rule of the Triune God. If the church grows as a result, so be it. God's reign is full and complete, an eternal and non-negotiable reality, not enlarged nor diminished by the number of people who believe it and yield to it. Our mission, then, is to alert people to this irrefutable reality, by both announcement and demonstration.

We agree with Bishop Lesslie Newbigin's description of the church as "sign, instrument, and foretaste of God's redeeming grace for the whole life of society."[2] That's another way of saying the church alerts others to the reign of God, but it spells out those three essential dimensions: the church points others to God's reign; the church is used by God to extend God's reign; and the church is a taste, or down payment, or firstfruits of the coming kingdom.

A core question for all missional Christians is to ask is what the reign of God through Christ looks like in their context? If the kingdom of God has come and is overlapping with the broken world in which we live, how can

---

1. Bosch, *Believing in the Future: Toward a Missiology of Western Culture*, 33.
2. Newbigin, *The Gospel in a Pluralist Society*, 232–33.

we alert people to it? What does it look like? Where do I see the evidence of it? In fact, it occurs to us that this is a far more legitimate and creative question to ask than the usual questions about how we can attract people to our church programs. Shaping churches that can do this work is the duty of missional Christian leadership. Equipping the laity to be able to both announce and demonstrate the reign of God in every aspect of life and society is now essential.

While it could be argued that many members of evangelical churches are in some measure competent to explain the gospel, where the gospel is taken to mean the way of salvation for an individual, we would contend that far fewer members could articulate what the reign or kingdom of God is, particularly to an outsider. Likewise, if the research of people like Robert Banks and Mark Greene is accurate, members of evangelical churches report that they receive little equipping in how to seek illumination for their daily secular duties in the light of the gospel.

We fear much equipping of the laity in recent decades has been based on an understanding of mission that emphasizes personal evangelism and recruitment. A broader definition of mission, along the lines that we've briefly discussed here, will necessitate a new missional form of leadership. We believe the distinguishing contours of a distinctly missional approach to leadership include the need for leaders to help churches shift from an internal to an external focus; from program delivery to disciple-making; and from a spirituality of retreat to a spirituality of engagement.[3] When these shifts are properly understood they have significant implications for the kind of theological education needed for developing missional leaders.

A New Kind of Leadership

In brief, the primary shift required in the development of missional leaders is to equip them to move from a traditional church-based leadership model to a more apostolic understanding of leadership. J. R. Briggs and Bob Hyatt define the work of apostolic leadership this way:

> ... to model a humanity that is broken yet redeemed and given incredible value (imago Dei) while reflecting the sending/sent heartbeat of a missioning God in the world (missio Dei). They see themselves not as preservers of tradition, but instead as shepherds of God's people, image bearers aligned with God's mission and cultivators within his kingdom. The call of [missional

---

3. McNeal, *Missional Renaissance: Changing the Scorecard for the Church*.

leaders] in a local church context is to *faithfully lead God's people by imaging the character of a missioning God.*[4]

Missional leaders are required to provide oversight to a community of missionaries who are themselves pursuing the heart of God, seeking his kingdom, and joining faithfully in God's mission in their worlds. As Briggs and Hyatt say, "If mission is to be pursued, elders must make a wholehearted commitment to leading differently."[5]

This different kind of leadership will require at least three fundamental shifts.

From an Internal to an External Focus

If the mission of the church is to alert others to the reign of God by both announcement and demonstration it follows that churches need to be equipped to join God's mission beyond the walls of the church. This is in fact a monumental shift for many churches to undertake. Many church members were raised in a church environment that emphasized the internal life of the faith community. In saying this, we don't suggest that the internal life of the church isn't important. Churches need to fashion an alternative society to their world. We need to live out the commands to fellowship, worship, and for spiritual formation. But a shift to an external focus sees the mission of God as the catalytic function of the church. As stated earlier, mission is reduced to recruitment of outsiders to the internal life of the church. Rather, mission energizes and refreshes the internal life of the church. Missional churches, then, are those faith communities for which mission has become their organizing function. Transitioning existing churches to this paradigm requires sensitive and distinctly missional leadership. Some have referred to this as creating a missional culture, most notably J. R. Woodward in his book of that title. Following Lesslie Newbigin, Woodward writes,

> Creating a missional culture helps the church live out her calling to be a sign of the kingdom, pointing people to the reality beyond what we can see, a foretaste of the kingdom where we grow to love one another as Christ loves us, and an instrument in the hands of God to bring more of heaven to earth in concrete ways.[6]

---

4. Briggs and Hyatt, *Eldership and the Mission of God*, 26.

5. Ibid., 27.

6. Woodward, *Creating a Missional Culture: Equipping the Church for the Sake of the World*, 29.

From Program Delivery to Disciple-Making

An overreliance on the internal life of the church has led over time to a perspective on traditional leadership as program deliverers. Church leaders are familiar with the idea of tailoring ministries and programs to the perceived needs of their congregations. Indeed, this was a hallmark of the Church Growth Movement. But missional leaders must bear in mind that Christian ministry is concerned with supporting people as they journey to where God wants them to be. This is different to a paradigm of helping people to undertake a journey to where they want to be. If God's mission is to unfurl his reign as a place of reconciliation, truth, healing, beauty and justice, and to call others to come under that reign, it follows that God wants us to live *in* the world for the *sake* of the world, without being *of* the world. In short, missional leadership focuses on people development, the shaping of followers of Christ into an ever more radical obedience to him. Increasingly, missional literature has developed its focus from emphasizing an outward orientation to also promoting personal and collective discipleship. Neil Cole bluntly points out,

> Ultimately, each church will be evaluated by only one thing—its disciples. Your church is only as good as her disciples. It does not matter how good your praise, preaching, programs or property are; if your disciples are passive, needy, consumeristic, and not moving in the direction of radical obedience, your church is not good.[7]

From a Spirituality of Retreat to a Spirituality of Engagement

In saying this we are not suggesting that traditional churches have not made discipleship a priority. But we fear that traditional understandings of discipleship have fostered a spirituality of retreat, emphasizing such things as personal piety and spiritual disciplines such as private and group Bible study, prayer, and worship. It could be argued that there has been an emphasis on the inner life of a Christian. Missional leadership seeks to foster *a spirituality of engagement*, an ability to seek and sense God's presence in the activity of work, service and evangelism. This was a focus in designing the Master of Missional Leadership and particularly with one of the core units, Missional Spirituality. We explore this further below.

---

7. Cole, *Ordinary Hero: Becoming a Disciple Who Makes a Difference*, 185.

Broad Outline and Distinctives of the Masters of Missional Leadership

With this understanding of leadership in mind, we set about designing the Master of Missional Leadership (MML). Our goal was to form students so that they join with God on his mission in the world and help equip their churches to be a sign, foretaste and instrument of God's kingdom. As Robert Banks writes in his now classic book *Reenvisioning Theological Education*, "By mission I mean not just 'mission-oriented,' but an education undertaken with a view to what God is doing in the world, considered from a global perspective."[8] In our view, this then implies and necessitates a particular way of imagining theological education as well as the expected learning that comes from teaching on the particular topic of missiology. Again, Banks is helpful here:

> I'm thinking rather of reflection, training, and formation for work on the mission field, whether the latter takes place overseas or locally . . . By "missional" I mean theological education that is wholly or partly field based, and that involves some measure of doing what is being studied. This may take the form of action-reflection, distinctions that in any case are useful only up to a point, since effective action involves some element of or relationship with reflection, and effective reflection involves some element of relationships with action.[9]

By missional education then, we mean a pedagogy that has a specific purpose, method, structure and which can even offer a corrective to and critique of some other forms of Christian education. Missional education can be defined as:

> Christian education that specifically privileges the goal of helping Christians discover and live into their identity as God's cooperative partners in the *missio dei*. Missional education is generally required as a corrective to truncated approaches to Christian education that have omitted the missional dimension, emphasizing only personal relationship with God and/or spiritual formation in Christlike character.[10]

---

8. Banks, *Reenvisioning Theological Education*, 142.

9. Ibid.

10. James, "Education That is Missional: Towards a Pedagogy for the Missional Church," 145.

With this purpose as the foundation, the MML was then developed as a course composed of eight units; four core subjects, two electives, and a project. The structure was chosen so that it would be aligned to other Masters courses offered by the ACT. The four core units were chosen because of the crucial role that these subjects play in understanding and embodying a missional life. They are Missional Leadership, Missional Hermeneutics, Missional Spirituality and Cultural Exegesis. We thought that it was necessary for students to view leadership, Scripture, and also spirituality from a missional perspective, and cultural exegesis is a needed skill for contemporary leaders who must know their context before they apply what they have learnt. Scripture, leadership and spirituality are three areas of study which facilitate discipleship and formation in the student's learning experience, so these were prioritized along with cultural exegesis. Two electives can be chosen in the course which relate to mission, leadership and apologetics. The project that the students undertake must be documented in a 15,000-word essay based on a plan that they formulate to engage in a context missionally. This is a core part of the course which is interwoven into the structure of the MML and takes approximately two years to complete. This project component and the spirituality unit in the course display most strikingly the unique and broad vision we have outlined for a renewed missional theological education. These two components of the MML point to three distinctives of the course which reveal aspects of a reimagined missional theological education—a practitioner orientation, the use of action-research as a methodology, and a firm belief in the correlation between spiritual formation and theological study. Action research was chosen as a methodology because it is a helpful tool that social scientists use in order to assess and bring change to a particular context.[11] The methodology is useful in that it creates opportunities for the participants and researcher to work together in order to produce an outcome that is mutually agreed upon.

The course has a practitioner focus and this was intentional because the MML is aimed at people who have a primary degree and are currently working in their respective fields, be that church or non-church related. So, the course had to make ample room for practitioners to employ their field experience as they learned new information during the course. Moreover, the content presented needed to have relevance to the practitioners so that they could further apply what they learned to their workplaces and churches. Not only this, the teaching methodology had to be suitable for practitioners. Craig van Gelder, pointing to the positive re-visioning of theological

---

11. Reason and Bradbury, *Sage Handbook of Action Research: Participative Inquiry and Practice*.

education in Robert Banks's book, says "The proposed reconstruction was toward finding some way to reintegrate theological knowledge (*theoria*) with practical wisdom (*phronesis*) and for these to be shaped by personal and communal formation (*habitus*)."[12] All assessments in each of the core units of the MML aim to carry this mix of *theoria* and *phronesis*.

The interplay between theory and practice is most evident in the research methodology which is used for the project. Students must use action-research to observe a context such as a church, and then design an "intervention" with the cooperation of the people in that context in order to help facilitate a missional paradigm. Reggie McNeal in *Missional Renaissance* critiques seminary training and says that we "must abandon the train-and-deploy model" and instead use Jesus's model of "deploy and debrief."[13] Action-research helps develop skills of listening, reflection, debrief, and participation with people in a context for its potential transformation.

Another unique distinctive of the MML is its attempt to take seriously the connection between theological education and spiritual formation. The Missional Spirituality unit is key to this intention in that it is framed as a year-long unit in the attempt to form a cohort which has the purpose of forming the students. Even though the course has only been in existence for a short time, students have been conveying that the acts of seeing each other face to face, online, and practicing hospitality towards each other have been opportunities for God to shape them into disciples of Jesus. Online community, communal meals during intensives as well as assessments that involve reflection and missional disciplines are practiced. Time is left towards the end of the class in order to integrate learning with formation. Activities such as group work around spiritual reflection on assessments, designing prayers reflecting class content and devotions with a point of highlighting class material that day, are all methods used in the MML to forge theological reflection and formation. This interdependence between learning and spiritual formation is something that was implemented in a psychology course at Fuller Seminary.

> Faculty also emphasized in-class experiences. Several faculty use beginning-of-class devotionals in thoughtful and creative ways and weave these into the topic of that day's class. This creates not only an "integrative moment" but also a model of a practice for approaching psychology and theology. Other faculty members discussed incorporating spiritual disciplines into

---

12. Van Gelder, *The Ministry of the Missional Church: A Community Led by the Spirit*, 1614.

13. McNeal, *Missional Renaissance: Changing the Scorecard for the Church*, 2362.

the overall course experience. These practices are overtly linked to the content of the course in a variety of ways.[14]

Brian Edgar says "Theological education is thus not so much knowing about God as it is about *knowing* God. It is not primarily about *theology*, that is, the formal study of the *knowledge* of God, but it is more about what Kelsey calls *theologia*, that is, gaining the *wisdom* of God."[15] If this is the case then "holiness and moral, spiritual transformation are central to the educational task."[16]

Opportunities and Challenges for Further Developments in the Field of Missional Leadership Within an Academic Context

There are many opportunities for the development of training people for missional leadership. Theological institutions need to see these opportunities, reflect on them, and take action where they see possibilities for growth. One of the critiques of theological education institutions is that training reflects approaches which stem from within a context of Christendom. Darrell Guder says "Seminary training remains firmly committed to the model of preparing a professional clergy for a set of tasks considered to be "ministry" . . . in the twentieth century the clerical paradigm of Christendom has shaped and determined the curricula and ethos of seminaries."[17] What would it look like if we intentionally shaped courses for our post-Christendom context in the West? It at least involves further reflection on what it means to train ministers to be missionaries. Even though Lesslie Newbigin wrote this nearly three decades ago his words are still relevant for the academy today. He said " . . . it seems clear that ministerial training as currently conceived is still far too much training for the pastoral care of the existing congregation, and far too little oriented toward the missionary calling to claim the whole of public life for Christ and his kingdom."[18] Some change might be needed in the contemporary academic context because it faces the same concerns that the church does regarding responding appropriately to

---

14. Hammer, "Spiritual Formation Through Direction at Fuller Theological Seminary School of Psychology," 307.

15. Edgar, "The Theology of Theological Education," 209.

16. Ibid., 210.

17. Barrett and Guder, *Missional Church: A Vision for the Sending of the Church in North America*, 209.

18. Newbigin, *The Gospel in a Pluralist Society*, 231.

our changing times. If changes do not get implemented soon, the possibility is that people will search for alternate models of theological training so they can know what it means to flesh out the gospel in today's context. We see two opportunities for growth in the area of missional education within the academic context; further developing holistic and integrated learning, and secondly, promoting a deeper integration between spiritual formation and theological study.

As we mentioned, ideally missional education is not only aimed at transmitting knowledge about mission-oriented topics such as missional ecclesiology and the *missio Dei* for instance, it also involves a particular way of teaching which must be integrated and holistic. Perry Shaw is helpful here as he outlines the three areas that promote good theological education. He says that what is needed is "intentional promotion of; affective learning, shaping values, attitudes, emotions and motivations, behavioural learning through action and practice, cognitive learning that moves beyond the mere transmission of knowledge to the development of complex thinking skills."[19] In order to nurture missional reflective practitioners for the contemporary world, we will need to make a commitment to focusing on these key areas as we design learning outcomes and goals for units and courses. This includes paying more attention to how practitioners function in their workplace and then reflecting this style in the learning environment. Donald Schon says that this learning style can be described as "reflection-in action," rather than a "theory to practice," or even an "action-reflection" model.[20] How can we better train practitioners on the field rather than focusing primarily on what is learnt in the classroom context? This means clearly, making theological training more field-based so that students put into action and apply what they are learning. There is still a lot of research needed regarding how we can do this better, especially in a postgraduate setting.

Our view is that not only must theological training which is missional be holistic and integrated, it must also take more seriously the interdependence between learning and spiritual formation. Being missional is primarily an issue to do with identity and formation as we embody what it means to be "sent ones" into our world. So, mission and spirituality or formation are deeply connected. Roger Helland and Len Hjalmarson in their book *Missional Spirituality* say that the goal of theological education must be equipping "leaders who will also equip others in what it means to love God from all one's heart, soul, mind and strength, and to love one's neighbour

---

19. Shaw, *Transforming Theological Education*, 67.
20. Schon, *The Reflective Practitioner: How Professionals Think in Action*, 68.

as oneself."[21] We think that helping students become Christians who participate in God's heart for mission will mean "active partnerships between churches, seminaries and Bible colleges, with corresponding resolve, prayer, conversation and curriculum revision."[22] More and more the goal must be on formation, rather than primarily learning content.

One interesting question to explore is how to interpret teaching as a missional venture. This would include teachers and students showing hospitality and engaging in other missional practices that shape a Christian community. We can learn here from monastic communities which have a culture of communal learning and formation as habits are practiced in order for God's people be a witness to the gospel of good news. James K. A. Smith is especially helpful with his explanation of the relevance of embodied practices to the formation of Christians. He applies this to the theological training institution and says that if Christian worship attests to the fact that we are "embodied, liturgical animals whose desire is shaped by material practice" then "a liturgically informed pedagogy, assuming and drawing upon the 'education' that already takes place in the liturgy, will also seek ways to extend and improvise upon Christian practices in order to create a learning environment (in academia) that is animated by intentional practices that form the imagination and shape character."[23] Spiritual formation is crucial in missional theological education and this will require some imagination and creativity if we are to change current practice in academia.

Bibliography

Banks, Robert. *Reenvisioning Theological Education: Exploring a Missional Alternative to Current Models*. Grand Rapids: Eerdmans, 1999.

Barrett, Lois, and Darrell L. Guder. *Missional Church: A Vision for the Sending of the Church in North America*. Kindle ed. Grand Rapids: Eerdmans, 1998.

Bosch, David. *Believing in the Future: Toward a Missiology of Western Culture*. Valley Forge: Trinity Press, 1995.

Briggs, J. R., and Bob Hyatt. *Eldership and the Mission of God*. Downers Grove: IVP, 2015.

Cole, Neil. *Ordinary Hero: Becoming a Disciple Who Makes a Difference*. Grand Rapids: Baker, 2008.

Edgar, Brian. "The Theology of Theological Education." *Evangelical Review of Theology* 29, no. 3 (2005) 208–17.

---

21. Helland and Hjalmarson, *Missional Spirituality: Embodying God's Love from the Inside Out*, 2282.

22. Ibid., 2305.

23. Smith, *Desiring the Kingdom: Worship, Worldview and Cultural Formation*, 228.

Hammer, Brad Strawn, and Miyoung Yoon. "Spiritual Formation Through Direction at Fuller Theological Seminary School of Psychology." *Journal of Psychology and Christianity* 32, no. 4 (2013) 304–12.

Helland, Roger, and Leonard Hjalmarson. *Missional Spirituality: Embodying God's Love from the Inside Out*. Kindle ed. Downers Grove: IVP, 2011.

James, Christopher B. "Education That Is Missional: Towards a Pedagogy for the Missional Church." In *APM Annual Meeting. Social Engagement: The Challenge of the Social in Missional Education*. Wheaton, 2013.

McNeal, Reggie. *Missional Renaissance: Changing the Scorecard for the Church*. Kindle ed. San Francisco: Jossey-Bass, 2009.

Newbigin, Lesslie. *The Gospel in a Pluralist Society*. 1989. Reprint, Grand Rapids: Eerdmans, 2002.

Reason, Peter, and Hillary Bradbury, eds. *Sage Handbook of Action Research: Participative Inquiry and Practice*. London: Sage, 2013.

Schon, Donald A. *The Reflective Practitioner: How Professionals Think in Action*. New York: Basic, 1983.

Shaw, Perry. *Transforming Theological Education: A Practical Handbook for Integrative Learning*. Carlisle: Langham Creative, 2014.

Smith, James K. A. *Desiring the Kingdom: Worship, Worldview and Cultural Formation*. Grand Rapids: Baker Academic, 2009.

Van Gelder, Craig. *The Ministry of the Missional Church: A Community Led by the Spirit*. Kindle ed. Baker: Grand Rapids, 2007.

Woodward, J. R. *Creating a Missional Culture: Equipping the Church for the Sake of the World*. Downers Grove: IVP, 2012.

14

Developing Genuinely Reflective Ministry Practitioners

Peter Francis

Abstract

This chapter posits that to become an effective ministry practitioner, it is imperative that one appreciates the importance of becoming a genuinely reflective ministry practitioner. After considering the place of discernment in understanding one's gifting and call to ministry the inherent value of reflection for ongoing growth in that calling is considered. Here the emphasis is not only upon *doing* reflection as a "one-off" or occasional exercise, but *being* reflective. A proposal is then set forth which espouses the value of an integrative approach to ministry reflection which embraces the behavioral, cognitive and affective domains of learning. The proposed framework argues for a genuine "trialogue" between practical or situational reflection, theological reflection and personal reflection, which sees the ministry practitioner developing not just the requisite skills for ministry, but a deep personal relationship with God which fuels and sustains ministry for the long haul.

The Goal of Ministry Formation

ONE THE GREATEST CHALLENGES that many students feel when preparing for ministry is the need to learn "how to do the stuff of ministry." They want to learn the "skills" of effective ministry. Many will even commence their theological studies with some reasonably well-defined ideas about what constitutes effective ministry practice based upon some model of ministry which they have observed in others. Sometimes this will be a ministry leader that they have had the opportunity of watching firsthand in a range of contexts—perhaps a pastor or a youth leader or some other influential leader whose ministry has impacted them personally. Sometimes it may be some "ministry hero" whose podcasts and/or blogs have captivated their imagination and they decide that this person is the kind of role model which they would like to imitate.

Yet, the goal of theological field education is to help students discover more than just the "how-tos" of ministry. Clinton asserts that "we minister out of who we are."[1] If this is the case then we must understand that effective ministry is much more than just fulfilling the tasks of ministry. We must also be committed to our own spiritual growth and understanding of who we are, both as children of God and servants of God. Indeed, Vos argues that "our effectiveness in leading others into spiritual growth is entirely dependent upon the extent of our own spiritual growth."[2] Thus, an integral part of the field education journey is not merely the development of the "skills" of ministry but the development of an ongoing commitment to one's personal spiritual growth and understanding of who they are as children of God and as servants of God. It is out of the depth of such understanding that truly effective ministry practices can develop and flourish.

So, what are the key components which might facilitate this ongoing spiritual growth in both personal awareness and ministry skills?

The Means of Ministry Formation

The approach adopted by many theological seminaries and colleges combines a mixture of instruction, observation, participation, and reflection. Indeed, as one contemplates the ministry of Jesus amongst his inner band of disciples, they are quickly able to identify each of these key components.

The Gospels record the many occasions on which Jesus invested personally in the training and instruction of his inner band of disciples. Whilst,

1. Clinton, *The Making of a Leader*, 32.
2. Vos, "The Spiritual Disciplines and Christian Ministry."

for example, Mark regularly draws our attention to the "crowds" who followed Jesus, he also records for us other occasions on which he sought to teach his disciples in a more closed environment, away from the gaze of the masses (Mark 3:13; 7:17–23; 9:28–31). Yet, within the busyness and press of ministry, he also ensured that his disciples had, as it were, "a front row seat" to ministry in action. Indeed, they were being invited to observe, think and learn. So often, it was their exposure to Jesus' public ministry that set the stage for their private "tutorials" (as in Mark 7:7–23).

But as Mark 6:7–13 indicates, an integral part of their learning, growth, and development was their own, hands-on participation in the work/ministry of Jesus. Thus, having invested deeply in their individual lives, Jesus sent his disciples out, with his authority, to engage in the task of ministry. Here was their opportunity to put theory into practice, to draw together what they had learned in their minds and seen practically demonstrated for them. Then, at the conclusion of such an exercise, we find that the disciples were encouraged to return to Jesus and reflect or debrief on their experiences (Mark 6:30–32). While we are not privy to the precise methodology which Jesus employed in helping his disciples to reflect upon their ministry experiences, we cannot miss his intention when the seventy-two, who were sent out in Luke 10, returned and reported all that had taken place. Jesus not only celebrated their successes with them (Luke 10:18–19) but also offered them another lens through which they might also reflect upon their experience (Luke 10:20–24). Jesus clearly wanted his disciples to not only engage in ministry but to grow in their ministry effectiveness as they reflected upon their ministry journey.

So, what does it take to become a truly reflective ministry practitioner?

The Value of Discernment

One of the greatest traps in ministry development can be the blind endeavor to simply model one's ministry practice on the performance of some other ministry leader that the ministry candidate has come to appreciate, whether that be their ministry mentor or another person whose ministry style they would long to emulate. This is in no way to devalue the role of faithful ministry mentors who invest their lives well into the development of up-and-coming ministry leaders. Indeed, the model of disciples making disciples has a strong biblical warrant (Matt 28:19).

To the extent that other ministry leaders are faithfully following the example of Christ, we might properly endorse the notion of looking for godly examples to follow in ministry. This was the essence of the Apostle

Paul's charge to the Corinthians, "Follow my example, as I follow the example of Christ" (1 Cor 11:1).

But here a note of caution is warranted. To simply seek to imitate another person's specific approach to ministry can be a significant trap. First, because Ephesians 4:11 reminds us that we are not all called to exercise precisely the same ministry, nor are we all endowed with the same spiritual gifts (1 Cor 12:1–12). As Romans 12:6 says, "We have different gifts, according to the grace given to us." And none of these gifts has been given to us for our own self-aggrandizement. They have been given so that we might have the spiritual resource necessary to exercise the specific ministry that God has prepared for us. But, the second trap into which we can easily fall is that some people, whilst having accurately identified their spiritual gifting and potential sphere of service, simply seek to imitate others in their ministry practice without recognizing that our spiritual gifts are to be developed through careful and reflective exercise. As previously mentioned, even as Jesus sent out the seventy-two in Luke 10 we see that he helped them, upon their return, to reflect deeply upon what they have seen and experienced.

The Value of Reflective Practice

In the busyness of ministry, it becomes extremely easy to run simply from one task to the next, seeking to synthesize and put into practice the diverse range of ministry knowledge and skills which we have acquired through both our informal and formal training. With the competing demands of life and ministry, we are often forced to move quickly from one sphere of ministry to another with little time in between our commitments. When we do finally have the opportunity to stop, many of us are then keen to reward ourselves with some well deserved "downtime." Yet, in the midst of the press of ministry many fail to see the value of the "pause," to stop and reflect upon not only the task of ministry but how they are seeking to integrate their understanding of who they are, what they believe, and how they serve in ministry.

Nash and Nash[3] posit that amongst the many valuable contributions that reflective practice provide are such things as:

- developing of our self-awareness;
- enabling us to see how we are integrating values and practice;
- empowering us as practitioners as we grow in confidence and have better understanding of what we do;

3. Nash and Nash, *Tools for Reflective Practice*, 23.

- liberating us for some of the preconceptions or assumptions about ourselves, others and our ministry;
- helping us solve problems in a creative rather than formulaic way;
- leading to action or decision;
- developing our capacity to deal with new situations as they arise.

However, Johns[4] reminds us that genuine reflection must not only be a matter of "*doing* reflection" as if reflection was just a tool or device, but "*being* reflective," helping us to move beyond simply thinking about "what we do," to "who we are." He further suggests that there are multiple layers of reflection which will help us to move from the more epistemological approach of just "*doing* reflection" to the deeper ontological approach of "*being* reflective." Johns' proposed typologies of reflective practices are illustrated in the table below:

Reflection on Experience	The practitioner reflects on a particular situation after the event in order to learn from it and to inform future practice.	*Doing* Reflection
Reflection in Action	The practitioner pauses to make sense of an experience as it is going on to reframe the situation to achieve desired outcomes.	
The Internal Supervisor	The practitioner dialogues with self while in conversation with another as a process of making sense and response.	
Reflection within the Moment	The practitioner is mindful of his/her pattern of thinking, feeling, and responding within the unfolding moment ensuring that responses are congruent and providing space to change his/her mind rather than being fixed about how to proceed.	
Mindful Practice	The practitioner sees things for what they are without distortion.	*Being* Reflective

Emily Click maintains that theological field education can help to build "habits of ministerial reflection" which will enable ministry students to "become more attuned to the multiple meanings embedded in [ministry] situations and the layers of interpretation."[5] Click asserts further that the goal of field education is to help students "integrate [these] multiple types of reflection into a coherent framework."[6]

4. Johns, *Becoming a Reflective Practitioner*, 4.
5. Click, "Ministerial Reflection," 31.
6. Ibid., 31.

The goal of quality theological education is clearly to develop those who can be reflective, and for this to be adequate the reflection needs to embrace the behavioral, cognitive and affective domains of learning. Thus, I would posit that good reflective practice in ministry will demand a suite of integrative and reflective practices which will include practical (behavioral), theological (cognitive), and personal (affective) reflection.

Developing a Framework for Reflective Practice

While many ministry students will acknowledge the potential value of reflective practice, I assert that without a suitable framework to engage in the task, the concept can easily become yet another aspirational ideal which sounds good in theory but gains little traction in practice.

As indicated above, there are multiple layers of both reflection and interpretation which need to be processed and synthesized for truly reflective practice to take place. For that reason, I posit below a threefold framework for establishing ongoing reflective ministry practice. The threefold loci which underpin this framework include practical or situational reflection, theological reflection, and personal reflection.

Before considering each of these in more detail it needs to be pointed out that none of these is intended to be considered in complete isolation. Truly reflective practice will demand an ability to genuinely integrate the various forms and levels of reflection thus ensuing personal growth which facilitates more "faithful practice" and "truthful action" into the future.

Practical/Situational Reflection

Perhaps the most obvious and seemingly simple form of ministerial reflection is that of practical or situational reflection. Here the ministry practitioner intentionally reflects upon a particular ministry activity or function. In this respect, Scharen[7] identifies three main postures from which this kind of reflection may take place. The first of these is "Observation and Reflection" where the student has been authorized to be an observer (for example, accompanying their ministry supervisor in any number of ministry contexts such as hospital visitation). "Being present together then provides the basis of a conversation about the 'whats' and 'whys' involved in the situation."[8] A

---

7. Scharen, "Vocational Formation for Ministry: The Need for Contextual Reflection," 408.

8. Ibid., 408.

second level of observation would involve "Participation and Reflection." Here the ministry supervisor will have agreed in advance on a specific ministry function in which the student will be engaged. Following on from this engagement the student and the mentor will then reflect on the dynamics of the ministry activity and the possible lessons to be learned from the experience. A third level of observation moves the student into a more responsible position of "Leading and Reflecting." In such cases, more autonomy is granted to the student, taking greater ownership of their preparation and execution of the ministry function. Yet, once again, the process demands intentional reflection, prior to, during and after the ministry activity.

Ballard and Pritchard[9] strongly advocate for the use of an "action-reflection" model when it comes to ministerial reflection. While such models have been posited in a variety of forms over recent decades the model they suggest is most helpful is known as the "pastoral cycle." In short, this model includes a four-step process:

1. Experience. The starting point is the present situation—the ministry setting in which one is called upon to either observe or function.

2. Exploration. Any considered response must be based upon an analysis of what was/is going on. This demands information and a consideration of the multiple perspectives of those who have been involved in the ministry activity, be they fellow ministry servants or those being ministered to.

3. Reflection. Information, by itself, does not give answers; it only indicates possibilities. There is a range of other matters which need to be taken into consideration: personal and communal beliefs about how the world works, the purpose of life, moral values, and religious/spiritual convictions.

4. Action. This comes out of the whole process based on good reflective practice which in turn informs and shapes future decisions and actions.

Yet, Ballard and Pritchard remind us that the cycle does not stop. Indeed, "the pastoral cycle is really a spiral, moving on all the time"[10] as it shapes and develops our thinking and our future ministry practice.

---

9. Ballard and Pritchard, "Tools for Practical Theology—Introducing the Pastoral Cycle," 81–95.
10. Ibid., 86.

So, what kinds of questions might best facilitate good practical/situational reflection? In the following sample exercise, I suggest a range of questions which may stimulate this kind of reflection.

While this kind of reflection is extremely helpful, as ministry practitioners there is another important dimension to our reflective process and that is our biblical/theological reflection, for out of this flows our deeper

---

Practical/Situational Reflection

Briefly describe the event, activity or ministry experience you have chosen to reflect upon. Be as specific as possible, identifying the context and purpose.

1. What were your specific responsibilities?
2. Were you required to or able to take initiative?
3. What went well? What did not go well? Why?
4. What would you do differently if you could engage in this ministry exercise again?

---

convictions about life, meaning, and purpose, and relationship with God and others.

Theological Reflection

As ministry practitioners, theological reflection ought to be an integral part of our reflective practice, since a failure to allow our theological convictions to guide and shape our actions runs the serious risk of rendering us as little more than ministry pragmatists. In that sense, as ministry practitioners we are to be "practical theologians"; that is, we are to be constantly relating our ministry practice to our theological understanding and convictions. Forrester suggests that "practical theology [is] a study which is concerned with questions of truth in relation to action."[11]

So, what are the sources of "truth" which may guide us in terms of our faithful action in ministry? Since the 1970s the concept of what became known as the "Wesleyan Quadrilateral" has provided a useful framework for many who have sought to develop a faithful hermeneutic which brings

---

11. Forrester, *Truthful Action: Explorations in Practical Theology*, 22.

critical theological reflection into dialogue with praxis, thus encouraging faithful action on the part of the ministry practitioner.

While Wesley did not use the term "quadrilateral" himself, Thorsen notes that the term, first coined by Albert Outler in the 1960s, was used to "refer to Wesley's understanding of religious authority. It affirms the primacy of scriptural authority along with the secondary, albeit genuine, religious authority of tradition, reason, and experience."[12] Conceptual diagrams to illustrate this "Wesleyan Quadrilateral" have variously been fashioned to convey the essential thrust of Wesley's proposition.

In essence, Wesley posited that true theological reflection must always be rooted back into the Scriptures since this is the source of what Schaffer called "true truth."[13] Notwithstanding, there is also truth to be discerned from wider spheres of inquiry, which often supplement and find strong correlation with the revealed truths of the Scriptures. Such truths, according to Wesley, can be gleaned from the spheres of experience, reason, and tradition.

While theological reflection, of necessity, takes us back to the Scriptures it also begs us to consider how these scriptural truths shape our assessment and use of a range of other spheres of enlightenment. Nash and Nash rightly warn that "there is a danger that theological reflection can degenerate into a simplistic version of 'what would Jesus do?' As well as engaging with our faith heritage, our experience needs to be understood in this context, which often means also drawing on social science disciplines for insight."[14]

So, what kinds of questions might best facilitate good theological reflection? Shaw[15] employs a range of questions which are designed to evoke deeper theological reflection amongst theological students. They are summarized in the following table of questions:

While these two forms of reflection are vital in the task of ministerial reflective practice, there is yet another form of reflection which is critical to the ongoing development of the faithful ministry practitioner, and that is "personal reflection."

---

12. Thorsen, "Solus Gratia, Solus Fide, and Solus Scriptura: Reforming Protestant Principles to Serve the Present Age."
13. Schaeffer, "Escape from Reason," 218–19.
14. Nash and Nash, *Tools for Reflective Practice*, 38.
15. Shaw, "Theological Reflection at ABTS."

> Theological Reflection
>
> Consider and respond to the following questions:
>
> 1. What aspects of God's character were revealed through your experience?
> 2. In what ways [and to what extent] was the missionary heart of God demonstrated within this context? Explain your thinking.
>
> A central theological lens is that of salvation history—creation, fall, redemption, consummation: humans are created in God's image but fallen, and consequently we can expect to see something of God's character and something of the fall in those we serve.
>
> 3. Without mentioning names how do we see this in action?
>
> The work of Christ has opened the way for redemptive responses to negative situations as we strive towards the consummate ideal. Consider at least one negative situation you observed.
>
> 4. How might this situation have been approached in a more redemptive way? What could you as a cross-bearing servant personally have done to promote redemption?
> 5. What other theological themes were apparent as you reflect on this experience? (e.g. the role of the church in building the kingdom of God on earth; the incarnation etc.)
>
> Reflecting on the church context where you served [if relevant]:
>
> 6. Name at least two ways that the church demonstrated sound biblical ecclesiology. Were there any ways in which the church context differed from what you see as the biblical idea of the church? Explain your response.
> 7. What do you think God would want to speak into the situation that you experienced to the various people/communities that were involved? How do you think he might seek to do this?

Personal Reflection

Patton maintains that "theological reflection should contribute to a wisdom that gains insight into situations of ministry, that creatively interprets the texts and traditions of faith, and that further develops the *person* and *practice* of the minister" (emphasis added).[16] Indeed, it is through the process of intentional, personal reflection that we can begin to more accurately assess both the effectiveness of our practice and the congruence between our stated beliefs and our praxis.

Hillier lauds the value of critical reflection amongst those who are engaged in the education arena. Her suggestion is that "when we reflect, we not only challenge our assumptions about why we do what we do, we can also help ourselves identify where we feel lacking."[17] To that extent, personal reflection can be a valuable tool in helping us to assess our performance in any set task or ministry context. However, Hillier's focus on personal reflection is essentially focused upon the individual's performance as a practitioner.

Within the context of ministry practice, this is an extremely important component of our development as reflective practitioners. In such a process, we are constantly reflecting on our performance as servants of God and of others. Typical questions which arise in such reflection are: What went well in this setting? What could I have done differently or better? What ministry skills do I need to continue working on? Where we identify a "lack," we are then able to take decisive remedial steps. While there is clearly a degree of overlap between this and "situational reflection" mentioned earlier, this goes to the development of our personal skills and competency in ministry. This is, at last in part, how we continue to grow in our ministry effectiveness.

Yet, my experience of the past few years has alerted me to another level of personal reflection which I suspect is all too often lacking in our personal reflection. This is our ability to reflect, not only upon who we are as ministry servants, but who we are as children of God. If, as was posited at the start, "we minister out of who we are,"[18] as opposed to just what we do, then this becomes a vitally important question.

Too readily we can use personal reflection to hone our ministry skills such that we can become well versed and well skilled in the "art of ministry." Yet, if that ministry is not being fueled and sustained by a deepening understanding of who we are as children of God, we can too easily develop an unhealthy dichotomy between our ministry and who we essentially are.

So, what kinds of questions might best facilitate good personal reflection? Once again, I have borrowed from some of the helpful suggestions posited by Perry Shaw[19]:

---

16. Patton, "Some Reflections on Theological Reflection," 2.
17. Hillier, *Reflective Teaching in Further and Adult Education*, 7.
18. Clinton, *The Making of a Leader*, 32.
19. Shaw, "Reflective Practice."

Conclusion

While this paper posits three main reflective foci for effective ministry practice, it needs to be affirmed that none of these foci can or should be

---

Personal Reflection

Consider and respond to the following questions:

1. What have you learned about yourself as a child of God?
2. What have you learned about God's calling on your life?
3. What have you learned about your role as a ministry practitioner?
4. Are there areas in which you feel God is challenging you at the moment?
5. Are there some changes which you need to make within your personal relationship with God and/or your ministry practice?

---

viewed in total isolation. Nash and Nash assert that a number of voices are needed to facilitate ministerial reflective practice. They contend that "for a theologically reflective practice and lifestyle two voices are not enough."[20] What is needed in their view is not merely a dialogue between theology and practice, but a "trialogue," a reflective conversation that embraces "the voice of God and our Christian heritage," "our own beliefs, personal and professional values and theory from our discipline," and "experience." I would posit that in the development of truly effective ministry practitioners, we need to develop a genuine "trialogue" between practical or situational reflection, theological reflection and personal reflection which sees the ministry practitioner developing, not just the requisite skills for ministry, but a deep personal relationship with God which fuels and sustains ministry for the long haul. For such an integrated reflection to yield its ongoing fruit in the life of the ministry practitioner, there needs to be a recognition that merely *doing* reflection as a "one-off" or occasional exercise, will never be sufficient. What is required is an ongoing commitment to a lifestyle of *being* truly reflective.

---

20. Nash and Nash, *Tools for Reflective Practice*, 41.

Bibliography

Ballard, Paul, and John Pritchard. "Tools for Practical Theology—Introducing the Pastoral Cycle." In *Practical Theology in Action: Christian Thinking in the Service of Church and Society*, 81–95. London: SPCK, 2006.

Click, Emily. "Ministerial Reflection." In *Welcome to Theological Field Education*, edited by Matthew Floding. Herndon, VA: Alban Institute, 2011.

Clinton, J. R. *The Making of a Leader*. Colorado Springs: Nav Press, 1988.

Forrester, Duncan. *Truthful Action: Explorations in Practical Theology*. Edinburgh: T & T Clark, 2000.

Hillier, Yvonne. *Reflective Teaching in Further and Adult Education*. London: Continuum, 2005.

Johns, Christopher. *Becoming a Reflective Practitioner*. West Sussex: Wiley-Blackwell, 2013.

Nash, Sally, and Paul Nash. *Tools for Reflective Practice*. London: SPCK, 2009.

Patton, John. "Some Reflections on Theological Reflection." *The Journal of Christian Ministry* 2 (2010): 1–23.

Schaeffer, Francis. "Escape from Reason." In *The Complete Works of Francis Schaeffer*. Wheaton, IL: Paternoster, 1982.

Scharen, Christian. "Vocational Formation for Ministry: The Need for Contextual Reflection." *Word and World* 3, no. 4 (2013).

Shaw, Perry. "Reflective Practice." Beirut, Lebanon: The Arab Baptist Theological Seminary, 2016.

———. "Theological Reflection at ABTS." Beirut, Lebanon: The Arab Baptist Theogical Seminary, 2017.

Thorsen, Don. "Solus Gratia, Solus Fide, and Solus Scriptura: Reforming Protestant Principles to Serve the Present Age." In *The Continuing Relevance of Wesleyan Theology*, edited by Nathan Crawford. Eugene, OR: Wipf and Stock, 2011.

Vos, Beverly. "The Spiritual Disciplines and Christian Ministry." *Evangelical Review of Theology*, 36, no. 2 (April 2012): 100.

15

Rethinking our Approach to Student Formation in Australian Theological Education

Diane Hockridge

Abstract

This chapter makes some practical recommendations for theological college leaders and educators looking for ways to contribute to student formation in the changing context of Australian theological higher education. It recommends that as an intended holistic outcome of theological education, student formation requires a holistic response which includes the entire institution, the entire learning experience, and addresses the whole person. Drawing on educational research and good practice, the chapter proposes ways in which colleges can intentionally recontextualize their formation strategies for the new learning contexts in which students are located, and suggests some ways of evaluating the impact of these strategies. It recommends some educational approaches, pedagogies and learning designs known to be particularly effective and beneficial for student formation. And it recommends colleges recognize the natural limits and boundaries of their contribution to student formation and engage in effective partnerships with others to further enhance and extend their impact.

Introduction

THEOLOGICAL EDUCATION IS INTENTIONALLY formative. A theological education is expected to be personally transformative of the whole person, to impact on "head, heart and hands." Yet a broad holistic goal like spiritual formation of students sits somewhat uneasily in the formal higher education environment in which Australian theological colleges find themselves. Along with rapidly changing learning and teaching contexts and modes of study this brings some unique constraints and challenges to the sector. How might Australian theological colleges and educators grapple with these challenges and constraints to encourage and support student formation?

Spiritual formation, in its broad sense, is usually understood as the lifelong journey of Christian discipleship. As such, it is a topic of significance and interest to Christians and church communities in general as well as to theological educators. Many traditions, practices, emphases and understandings of spiritual formation exist across the spectrum of Christian history and experience. While the term "spiritual formation" is often used in theological education, it usually refers to more than individual personal spirituality. This chapter uses the generic term "student formation" to refer to the holistic formative intentions of theological education.[1]

This chapter makes some practical recommendations for theological college leaders and educators looking for ways to contribute to student formation in our changing educational context. It recommends that as an intended holistic outcome of theological education, student formation requires a holistic response which includes the entire institution, the entire learning experience, and addresses the whole person. It suggests that addressing student formation is a complex or "wicked" educational problem[2] which requires a complex, thoughtful and educationally sound response using pedagogies and learning designs that are conducive to formation. It recommends that colleges intentionally recontextualize their formation strategies for the new learning contexts in which students are located, and suggests some ways of evaluating the impact of these strategies. It further suggests that colleges recognize the natural limits and boundaries of their contribution to student formation and engage in effective partnerships with others to enhance and extend their impact.

In summary, an effective approach to student formation will:

1. Articulate clear formational goals at an institutional level.

---

1. This usage is consistent with common practice in the context of theological education. See Hockridge, "Challenges for Educators," 149.
2. Knight and Page, "The Assessment of 'Wicked' Competencies."

2. Develop a whole-program approach to address student formation.
3. Use pedagogies and learning designs conducive to student formation.
4. Employ appropriate means of evaluating or assessing formation.
5. Work within and across the boundaries of theological education.

Each of the following sections identifies key challenges, provides examples of good practice or insights from research, and suggests some potential practical applications for colleges and individual educators.

Articulate Clear Formational Goals at an Institutional Level

There is little doubt that Australian theological colleges have formational aims. Sherlock has described Australian theological education as being "marked by a strongly formative ethos."[3] Theological programs of study aim to not only produce graduates who are competent for a profession, but who also have broader and deeper expectations of moral transformation, spiritual growth and the development of mature character as disciples of Christ. These are reflected in the Australian College of Theology graduate attributes which expect graduates to emerge from their courses as: 1) Christian people; 2) Christian scholars; 3) Christian professionals; and 4) Christian leaders.

While the formative intentions of theological education are widely agreed, there can be lack of clarity regarding particular formational outcomes sought by individual colleges. Colleges and educators use a variety of terms to describe formation including; spiritual, personal, ministry, pastoral, character, and leadership formation. The varying educational and denominational emphases of the individual institutions within the Australian College of Theology consortium impact on each institution's approach to formation. For example, a college that prepares students for ordination needs to meet relevant denominational expectations and is likely to have somewhat different formational emphases to a college that prepares students for overseas mission.

To effectively contribute to spiritual formation of students the first task of a theological college or faculty is to clearly articulate their formational goals. Colleges need to be clear about what they understand "formation" to mean, the formational outcomes they are seeking, and whether these are related primarily to personal or spiritual formation, ministry, pastoral or

---

3. Sherlock, *Uncovering Theology*, 13.

leadership formation. To identify formational goals colleges can ask questions such as: What is a "formed" person like? What are our expectations and aspirations for a "formed" person? What will they know? How will they act? What will they value? What will they be able to do? Who will they be? What are we forming them for?

Clearly articulated formational goals at an institutional level help set the direction and establish priorities which enable a consistent approach and commitment to student formation across all aspects of college life and teaching. Articulating such goals is a "big picture" exercise which is best done corporately, involving all relevant stakeholders who are likely to contribute to the overall formational outcomes the college wants to achieve. It can also be a helpful exercise for individual educators or teams who want to review desired formational outcomes for a specific subject or set of subjects.

APPLICATION

Guiding Question: What are our formational goals for students?

Suggested Actions:

Institutional level: Determine whether your college has clearly articulated its formational goals. Review existing statements such as your institutional mission and values statements. These are likely to already articulate and incorporate broad level formational goals. Are these adequate or might they need revision? Has your college developed graduate attributes statements and do these adequately address your formational goals?

Subject level: Faculty members could work individually or in small teams to identify or review specific ways in which subjects or sets of subjects are intended to contribute to formation of students.

Develop a Whole-Program Approach to Address Student Formation

In the formal higher education environment in which Australian theological education operates colleges need to develop an integrated whole-program approach to address student formation. Like many theological training institutions Australian theological colleges are subject to constraints including the accreditation requirements of Tertiary Education Quality Standards Agency (TEQSA) and the Australian Qualifications Framework

(AQF) standards. Colleges are expected to meet certain quality standards for teaching, learning and assessment and provide evidence of how they do so. Operating in this formal higher education environment introduces a tension for theological colleges seeking to address student formation. To what extent should spiritual formation be included in our formal educational goals, or in our curriculum? Is it possible to "teach" formation? Or to "assess" it? Historically, Australian theological institutions have tended to deal with this tension by addressing formation in a variety of *informal* ways, through cocurricular or extracurricular activities such as communal meals, chapel services, or student small groups. There are however some problems with this approach.

One problem is that while there is often great value in such informal activities it can be difficult to evaluate their impact and effectiveness. Colleges may assume they are addressing formation by offering such activities, but are they able to clearly articulate their formative purpose and impact? Another problem is that if colleges' approach to student formation is heavily dependent on cocurricular or extracurricular activities, they risk not actually reaching large parts of their student cohorts as students increasingly study part-time, at a distance and in mixed mode. Colleges need to consider how to address the formational needs of students who aren't able to participate in these campus-based activities. This can be done by addressing formation in students' formal learning experiences, whether these are online, on campus or a mix of both, as well as via informal experiences and activities. Indeed, we are selling ourselves short if we don't plan to address formation via our formal curriculum.

There remains an important place for colleges to include campus-based cocurricular or extracurricular activities as part of their formation strategy, however, in order to be effective in encouraging student formation we need to do more. As Ball's 2012 report noted, Australian theological colleges need to take an integrated approach to addressing student formation which includes the entire student learning experience; curricular, cocurricular and extracurricular formational activities.[4]

A relatively simple means of addressing formation in the formal curriculum is for colleges to mandate or recommend particular units of study with a formational focus, such as *Guided Spiritual Formation*, or *Ministry Formation*,[5] within student's programs. It is not, however, necessary to include specific units of study with a formational focus in order to encour-

---

4. Ball, *Transforming Theology*, 126. See also "Where Are We Going?"

5. The Australian College of Theology curriculum includes a range of units of study with formation-specific content.

age student formation. Nor should colleges assume that by offering formal units of study in formation that they are necessarily adequately addressing formation. Hussey's research indicates that such units may have a relatively low formational impact and that students attribute their spiritual formation to a range of educational experiences.[6]

To plan an integrated approach to address student formation colleges can undertake a *formation mapping* exercise. Similar to curriculum mapping, formation mapping aims to map out how formational goals can be addressed in curricular, cocurricular, and extracurricular activities. Again, this is an exercise best undertaken corporately and involving relevant stakeholders, such as teaching faculty, and other relevant academic and support staff. The mapping exercise has two main stages. In the first stage colleges ask what is currently being done to foster and support student formation. The aim is to record, preferably in a visually accessible manner, all the ways in which formation is being addressed. The second stage is evaluative and forward-looking. Colleges can ask themselves whether their current approach is effective, and how they know it is effective. They can identify gaps in their approach and consider whether they need to do anything differently. Depending on the answers to these questions, a new approach can be mapped out, which takes into account the student body, their needs, the formational aims of the college and the resources available.

As well as considering how to address formation in the formal curriculum and via cocurricular and extracurricular activities colleges should take into account the impact on student formation of the ethos or culture of the college, or what is sometimes referred to as "the hidden curriculum." The term "hidden curriculum" can be used in a negative way to describe "the shadowy, ill-defined and amorphous nature of that which is implicit and embedded in educational experiences"[7] or to suggest the existence of lurking hidden agendas. However, it can be helpful for colleges to evaluate the hidden curriculum to assess whether the desired messages, values and ethos are communicated and encouraged. Research shows the culture/ethos of an institution has a formative impact on students[8] and that effective student support positively impacts student engagement and satisfaction.[9] Our college websites might declare our commitment to forming mature Chris-

---

6. Hussey, "Spiritual Formation in an Australian Baptist Theological College."

7. Sambell and McDowell, "Construction of the Hidden Curriculum," 391.

8. Hockridge, "Challenges for Educators," 149; Reed and Balzer, *Building a Culture of Faith*, 15.

9. Coates, "Development of the Australasian Survey of Student Engagement (AUSSE)"; Kahu, "Framing Student Engagement in Higher Education"; Peach, "Ensuring Student Success."

tians but is this goal consistently demonstrated and supported across all elements of student experience, in all aspects of our college life? What does our college culture reveal about what our priorities are? What values and behaviors do our management, academic, and support staff model? How does the college as a whole demonstrate care for its students? How does it contribute to their spiritual growth? These questions can also be asked as part of a formation mapping exercise designed to develop an integrated whole institution, whole-program approach to formation.

As colleges consider how to develop an integrated whole-program approach to formation they need to do so in a way that is appropriate for today's new learning and teaching contexts and modes of study. Australian theological students come from increasingly diverse backgrounds and the proportion of students studying at a distance or part-time continues to increase.[10] With the expansion of online learning there has been a corresponding increase in students studying in "mixed mode" (taking some subjects on campus and some online); as well as an increase in the number of subjects offered in "blended" mode (a combination of face-to-face and online learning within the one subject), with the result that boundaries between modes of study are becoming increasingly blurred. In the past theological colleges developed ways of addressing formation that were appropriate for the learning and teaching contexts of their time. Similarly, today's theological colleges need to work out ways to continue to address the heads, hearts and hands of students in current learning and teaching contexts by recontextualizing their formation strategies.

Colleges can recontextualize their approach by identifying the *function* of existing (or proposed) programs or activities in relation to formation, which enables existing activities to be reconfigured for new contexts. Take for example chapel or worship services, which are part of the daily or weekly fabric of many theological colleges. As part of a mapping exercise a college might identify that chapel services on campus contribute to student formation, but it is more helpful (for mapping and strategy purposes) to identify the *function* of those chapel services in relation to formation. Amongst other things chapel services allow students to engage in corporate worship, to see good preaching modeled, to practice preaching themselves, or to practice leading services. A college may decide some or all of these are good reasons for running regular chapel services. And a college might also decide that as well as running chapel it will address the need for student preaching practice in other ways such as through preaching workshops, or through supervised ministry experience in students' own church contexts.

10. Sherlock, *Uncovering Theology*, 44–45.

Or it might seek to connect with students' worship experience in their local church contexts by including intentional reflection on it within their learning experience. Decoupling the desired functions of a particular activity in relation to formation from the activity itself thus enables us to work out ways to include these desired functions in other educational contexts or modes of study.

An effective formation strategy will consider ways in which the whole program (institutional culture, the formal curriculum, and the less formal cocurricular and extracurricular activities) contributes to student formation. And it will do so in a way that is appropriate to current learning and teaching contexts.

APPLICATION

Guiding Questions: How is your college currently addressing student formation? How else might you do it?

Suggested Actions:

Undertake a functional review of existing cocurricular and extracurricular activities to identify how you expect them to contribute to student formation. How else might you address those formational goals? Undertake a formation mapping exercise (contact the author for a formation mapping template).

Use Pedagogies and Learning Designs Conducive to Student Formation

Addressing formation of students is a complex educational problem which requires a complex and thoughtful educational response. An effective formation strategy will intentionally include pedagogies and teaching practices that allow, foster and encourage formation appropriate to the range of learning contexts in which students are engaged. An effective approach to formation will also be intentionally learner-centered, in that it focuses on the intended experience of the learner. What educational approaches, practices and pedagogies are known to be particularly effective and beneficial for student formation?

The Formational Learning Design research project being conducted by the author aims to identify learning design principles and pedagogies that are conducive to formation, particularly in online learning contexts. To do so, the project is working on identifying and describing helpful pedagogies in a *decontextualized* way, which means they can be applied to any learning context, regardless of the mode of study. Preliminary conclusions from this research[11] indicate that formation of students can be fostered where learning contexts (curricular, cocurricular and extracurricular) are designed to:

- allow the development of meaningful relational connections between students, and between students and teachers;
- help students to develop frameworks to assist them in reflecting on and in practice, and include opportunities for supervised practice (e.g. through field education, internships);
- include opportunities for students to engage in spiritual practices and personal reflection;
- provide opportunities for formal and informal mentoring, with teaching staff, peers and mentors external to the college;
- expose students to, and ask them to engage with different perspectives;
- include learning activities and assessments that require students to apply their understanding to real contexts (authentic learning and assessment);
- include intentionally formative outcomes and content (in all subjects).

These pedagogical approaches can be applied in a range of learning modes and contexts. Preliminary data from the Formational Learning Design project indicates that these pedagogies can be successfully applied online to increase the formative impact of online learning for students.

As an educational problem for theological colleges, formation of students deserves an educationally sound response. Theological colleges should therefore continue to develop the quality of their scholarship of teaching and learning. Recent initiatives that support professional development for teaching and learning within the Australian College of Theology have provided helpful platforms for colleges to share and discuss solutions to pedagogical and technological challenges and should be continued. Colleges and educators will also benefit from building professional expertise in the areas of learning design, effective use of educational technologies and learning data analysis.

---

11. This is a partial and preliminary sketch of findings from the Formational Learning Design Project. A full report will be available at the completion of the project.

Employ Appropriate Means of Evaluating or Assessing Formation

Evaluating student formation presents a significant challenge to theological educators. Is it even possible to assess or measure formation? And if it is, do we want to? Theological colleges are rightly wary of superficial or reduction-

> **APPLICATION**
>
> **Guiding Questions:** What pedagogies and learning design practices are conducive for formation and how might you include these in your programs?
>
> **Suggested Actions:**
>
> *Institutional level:* How can your college support the scholarship of learning and teaching and the professional development of your academic staff?
>
> *Individual level:* Review your own teaching practice and identify ways in which it contributes to student formation. Identify any professional development needs in terms of your own learning and teaching practice.

ist forms of assessment relating to student formation. Measures of spiritual growth or maturity are often thought to be overly subjective, and we hesitate about grading spiritual formation. It is, however, beneficial to have some means of assessing formation not only for the benefit of the student but also for reporting to external bodies, such as ordaining committees, and for evaluating and improving our formational approach. But what should we actually be assessing or evaluating? And how should we do it?

Evaluation requires intentionality. Colleges need to clearly communicate formational intentions and expectations and also provide a means of mapping and recording the formational progress of students. Where a college is clear about its desired formational outcomes evaluation will be easier because those outcomes can be turned into a set of indicators, which can then be used by college and students to evaluate their formational journey. The first section of this chapter explained that colleges can set formational goals by asking what a "formed" person is like: What will they know? How will they act? What will they value? What will they be able to do? Who will they be? What are we forming them for? The answers to these questions can help colleges identify a set of "formation indicators" or descriptors of the actions, attitudes, and characteristics that "formed" students are expected to display and practice.

Formation indicators might vary to some extent across theological institutions, but we might expect some commonality at a broad level that formation indicators for theological students would relate to: developing and applying theological understanding; developing dispositions and patterns of behavior helpful for lifelong personal spiritual growth and maturity, and for Christian leadership and ministry; developing skills and proficiencies for Christian leadership and ministry. Within these broad categories colleges can identify specific indicators of formation appropriate to their institutional goals, and learning and teaching context. Having identified the desired indicators, colleges can then look for ways in which these are evidenced or expressed by students. In this way "formation indicators" serve as a proxy for student formation and can be used in evaluation.

Evaluating or assessing individual student formation is best done in partnership with the student and, where possible, in partnership with others who know the student. The college's role is to advise students of its expectations around formational outcomes; to encourage students to take control of the process by equipping them to set their own formational priorities and goals; and to enable opportunities for staged self-assessment at key points. Rather than "grading" formation our evaluation should focus on the overall trajectory or direction in which a student is heading and the progress they are making towards appropriate goals.[12] Staged self-assessment might involve submission of reflective reports by students at key points such as entry and exit points, or annually, or take the form of student self-reflective portfolio over the entire student journey. In addition to self-assessment, input from appropriate third parties (such as ministry supervisors, mentors, local church ministers) can provide additional evaluative information.

APPLICATION

Guiding Questions: How do you know whether your formational strategy works? How could you improve it?

Suggested Actions:

Workshop these questions: Does your college have a set of formation indicators (or equivalent)? How do you communicate these to students? Can you identify key points or milestones for evaluation of student formation? Do you have a plan for staged self-assessment of student formation? Is there existing data that you could use to help evaluate student formation? What other data might you need to collect?

---

12. Shaw, *Transforming Theological Education*, 21, 56.

The emerging field of Learner Experience Design[13] employs a variety of learner-centered strategies such as "Learner Journey Mapping" and learner-controlled use of data, some of which might be helpfully applied in theological colleges to map and record the formational progress of students.

Work Within and Across the Boundaries of Theological Education

Whether articulating goals, developing strategies, or evaluating progress, theological colleges and educators need to keep in mind the limitations and boundaries of the theological student experience. As Shaw points out, the student's experience of theological education is only one element of their lifelong journey to spiritual maturity, and theological educators are not responsible for delivering everything a student needs for the rest of their life.[14] As theological educators our contribution to the formation of students, though it may be significant, is limited. Ultimately, we need to remember that formation is the result of the work of God's Spirit among his people.

What contribution can theological educators realistically make towards student formation? Educators can firstly focus on preparing students as best they can for the long haul; for the actual world in which they live, work and minister. Statistics on burn out of ministers and an increasing demand for post-theological college mentoring indicate colleges may not be successfully forming students for the current demands of Christian ministry.[15] Educators can better prepare students by ensuring theological programs don't just fill students' heads with knowledge but enable them to develop helpful spiritual practices and habits, and equip them with skills for lifelong learning and tools for resilience.[16] Since we know that a significant proportion of Australian theological students do not intend to engage in full-time ministry or to work in church or Christian contexts,[17] we also need to consider how we might better equip and form students who choose to work primarily in non-church contexts.

Second, educators can help students make meaningful connections between their learning and their real life, work and ministry experiences by using authentic means of learning and assessment. Nichols' research

---

13. For example, Seitzinger, "Learner Experience Design." Formation by Design Project, "Formation by Design Project Progress Report 2014–15."

14. Shaw, *Transforming Theological Education*, 20–21.

15. One example: Croucher, "Pastor Burnout Statistics."

16. Ball, *Transforming Theology*, 135–36.

17. Sherlock, *Uncovering Theology*, 44–45.

indicates that students are better formed where their study experience connects with and draws on their real life and ministry setting for learning.[18] Similarly Lowe and Lowe suggest the student theological education experience should utilize the wider context of the larger macro system or ecology of the student for learning.[19] Including authentic assessment which asks students to apply their learning to real contexts is a simple way of meaningfully connecting learning to the student's wider context. Taking the student's broader life context into account can also help theological colleges and educators not to overburden students with unnecessary expectations or overloaded courses.

Third, as colleges and educators recognize the boundaries and limits of their contribution to formation they can seek to work with others across those boundaries. Sadly, there is often a disconnect or gap between theological colleges and churches. How might theological colleges and churches partner with each other in more productive ways? This is clearly a large and complex topic, however, a relatively simple and strategic step would be for theological colleges to encourage or require students to include more work and ministry-based learning experiences in their programs. Australian College of Theology accredited study programs already include a variety of accredited elective field education units which are designed to incorporate practical experience in programs of study. The field education and other practically oriented units in the developmental ministry and pastoral and church-focused ministry fields provide great opportunities for students to be formed through mentored experience, receiving feedback and engaging in reflective practice, as part of their formal study program. Unfortunately, these are underutilized. In 2016, only 8 percent of the total student body enrolled in a field education unit, and this represented only 2.3 percent of the total EFTSL for the ACT.[20]

Offering such units may help to establish good ongoing working partnerships between colleges and local churches and the wider Christian community. The Australian public university sector is currently working to develop community and industry partnerships that enable work-integrated learning and establish partnerships of value to the broader community. There is great potential for theological colleges to similarly pursue productive partnerships with church and parachurch groups that engage students

---

18. Nichols, "A Comparison of Spiritual Formation Experiences," 193.

19. Lowe and Lowe, "Spiritual Formation in Theological Distance Education," 98–99.

20. Enrollment statistics provided by the ACT Registrar's Office.

in hands-on learning and reflection in and on action[21] and help to enhance and extend the formative impact of theological education.

> **APPLICATION**
>
> **Guiding Questions:** How might your college partner more productively with relevant churches and other organizations? What opportunities for supervised practical ministry experience does your college currently offer? How might your college better prepare students to live and work as effective Christians in diverse work contexts?

Conclusion

Theological colleges and educators desire to offer their students more than an academic qualification. We seek to form not only head, but hearts and hands as well, to prepare people as faithful Christian disciples, as leaders for our churches, and as evangelists who will continue to teach the gospel. To do so, we need to recognize and respond to the realities of our current educational context and the associated challenges for addressing student formation. Formation of students will continue to be well served where colleges articulate their formational goals at an institutional level, and respond with a whole of institution approach and commitment to formation. Colleges can work towards recontextualizing their formation strategies for new learning contexts by identifying the functions of existing formational strategies and activities and by addressing these in the formal curriculum as well as through cocurricular and extracurricular activities. We can use pedagogies and learning designs for classroom and online learning contexts that we know to be conducive to formation. We can be more intentional about communicating our formational goals and the ways in which we work with students to evaluate progress towards these. And we can explore opportunities to work with others within and across the boundaries of theological education to continue to enhance student formation.

---

21. Banks, *Reenvisioning Theological Education*, 157–68.

Bibliography

Ball, Les. *Transforming Theology: Student Experience and Transformative Learning in Undergraduate Theological Education.* Preston, VIC: Mosaic, 2012.

———. "Where Are We Going?" In *Learning and Teaching Theology: Some Ways Ahead,* edited by Les Ball and James R. Harrison, 11–20. Northcote: Morning Star, 2014.

Banks, Robert. *Reenvisioning Theological Education: Exploring a Missional Alternative to Current Models.* Grand Rapids: Eerdmans, 1999.

Coates, Hamish. "Development of the Australasian Survey of Student Engagement (AUSSE)." *Higher Education* 60, no. 1 (2010): 1–17.

Croucher, Rowland. "Pastor Burnout Statistics." http://www.jmm.org.au/articles/27347.htm.

Formation by Design Project. "Formation by Design Project Progress Report 2014–15." https://futures.georgetown.edu/formation/.

Hockridge, Diane. "Challenges for Educators Using Distance and Online Education to Prepare Students for Relational Professions." *Distance Education* 34, no. 2 (2013): 142–60.

Hussey, Ian. "Spiritual Formation in an Australian Baptist Theological College: A Survey-Based Case Study." *Journal of Adult Theological Education* 12, no. 2 (2015): 137–52.

Kahu, Ella R. "Framing Student Engagement in Higher Education." *Studies in Higher Education* 38, no. 5 (2013): 758–73.

Knight, Peter, and Anna Page. "The Assessment of 'Wicked' Competences: A Report to the Practice-Based Professional Learning Centre for Excellence in Teaching and Learning in the Open University." 2007.

Lowe, Stephen D., and Mary Lowe. "Spiritual Formation in Theological Distance Education: An Ecosystems Model." *Christian Education Journal* 7, no. 1 (2010): 85–102.

Nichols, Mark. "A Comparison of Spiritual Formation Experiences between On-Campus and Distance Evangelical Theological Education Students." PhD diss., University of Otago, 2014.

Peach, D. "Ensuring Student Success: The Role of Support Services in Improving the Quality of Student Learning Experience." *Studies in Learning, Evaluation, Innovation and Development* 2, no. 3 (2005): 1–15.

Reed, Rod, and Cary Balzer. *Building a Culture of Faith: Campus-Wide Partnership for Spiritual Formation.* ACU Press, 2012.

Sambrell, Kay, and Liz McDowell. "The Construction of the Hidden Curriculum: Messages and Meanings in the Assessment of Student Learning." *Assessment and Evaluation in Higher Education* 23, no. 4 (1998): 391–402.

Seitzinger, Joyce. "Learner Experience Design." http://www.lxdesign.co/.

Shaw, Perry. *Transforming Theological Education: A Practical Handbook for Integrative Learning.* Carlisle: Langham Creative, 2014.

Sherlock, C. *Uncovering Theology: The Depth, Reach and Utility of Australian Theological Education.* Adelaide: ATF Press, 2009.

16

Theological Education for Cross-Cultural Ministry

Phillip Scheepers

Abstract

Most theological educators would agree that developing the cross-cultural competence and understanding of students are highly desirable as educational outcomes. Unfortunately, these outcomes are not always achieved. The twin purposes of this chapter are to explore why developing solid cross-cultural skills and awareness can sometimes be a challenging task, and also to provide some suggestions for best practice for theological educators working in this field. It is shown that effective cross-cultural training is about much more than offering specific units dealing with culture. Instead equipping students to be effective in this area will require a multi-disciplinary and comprehensive approach.

Reasons for Strengthening Training for Cross-Cultural Ministry

IT IS PROBABLY FAIR to suggest that the idea that culture should be taken seriously in theological formation will be seen as fairly uncontroversial by most theological educators in twenty-first-century Australia and around the world. In fact, the recent *Global Survey on Theological Education* found that cross-cultural communication is one of the subjects that respondents would most like to see added or strengthened in theological education.[1]

While many streams have fed into this broad-based consensus, two contributing factors, one theological and the other practical, should be noted.

Rediscovering the World

Many in the Western Christian church entered the twentieth century with the deep, some might say triumphalist, conviction that the world will be reached for Christ through the methods and institutions that they were familiar with.[2] This optimism was quickly shattered by a series of events (WWI perhaps chief among them) that showed that Western Christians had a fairly rose-tinted view of how deeply the gospel penetrated their culture.[3] This waning of optimism was significantly sped up by the realization that some non-Western cultures are deeply resistant to the gospel and that this resistance cannot be broken by merely throwing more resources at the problem.[4] Cultures had to be reached at a deeper level. It would, of course, be facetious to suggest that twentieth-century Western Christians were the first to realize this but it can be suggested that the Western cultural captivity of the early twentieth-century church obscured this insight from many, leading to a kind of cultural and ecclesiastical imperialism. The world had to be rediscovered as it were. Not in terms of its geography, but in terms of how the astonishing variety of human culture shapes lives and societies. This is, of course, an ongoing journey of discovery with significant implications for gospel ministry. What is heartening to see is that different Christian traditions took this process of discovery seriously during the in-

---

1. Institute for Cross-Cultural Theological Education, "Global Survey on Theological Education 2011–2013."

2. According to Brian Stanley the delegates at the seminal World Missionary Conference (held in Edinburgh in 1910) arrived with: "... the anticipation that, through the redoubled missionary endeavours of the non-Roman churches of the west, the world was on the eve of a new transfiguration destined to inaugurate the kingdom of God in its fullness and glory." Stanley, *The World Missionary Conference, Edinburgh 1910*, 2.

3. For an excellent analysis of the spiritual impact of the Great War see Jenkins, *The Great and Holy War: How World War I Became a Religious Crusade*, 217–34.

4. This realization was especially strongly tied to the situation in India where centuries of missionary work had produced remarkably little fruit by the beginning of the twentieth century. See Neill and Chadwick, *A History of Christian Missions*, 479–85.

terwar period and beyond. Evidence of this can be seen at the highest level in the proceedings of Vatican II[5] and the Lausanne Conference on World Evangelization (1974)[6] and also in the way mission organizations grappled with the reality of training workers for cross-cultural ministry. Efforts such as these gradually percolated throughout the Western church to the extent that most Christian people in Australia will, at the very least, verbally assent to the importance of recognizing the effects of culture when engaging in Christian ministry.

Welcoming the World

The story of Australia's transformation into a multicultural society hardly needs retelling here. The reality is that in twenty-first-century Australia we are likely to encounter people from very different cultural backgrounds on a daily basis (including in our churches). This fact placed cross-cultural awareness on the agenda in a very real and practical way as something that is not only relevant for "over there." It also alerted the church to the fact that a bit more than verbal assent to the importance of cross-cultural sensitivity might be needed right here in Australia.[7] Unfortunately in many churches efforts at reaching across cultures are often bedeviled by a lack of knowledge or an unwillingness to engage with different cultures at anything beyond the surface level. This reinforces the need for the inclusion of cross-cultural understanding in theological formation as changes in this area will, more often than not, have to be led by leaders who have received some level of theological education.[8]

Pressures Working Against Effective Training for Cross-Cultural Ministry

It follows from the above that there is both awareness of the need for training for cross-cultural ministry and a stated desire to be active at this level

---

5. Markey, "The Making of a Post-Vatican II Theologian: Reflections on 25 Years of Catholic Education," 3–4.

6. Ott, *Beyond Fragmentation: Integration Mission and Theological Education*, 80.

7. Scheepers, "Migration: An Opportunity for the Gospel," 71.

8. Such leaders should be able to at least attempt to provide answers to the vital question posed by Darrell Guder: "How does the vital dialogue of theological education and missional practice contribute to the church's witness to its God-given unity, in all of its cultural and contextual diversity?" Guder, "Theological Formation for Missional Faithfulness after Christendom."

at many theological education institutions in Australia. It is, however, an area where constant efforts will have to be made to improve. A quick survey of the curricula of theological colleges will leave the impression that many institutions are still fairly narrowly focused on equipping students to minister in a broadly Western context.[9] Although training for cross-cultural ministry is sometimes available (e.g. through courses specifically focused on the preparation of missionaries) there remains a real danger that the average Australian theological student will often leave his or her institution ill-prepared to face up to the realities of ministering in a multicultural society. Ways will therefore have to be found for strategies for improving cultural awareness and intelligence to be incorporated into theological education courses, not only for those seeking to serve overseas but also for all who take the call to missional Christianity in our own communities seriously.[10]

It has to be acknowledged that there are some powerful pressures working against effective training for cross-cultural ministry. Here are some of them:

Non-Reflective Attitudes towards Culture

It is a common human foible to view our own cultures as normative and those of others as strange and deviating from the norm. This is evident in the many cultures around the world whose names mean something along the lines of "the people." The subtext to this is that those who do not share in this culture are somehow falling short of the ideal of what it means to be fully human. We should be careful, as worldly-wise Westerners, to sneer at such attitudes as plenty of evidence could be marshalled to show that these kind of attitudes are not merely the preserve of those in traditional tribal societies. The truth is that most people, and this includes theological students, do not tend to reflect deeply on cultural differences and the importance of

---

9. For a discussion of this phenomenon and ways in which curricula can be broadened to truly serve "World Christianity" see Kang, "Envisioning Postcolonial Theological Education: Dilemmas and Possibilities," ibid.

10. This is especially important in helping those who come to faith from non-Western backgrounds to find culturally appropriate expressions of the Christian faith within their context. As J. D. Payne says, "Since sometimes the novelty of Western Christian culture is attractive we must be prepared to respond appropriately. While teaching from the Scriptures on the doctrine of the church, we need to instruct others that our culturally preferred ways are not the only ways and simultaneously help those we are teaching to think how they will apply biblical church planting principles to their own contexts." Payne, *Strangers Next Door: Immigration, Migration, and Mission*, 144.

attempting to understand those belonging to another culture on their own terms. As Paul Hiebert says:

> Clearly we need to understand the gospel in its cultural and historical settings. Without this, we have no message. We also need a clear understanding of ourselves and the people we serve in diverse historical and cultural contexts. Without this, we are in danger of proclaiming a meaningless and irrelevant message.[11]

It is important, in this context, to distinguish between what might be termed surface level and deeper level culture. It is often exciting and new to learn about things like the food, dress and festivals associated with other cultures. We should not make the mistake, however, to think that this is all that is required for cross-cultural understanding. Cultural differences will often go much deeper than these surface-level expressions of diversity.[12] The hard work of cultural awareness and competence must, therefore, necessarily involve asking the difficult worldview questions about what "makes the other culture tick." This does not mean that we are all to turn into amateur anthropologists. It does mean that we should be prepared to deal with culture at a deeper level than what most people are familiar, or perhaps comfortable, with.

Unhelpful Models of Cultural Engagement

Ignorance about other cultures is not the only problem that we will have to face when it comes to training for cross-cultural ministry. It is also the case that we will often have to confront deeply ingrained and unhelpful models and methods of cultural engagement. These may not always be explicitly articulated but they can be foundational to the way in which people think about how the gospel should interact with cultures different from their own. Such models can range from the belief that there is a particular human culture (e.g. Western culture) that is inherently better suited to Christianity to the belief that elements from every culture should simply be incorporated into the life of the church without asking too many questions.[13] The fact is that the Bible affirms and challenges aspects of all human cultures. As Lamin Sanneh reminds us:

---

11. Hiebert, *Anthropological Insights for Missionaries*, 14.

12. For a helpful discussion of the "layers of culture" see Hesselgrave, *Communicating Christ Cross-Culturally: An Introduction to Missionary Communication*, 14.

13. For a discussion of different models of cultural engagement, see Moreau, *Contextualisation in World Missions: Mapping and Assessing Evangelical Models*, 32–47.

> Christianity affects cultures by moving them to a position short of the absolute, and it does this by placing God at the center. The point of departure for the church in mission is Pentecost, with Christianity triumphing by relinquishing Jerusalem or any fixed universal center, be it geographical, linguistic or cultural, and with the result of there being a proliferation of centers, languages and cultures within the church.[14]

We should, in light of this, always attempt to steer clear of the extremes of cultural imperialism and uncritical acceptance. This brings us to the next point, the fact that a biblical understanding of culture is often sorely lacking, even among the theologically informed.

Lack of a Biblical Understanding of Culture

Much can be said about the helpful ways in which the Bible illuminates human culture and in which it can help believers to minister to and live in community with those who are different from us. Suffice it to say for the purposes of this chapter that deep and valuable lessons can be learned from Scripture when it comes to cross-cultural communication.[15] Yet, some believers do not think about the Bible as being particularly helpful in this area (or think that the biblical truths in question only apply to those preparing for overseas missionary service). Theological education institutions will have to find ways in which to communicate biblical perspectives on culture in ways that not only inform but that will also demonstrate why we need these perspectives in order to minister effectively in twenty-first-century Australia.

Curriculum Pressures

Most theological educators will agree that including material on cross-cultural effectiveness is a good thing to do. It is, however, not the only "good thing" that we have to achieve through our programs of theological education. Even a casual glance at material on course design and unit descriptions

---

14. Ott, Strauss and Tennent, *Encountering Theology of Mission: Biblical Foundations, Historical Developments and Contemporary Issues*, 272.

15. The first part of David Bosch's classical work 'Transforming Mission' is devoted to a discussion of a biblical theology of mission. Upon reading this survey one is reminded again and again of the riches of Scripture when it comes to the message of Christ crossing borders and boundaries to reach different cultures. See Bosch, *Transforming Mission: Paradigm Shifts in Theology of Mission*, 15–170.

will quickly make it clear that curriculums are chock-full of other "good things" that have to be covered in order to meet learning outcomes and to facilitate desired graduate attributes. It is easy to see, in this context, why cross-cultural training tends to be relegated to units specifically aimed at those preparing for overseas missionary service. The challenge of "no room to fit this in" illustrates the need for creative approaches to ensure that this very important part of ministry formation is not simply crowded out by seemingly more pressing priorities.

Lack of Interest

A final barrier to effective cross-cultural formation in theological education is the fact that this is an emphasis that may sometimes be resisted by students themselves. Some students may be convinced that they are destined to serve in essentially monocultural contexts and that preparation for cross-cultural ministry would, therefore, essentially be wasted effort (although few students would be willing to articulate it in this way). In such cases, it is important to emphasize the fact that there can be no such thing as monocultural ministry in twenty-first-century Australia, and secondly, that life in Christian ministry can sometimes go through some very interesting twists and turns (including people ending up in ministry contexts that they would never have imagined).

Increasing Effectiveness in Preparing Students for Cross-Cultural Ministry

It would be easy to become discouraged whilst reflecting on some of the obstacles and challenges mentioned above. However, they also emphasize the need to engage in cross-cultural ministry formation with creativity and determination. This is simply not an area that can or should be left to chance or approached in a half-hearted fashion. Doing so will result in us sending theological graduates to minister in a context for which they are ill-prepared. I would, in fact, go as far as to suggest that not prioritizing cross-cultural formation will cause theological institutions to miss out on what I believe should be one of our primary callings: preparing graduates (regardless of whether they go on to serve here or overseas) for effective missional understanding and service. As Darrell Guder reminds us:

> Missional practice is the action of the missional community that knows that it exists to serve God's mission in the world—rather

than its own maintenance. The theological education that informs such missional practice, through the service rendered by those at schools, should be defined by the same understanding of the *missio Dei*. On that common ground the vital dialogue can take place that will result in the continuing conversion of late Christendom communities to their missional vocation.[16]

It is heartening to see that conversations about increasing our effectiveness in preparing students for cross-cultural ministry are indeed happening at many institutions and in several networks. Pending the outcomes of these conversations the following can be offered as some tentative suggestions for a possible way forward:

Create Opportunities for Students to Learn from Other Cultures

When it comes to cross-cultural formation, exposure and investigation are essential first steps. These are not things that can happen through merely reading about different cultures. Students will have to actively rub shoulders and converse with people with different worldviews, customs and "ways of being." These interactions should go much deeper than merely getting to know what might be termed "surface culture" (e.g. food, dress, games) but should ideally include attempts to come to terms with those aspects of culture that would most likely be significant in terms of gospel ministry.[17] This presupposes that the cultural interactions that are in view here should ideally be long-lasting (it is unlikely that any significant level of understanding will be achieved in a meeting or two) and geared towards the specific outcome of increasing cultural fluency. Here are some ways in which this could possibly be achieved:

- Regularly invite people from non-majority cultures to contribute to community life. A necessary first step to cross-cultural understanding is simply for students to hear from people who may be different from them. In most cases, Australian theological institutions do not have to go far to look for such people as most will have students who hail from non-Western cultures. The question is how we can utilize the presence

---

16. Guder, "Theological Formation for Missional Faithfulness after Christendom," 55.

17. For a helpful discussion of the importance of going beyond surface culture towards engaging with different worldviews, see Ott, Strauss, and Tennant, *Encountering Theology of Mission: Biblical Foundations, Historical Developments, and Contemporary Issues*, 267.

of such students without them feeling that they have entered a kind of cultural fishbowl. I would suggest that it should be done as naturally as possible through making sure that such students are effectively "dispersed" throughout the student body instead of forming their own subgroup within college life. How this can be done should obviously be worked out at the local level but there are certainly implications for the way in which things like small groups, "discipleship pairs," and devotions rosters are designed. Beyond this, care should also be taken to extend invitations to leaders, teachers, and preachers from different cultures to participate in the preaching, teaching, and community life of institutions. In this instance, it would be particularly beneficial to build links with people who are skilled in understanding their own as well as broader Australian culture. Such leaders can act as very valuable bridge-builders and as explainers and interpreters of culture.[18]

- Create formal opportunities for cross-cultural exposure and learning. While formal text-based study of culture has its place, it should be emphasized once again that this is an area where face-to-face contact and conversations are vitally important. Efforts should, therefore, be made to create opportunities for cultural learning outside of the classroom. These can range from things that institutions might be doing already (e.g. missions weeks) to more focused activities for cultural learning (e.g. visiting cultural centers or non-Christian places of worship). For those students who are particularly keen to get to know other cultures it would in many cases be possible to design a cross-cultural learning experience as part of their curriculum (e.g. through the ACT's "Cross-Cultural Field Education" unit).[19] Whatever route is followed it is vitally important that students are given the opportunity to reflect on and process what they are feeling, seeing, and hearing upon encountering the other culture. If ample opportunity for this is not provided there is a real danger that cross-cultural exposure can turn into just another "experience" instead of an opportunity for growth in understanding and effectiveness.

- Make use of interdisciplinary studies. In some cases, there may be scope for designing units with an interdisciplinary focus. This may present a great opportunity to include lectures and/or content that would normally be seen as belonging to the Missiology Department in settings where this is not the main area of study. Whether this would

18. For more on the importance, role and task of "bridge builders," see Scheepers, "Migration: An Opportunity for the Gospel," 80.

19. Australian College of Theology, *Undergraduate Handbook*, 351.

be possible will obviously depend on local circumstances but an interdisciplinary unit which brings cultural insights to bear on the topic being studied can prove a valuable addition to a course of theological study.

Make Use of a Range of Cultural Perspectives in Curriculum Design

One of the striking facts about the twenty-first-century church is the way in which the center of gravity of worldwide Christianity has significantly shifted towards the so-called two-thirds world.[20] This means that the majority of Christians now live in societies where Western culture does not predominate. One result of this is that a great deal of theological reflection now occurs in cultures where very different questions and perspectives are brought to bear on Scripture and on the nature of gospel ministry. Bringing the insights thus gained into Australian theological classrooms will not only prove stimulating for all concerned. Almost certainly it will also contribute to increased cultural sensitivity in the way the Bible is applied in the context of life and ministry. Some basic resources that can prove valuable in this area include the *Africa Bible Commentary*[21] and the *South Asia Bible Commentary*.[22] Another resource that can bring some profound and surprising majority world insights to bear on theological and ministry discussions is the *Global Church Project*. This is a resource (developed under the leadership of Graham Hill at Morling College in Sydney) that does an excellent job at presenting a wide range of voices from all around the world on a variety of theological and practical issues.[23]

Invest in the Cross-Cultural Competency of Lecturers

It goes without saying that lecturers will have to play a pivotal role in the process of preparing students for cross-cultural ministry. This means that

---

20. For one of the best discussions of the trend, see Jenkins, *The Next Christendom: The Coming of Global Christianity.*

21. Adeyemo, *Africa Bible Commentary.*

22. Wintle, *South Asia Bible Commentary.*

23. The website of the project can be found at https://theglobalchurchproject.com/. See also Hill, *Global Church: Reshaping Our Conversations, Renewing Our Mission, Revitalizing Our Churches.*

attention will have to be paid to the process of adequately preparing them for this task. This can be a significant challenge given the general level of busyness that most (probably the majority) of Australian theological educators have to contend with. The question must, therefore, be asked on how the level of cultural literacy can be raised without adding significantly to lecturer workloads. Part of the answer is probably to be found in encouraging lecturers and colleges to include cross-cultural elements to activities and programs that they are already committed to. This may include the inclusion of sessions on cross-cultural skills in professional development seminars. On a more individual level lecturers should also be strongly encouraged to include short overseas teaching stints as part of study leave programs. Not only will this very likely contribute to the sharpening of their teaching practice but it could also be of immense benefit in equipping them to be more effective in imparting skills for cross-cultural ministry.

Strengthen and Value "Mission Departments"

Within the context of theological colleges it will be lecturers in Missiology who will be most likely to have the skills and knowledge to train people for cross-cultural ministry. It is also within this field of study where units dealing with culture are likely to be found. It would be excellent if more colleges could review what is being offered in the area of missions and increase the focus on cross-cultural skills if necessary. Very often missions units major on the theology of mission and the "nuts and bolts" of missionary service. By making sure that a focus on the teaching of cross-cultural skills is established or maintained colleges will create (or maintain) capacity in an area that will become increasingly important in the equipping of students for ministry in the twenty-first-century world.

Conclusion

With this chapter I have attempted to highlight the importance of training theological students for cross-cultural ministry before discussing some barriers that could prevent this goal from being realized. We then looked at some possible cross-cultural training strategies for theological education institutions. These strategies are obviously not the last word that could be said in preparing students for cross-cultural effectiveness but they are offered with the hope that they will make some contribution to equipping Australian theological students for service in God's church: a church that will ultimately be made up of people from "every tribe and language and people and nation" (Revelation 5:9).

Bibliography

Adeyemo, Tokunboh. *Africa Bible Commentary*. Grand Rapids: Zondervan, 2006.
Australian College of Theology. *Undergraduate Handbook*. Sydney: Australian College of Theology, 2016.
Bosch, David Jacobus. *Transforming Mission: Paradigm Shifts in Theology of Mission*. American Society of Missiology Series. Maryknoll: Orbis, 1991.
Guder, Darrell. "Theological Formation for Missional Faithfulness after Christendom." In *Handbook of Theological Education in World Christianity*, edited by Dietrich Werner et. al., 51–56. Oxford: Regnum, 2010.
Hesselgrave, David J. *Communicating Christ Cross-Culturally: An Introduction to Missionary Communication*. 2nd ed. Grand Rapids: Zondervan, 1991.
Hiebert, Paul G. *Anthropological Insights for Missionaries*. Grand Rapids: Baker, 1985.
Hill, Graham. *Global Church: Reshaping Our Conversations, Renewing Our Mission, Revitalizing Our Churches*. Downers Grove: IVP Academic, 2016.
Institute for Cross-Cultural Theological Education. "Global Survey on Theological Education 2011–2013." Report Presented to the World Council of Churches Assembly, Busan, 30 October–8 November 2013.
Jenkins, Philip. *The Great and Holy War: How World War I Became a Religious Crusade*. San Francisco: HarperOne, 2014.
———. *The Next Christendom: The Coming of Global Christianity*. 3rd ed. Oxford: Oxford University Press, 2011.
Kang, Namsoon. "Envisioning Postcolonial Theological Education: Dilemmas and Possibilities." In *Handbook of Theological Education in World Christianity*, edited by Dietrich Werner et. al. Oxford: Regnum, 2010.
Markey, John. "The Making of a Post-Vatican II Theologian: Reflections on 25 Years of Catholic Education." America, 1994.
Moreau, A. Scott. *Contextualization in World Missions: Mapping and Assessing Evangelical Models*. Grand Rapids: Kregel, 2012.
Neill, Stephen, and Owen Chadwick. *A History of Christian Missions*. The Pelican History of the Church. Rev. ed. Harmondsworth, New York: Penguin, 1986.
Ott, Bernhard. *Beyond Fragmentation: Integration Mission and Theological Education*. Wipf & Stock, 2011.
Ott, Craig, Stephen J. Strauss, and Timothy C. Tennent. *Encountering Theology of Mission: Biblical Foundations, Historical Developments, and Contemporary Issues*. Encountering Mission. Grand Rapids: Baker, 2010.
Payne, Jervis David. *Strangers Next Door: Immigration, Migration, and Mission*. Downers Grove: IVP, 2012.
Scheepers, Phillip. "Migration: An Opportunity for the Gospel." *Vox Reformata* 77 (2011), 71–85.
Sfar, Mondher. *In Search of the Original Koran: The True History of the Revealed Text*. Amherst: Prometheus, 2008.
Spencer, Robert. *The Complete Infidel's Guide to the Koran*. Washington, DC; New York: Regnery, 2009.

Stanley, Brian. *The World Missionary Conference, Edinburgh 1910*. Studies in the History of Christian Missions. Grand Rapids: Eerdmans, 2009.
Wintle, Brian C. *South Asia Bible Commentary*. Grand Rapids: Zondervan, 2015.

17

Student Attrition in Theological Education
Empirical Research from Australia

DELLE MATTHEWS

Abstract

Attrition represents a significant challenge for theological colleges and seminaries. Through an exploration of data drawn from a large sample of Australian students, this chapter identifies nine reasons why students tend to discontinue their studies. In doing so, it draws comparisons with trends present in the Australian university sector, and some implications for institutions providing theological education.

Introduction

STUDENT WITHDRAWAL AND SUBSEQUENT non-completion of their studies has recently become a concern of theological educators. Every year a significant proportion of students of the Australian College of Theology discontinue their studies.[1] Comparison with the Australian university sector raises a number of questions as to why the attrition rate among ACT

---

1. Either having withdrawn totally from their course or taken leave for a semester or more with the intention of returning to studies in the future.

students is significantly higher than the 21 percent considered acceptable in the Australian tertiary sector and why students have not returned to study.[2]

Attrition is a cost to both the institution and the student, and in the case of theological students, to the Christian community. For the institution there is the loss of tuition income and the waste of resources invested in students' recruitment, teaching, support and administration. The report of the Hobsons project estimated the loss to an Australian institution in 2010 was as high as $8,000 per student who withdrew[3] and the measure now used by TEQSA[4] for institutional risk assessment includes reference to attrition rates.[5] Financial loss is only one of the costs to the student. Other costs to the student include the loss of occupational and other societal rewards given graduates,[6] and a sense of disappointment and at times failure. Every student who drops out represents one less fully trained leader within the Christian community and one less trained voice within the wider society, a cost to the church and beyond.

There is usually a complex network of factors that lead to a student discontinuing studies. Different student groups leave for different reasons. This chapter explores those factors and reasons in order to provide some suggestions to theological institutions wanting to minimize attrition.

Methodology

The participants in this study were students enrolled in a coursework award of the ACT between 2013 and 2015. The students were enrolled through one of the seventeen Bible and theological colleges affiliated with the ACT across Australia. Student enrollment patterns were first analyzed using data from the student management system, TAMS. There were a total of 4,701 students enrolled in a unit between Semester 1, 2013 and Semester 1, 2015 inclusive. Enrollment status was taken to mean the student's subsequent enrollment status in Semester 2, 2015, that is, enrolled, not enrolled, or graduated.

A survey was then sent to these students resulting in 957 usable responses (21 percent of students who received the email). A number of

---

2. Penn-Edwards, *An Overview of the Literature of the First Year Experience*, 12.

3. Adams et al., "The Hobsons Retention Project: Context and Factor Analysis Report," 16.

4. The Tertiary Education Quality and Standards Agency (TEQSA) is Australia's independent national regulator of the higher education sector.

5. TEQSA, "Risk Assessment Framework," 11.

6. Tinto, *Leaving College: Rethinking the Causes and Cures of Student Attrition*, 1.

questions on the survey were taken from the US National Survey of Student Engagement (NSSE).[7] Those questions have been validated in the United States and Canada where the survey is used extensively,[8] and in Australia where they form the basis of the Australasian Survey of Student Engagement (AUSSE).[9] Students were asked demographic information, their engagement in college life, and if relevant, reasons for attrition either temporary or permanent.

A quantitative approach was taken to analyze the survey responses along with data from the student database. Factors possibly associated with student attrition were examined using Chi-square tests for independence. This was followed by a logistic regression analysis to determine the predictors of attrition. All results reported were considered statistically significant to a level of $p<0.05$ unless otherwise indicated.

Reasons for Attrition

The students who had not graduated and were not enrolled as expected in Semester 2, 2015 were asked the reason for their non-enrollment. Students could select as many reasons as relevant and were also given an open-ended "Other" category. The responses in "Other" were reclassified into existing options. Seventy percent of students selected one reason only. Reasons given by more than 10 percent of students included study/work/life balance, paid work responsibilities, difficulty with the workload, health or stress, personal reasons, the need to do paid work, the need for a break, family difficulties and lack of career prospects. Perhaps one of the most noticeable aspects of this list is that the majority of reasons apart from "difficulty with workload" are largely outside of the control of theological institutions.

This outcome was compared with Australian university students studying in undergraduate awards in 2010 who had been given the same list of reasons.[10] Unlike ACT students who were asked for reasons for actually not enrolling, university students surveyed were studying at the time and asked to give their reasons for considering potentially not enrolling in the following semester. However, despite the fact that the two groups cannot

---

7. Used with permission from *The College Student Report*, National Survey of Student Engagement, Copyright 2001–15 The Trustees of Indiana University.

8. Pike, "The Convergent and Discriminant Validity of NSSE Scalelet Scores," 557; Pascarella, et al., "How Effective Are the NSSE Benchmarks in Predicting Important Educational Outcomes?", 7.

9. Coates, "Students' Early Departure Intentions and the Mitigating Role of Support," 21.

10. Ibid., 56.

be considered exactly comparable there are two striking differences in the reasons reported for either actually or intending to discontinue studies. The top reason given by university students for intending to discontinue their studies was "Boredom" (22 percent) while only 2.8 percent of ACT students discontinued studies due to boredom. However, 26.2 percent of ACT students cited "Paid Work Responsibilities" as a reason for non-enrollment compared to only 7 percent of university students claiming it to explain their intentions. That discrepancy and other differences between groups can best be explained by the demographics and motivations of theological students as discussed below. Based on analysis of data from TAMS and the survey a number of factors were found to have a significant association with attrition.

Profile of Students at Risk of Attrition

According to the TAMS data 18.8 percent of students studying between 2013 and 2015 had graduated before Semester 2, 2015. A further 41.1 percent of students enrolled as expected in Semester 2, 2015 while 38.2 percent did not enroll. Over half the students who did not enroll reported taking leave with the intention of returning. Of course, there is always the possibility that students won't return after having taken leave. The most common reasons given for taking leave from studies were the need for a break or that they were struggling with study/work/life balance. That left only 14 percent of all respondents having withdrawn totally. However, there was no one dominating reason why ACT students chose to withdraw totally.

Load of Study

Of all the students studying during the time period, students studying part-time were 2.3 times more likely to either have taken leave from their studies or withdrawn completely in Semester 2, 2015, compared to full-time students. Since 69.4 percent of ACT students in 2015 studied part-time compared to only 29 percent of Australian university students in the same year this factor alone may explain the high percentage of ACT students not enrolled compared to university students.[11] Part-time students in Australian universities are also at a higher risk of attrition and report similar reasons

---

11. Australian Government: Department of Education and Training, "Selected Higher Education Statistics—2015 Student Data."

to ACT students for discontinuing studies.[12] Many work full-time or have significant carer responsibilities making them time poor when it comes to fulfilling academic requirements and having reduced opportunity for social integration in college, both important for persistence. Study is often not their primary responsibility so it is not surprising that part-time students were most likely to report paid work responsibilities as the reason for not enrolling. Their greatest challenge is in balancing their life as a student with other external commitments.[13] In addition, part-time students often have limited access to administrative and academic support as they tend to access the campus after business hours or study externally.

Academic Progress

ACT students with a grade point average (GPA) below 2.0 were 1.9 times more likely to discontinue their studies compared to students with a higher GPA. In general, ACT students' GPA followed a normal distribution in 2015, peaking at a credit grade average. However, a large number of students had a GPA of zero with over half of those having withdrawn from their units after the withdrawal date,[14] or they simply did not submit all the assessment pieces required rather than having attempted and then failed their units. It is unclear, therefore, whether poor GPA was a result of academic difficulties or some other factor preventing them from achieving the grade they were capable of. This phenomenon is not unique to the ACT. Harvey also found this a problem among first year Bachelor of Arts students at LaTrobe University, Australia.[15] Nevertheless, a zero GPA should communicate to institutions that a student is at risk of discontinuing their studies. Research in general agrees that academic progress is the most important predictor of

---

12. Cao and Dabb, "Student Attrition at a New Generation University," 9; "Students' Early Departure Intentions and the Mitigating Role of Support," 23–4; Grebennikov and Skaines, "University of Western Sydney Students at Risk: Profile and Opportunities for Change," 64; Jacobs and Berkowitz King, "Age and College Completion: A Life-History Analysis of Women Aged 15–44," 225.

13. Gilardi and Guglielmetti, "University Life of Non-Traditional Students: Engagement Styles and Impact on Attrition," 36.

14. Within the ACT, withdrawal before the withdrawal date each semester does not impact a students' GPA. Withdrawal after the withdrawal date, except for compassionate reasons, is considered equivalent to a failure and given a zero GPA.

15. Harvey and Luckman, "Beyond Demographics: Predicting Student Attrition Within the Bachelor of Arts Degree," 26.

persistence with a student's performance in their first year and even in their first piece of assessment is found to be highly predictive of retention.[16]

Mode of Study

Distance students had lower enrollment and graduation rates but interestingly students who had studied by mixed mode[17] had the highest participation rate. These may be the students who are able to take advantage of the flexibility offered by colleges to balance their lives and maintain momentum with their studies. Other Australian studies also found attrition to be higher among distance students but did not also find higher retention among students studying by mixed mode.[18] Students studying by distance and mixed mode were also more likely to report paid work responsibilities as their reason for discontinuing studies. Since the majority of distance students were also studying part-time, this is not surprising. The most pressing responsibilities in the lives of distance students are often unknown to college staff and with significantly less reported interaction with college staff compared to students studying on campus persistence is a challenge.

Gender

Females were more likely to discontinue their studies compared to males. In general, women had a higher GPA compared to males but they were more likely to be studying part-time. Some research with university students, particularly with mature-age students, also found that females had a higher attrition rate[19] while other research found the attrition rate to be higher among males.[20] ACT female students were most likely to report study/work/life balance as the reason for not enrolling while men were more likely to report workload difficulties or difficulty paying fees as the reason for not enrolling. The results of the Australian Work and Life Index supports the finding that females are more likely to report feeling under pressure or

16. Coates and Ransome, "Dropout DNA, and the Genetics of Effective Support," 6; Whannell, "Predictors of Attrition," 291.

17. A student who had studied at least one unit on campus and one unit by distance was considered to have studied by mixed mode.

18. Coates, "Students' Early Departure Intentions and the Mitigating Role of Support," 23.

19. Alarcon, "Ability and Motivation: Assessing Individual Factors That Contribute to University Retention," 135.

20. Penn-Edwards, *An Overview of the Literature of the First Year Experience*, 9.

pressed for time and face greater challenges gaining higher qualifications.[21] Stone and O'Shea found Australian university female students were more likely to make sure studies fit around family responsibilities, while for a male student the family had to fit around his studies. Women were more likely to accept traditional expectations on their role including a denial of personal time and time for study.[22]

Level of Study

ACT undergraduate students were more likely to discontinue their studies compared to students enrolled in graduate level awards. Students studying in one of the diploma courses (AQF[23] Level 5) had the highest attrition rate and those undertaking a graduate diploma (AQF Level 8) had the highest graduation rate. Compared to undergraduate students those studying in the graduate level awards were more likely to report paid work responsibilities and workload difficulties as their reason for not enrolling. This may reflect the age and stage of career of the majority of graduate students who already having a degree are often established in a career. In 2015, 40 percent of ACT students were enrolled in a graduate level course while only 20.1 percent of university students were.[24] The majority of research undertaken in the university sector has focused on the undergraduate student and when research does target the graduate coursework student it focuses on one particular cohort.[25] So there is no data available to compare ACT students with university students when it comes to level of study.

Student Age

Students under twenty-four years of age had a higher attrition rate and lower graduation rate compared to older students. By virtue of their age they were generally enrolled in undergraduate awards. However, although the diploma courses had the highest level of attrition it was diploma students over forty-four years of age who were most likely to discontinue studies,

21. Pocock et al., "Work, Life and Workplace Flexibility: The Australian Work and Life Index 2009," 2, 6.

22. Stone and O'Shea, "Time, Money, Leisure and Guilt—the Gendered Challenges of Higher Education for Mature-Age Students," 97, 104.

23. Australian Qualifications Framework.

24. Australian Government: Department of Education and Training, "Selected Higher Education Statistics—2015 Student Data."

25. For example, students studying in a particular degree or faculty.

not the younger students. Research from Australian universities also shows that students under twenty years of age have a higher risk of attrition.[26] Although not statistically significant, there was a tendency for younger ACT students to report personal reasons and lack of career prospects as their reason for discontinuing studies. Attrition levels and the reasons for it tend to reflect students' stage of life. For example, students aged 24–29 years have a higher retention rate compared to other age groups. They are an age group less likely to have family concerns or to be established in a career. Students 30–44 years, who are more likely to be established in a career, reported paid work responsibilities as a reason for attrition. Although not statistically significant, students over forty-four years of age were more likely to report health and stress as their reason for not reenrolling.

Motivation for Study

While it is generally acknowledged that students enroll in university for career reasons[27] that is not necessarily true of ACT students. Most of the students reported a strong commitment to their own spiritual formation when they started theological studies but only a weak commitment to train for ordination or ministry. Commitment to spiritual formation did not impact persistence in studies but commitment to train for ordination did have a positive impact on retention. In addition, students who persisted with their studies were more likely to be enrolled in one of the ACT three-year degrees that potentially lead to a paid career. However, only 45.9 percent of ACT students were enrolled in a three-year degree compared to 80.7 percent of university students.[28]

Students with a strong commitment to graduate were those most likely to continue their studies to completion. Having a clear goal, especially a career goal and intention to complete have also been found to be important for persistence in among university students.[29] ACT students who were not

---

26. Australian Government: Department of Education and Training, "Selected Higher Education Statistics—2015 Student Data"; Adams et al., "The Hobsons Retention Project: Context and Factor Analysis Report," 6; Olsen et al., "Staying the Course: Retention and Attrition in Australian Universities," 9; Marks, "Completing University: Characteristics and Outcomes of Completing and Non-Completing Students," 2.

27. Penn-Edwards, *An Overview of the Literature of the First Year Experience*, 7.

28. Australian Government: Department of Education and Training, "Selected Higher Education Statistics—2015 Student Data."

29. Carroll et al., "Strategies to Improve Retention of Postgraduate Business Students in Distance Education Courses: An Australian Case," 149; Cohen, "What About Master's Students? The Master's Student Persistence Model," 29.

enrolled were also more likely to report that their studies had little relevance to their ministry, paid work, and other life responsibilities. Without a goal to work towards and studies not proving useful in their current responsibilities students found it harder to persist.[30]

Support from Others

Students who were not enrolled in Semester 2, 2015 were more likely to report having had little interaction with administrative staff, support services, lecturers and fellow students, and little support from friends and family when they had been enrolled. The importance of interaction between the student and others on campus for retention has been well documented in the university sector.[31] Wong, conducting a qualitative study in a theological college also found connectedness with other students and staff to be important to the persistence of theological students.[32]

Student Engagement

Students not enrolled in Semester 2, 2015 were also less likely to be engaged and spent less hours per week on college related activities when they were enrolled. While the term "engagement" can take on a variety of meanings the most common applied to Australian research and that best fits this study is that "Student Engagement represents both the time and the energy students invest in educationally purposeful activities and the effort institutions devote to using effective educational practices."[33] In this study it was found that students not enrolled were less likely to:

- keep up to date with their studies;
- work together with other students on assignments;
- put together ideas or concepts from different subjects;
- talk to lecturers about career or ministry plans;

30. Penn-Edwards, *An Overview of the Literature of the First Year Experience*, 12.

31. Whannell, "Predictors of Attrition," 295; Coates and Ransome, "Dropout DNA, and the Genetics of Effective Support," 11–14; Penn-Edwards, *An Overview of the Literature of the First Year Experience*, 12; Pascarella and Terenzini, *How College Affects Students: A Third Decade of Research*, 2, 417–20.

32. Wong, "What Factors Help Seminary Students Continue in Their Academic Programs? A Qualitative Case Study," 155–7.

33. Kuh et al., "Unmasking the Effects of Student Engagement on First-Year College Grades and Persistence," 542.

- discuss ideas from readings or classes with teaching staff outside of class;
- receive prompt feedback from teachers;
- work harder than they thought they could or work hard to master content;
- use the library;
- work on an essay or assignment that required integrating ideas or information from various sources; and
- blend academic learning with workplace or ministry.

Research tells us that student engagement with their studies is the most important factor impacting retention that lecturers can influence. Lecturers can influence engagement by facilitating competence, relating well to students and being well prepared, and teaching with enthusiasm.[34]

Summary

The two factors found to be most significant in predicting retention include load of study and student GPA. Students studying part-time with a low GPA are those most likely to withdraw or take leave from their studies. Adding any of the following factors increases the risk of a student not enrolling: female gender, studying by distance, enrollment in an undergraduate award (particularly a diploma), age under twenty-four years, poor support, weak commitment to graduate or to a career outcome, and weak engagement in college activities.

Limitations

It should be noted that the factors discussed in relation to attrition are not necessarily causal and relate to a single semester in time. No sample weights were applied to the survey data and since students who had not reenrolled in Semester 2, 2015 were underrepresented in the sample there are some limitations in the generalizability of the findings. The survey questions did not explore career aspirations thoroughly and only asked for ordination or ministry commitment at the commencement of studies. It is also possible that students changed their goals throughout their time of studies.

---

34. Groves et al., "Factors Affecting Student Engagement: A Case Study Examining Two Cohorts of Students Attending a Post-1992 University in the United Kingdom," 33.

Conclusion

There are many similarities between Australian university students and ACT theological students when it comes to attrition and the reasons for discontinuing studies. However, differences in demographics and motivation between the two groups have the effect of increasing the attrition rate of theological students and impacting their reasons for discontinuing studies. In particular, the greater proportion of part-time students, more mature students, and students without clear career or graduation goals presents a challenge to theological institutions.

Some practical implications for colleges include developing a greater awareness of students' non-college lives, motivation and needs in order to provide a more responsive and meaningful experience for theological students. Curriculum changes and ensuring greater access to services would be a good start to meet the needs of part-time students. Colleges can intentionally work to improve support and relationships with and between students. Monitoring students at risk of attrition will give institutions the opportunity for early intervention with such services as academic support, counselling, assistance with time-management, and career guidance. Finally, following up those students who have taken a break, taking an interest in their lives and encouraging them to return might begin to redress attrition in theological institutions.

Bibliography

Adams, Tony, et al. "The Hobsons Retention Project: Context and Factor Analysis Report," 2010.

Alarcon, Gene, and Jean M. Edwards. "Ability and Motivation: Assessing Individual Factors That Contribute to University Retention." *Journal of Educational Psychology* 105, no. 1 (2013) 129–37.

Australian Government: Department of Education and Training. "Selected Higher Education Statistics—2015 Student Data." http.//www.education.gov.au/selected-higher-education-statistics-2015-student-data.

Cao, Zhongjun, and Roger Gabb. "Student Attrition at a New Generation University." In *AARE Annual Conference*, edited by P. Jeffrey. Adelaide: Australian Association for Research in Education, 2006.

Carroll, David, et al. "Strategies to Improve Retention of Postgraduate Business Students in Distance Education Courses: An Australian Case." *Turkish Online Journal of Distance Education* 14, no. 1 (2013).

Coates, Hamish. "Students' Early Departure Intentions and the Mitigating Role of Support." *Australian Universities' Review* 52, no. 2 (2014) 20–9.

Coates, Hamish, and Laurie Ransome, "Dropout DNA, and the Genetics of Effective Support." Australasian Survey of Student Engagement Research Briefing. Vol. 11. Camberwell, Victoria: Australian Council of Educational Research, 2011.

Cohen, Kristen E. "What About Master's Students? The Master's Student Persistence Model." In *Annual Meeting of the Association for the Study of Higher Education*. Las Vegas, NV: 2012.

Gilardi, Silvia, and Chiara Guglielmetti. "University Life of Non-Traditional Students: Engagement Styles and Impact on Attrition," *The Journal of Higher Education* 82, no. 1 (2011) 33–53.

Grebennikov, Leonid, and Ivan Skaines. "University of Western Sydney Students at Risk: Profile and Opportunities for Change." *Journal of Institutional Research* 14, no. 1 (2009) 58–70.

Groves, Mark, et al. "Factors Affecting Student Engagement: A Case Study Examining Two Cohorts of Students Attending a Post-1992 University in the United Kingdom." *International Journal of Higher Education* 4, no. 2 (2015) 27–37.

Harvey, Andrew and Michael Luckman. "Beyond Demographics: Predicting Student Attrition Within the Bachelor of Arts Degree." *The International Journal of the First Year in Higher Education* 5, no. 1 (2014) 19–29.

Jacobs, Jerry A., and Rosalind Berkowitz King. "Age and College Completion: A Life-History Analysis of Women Aged 15–44." *Sociology of Education* 75, no. 3 (2002) 211–30.

Kuh, George D., et al. "Unmasking the Effect of Student Engagement on First-Year College Grades and Persistence." *The Journal of Higher Education* 79, no. 5 (2008) 540–63.

Marks, Gary. "Completing University: Characteristics and Outcomes of Completing and Non-Completing Students." In *Longitudinal Surveys of Australian Youth*, edited by ACER. Melbourne: ACER, 2007.

Olsen, Alan, et al. "Staying the Course: Retention and Attrition in Australian Universities." Australian Universities International Directors Forum. Hong Kong, 2008.

Pascarella, Ernest T., et al. "How Effective Are the NSSE Benchmarks in Predicting Important Educational Outcomes?" *Change* 42, no. 1 (2010) 16–22.

Pascarella, Ernest T., and Patrick T. Terenzini. *How College Affects Students: A Third Decade of Research*. Vol. 2. San Francisco: Jossey-Bass, 2005.

Penn-Edwards, Sorrel. *An Overview of the Literature of the First Year Experience in Australian Higher Education 2000–2010: Defining Attrition, Reviewing Solutions and Planning for Improved Retention*. Ace Occasional Paper Series. Mawson, ACT: Australian College of Educators, 2010.

Pike, Gary R. "The Convergent and Discriminant Validity of NSSE Scalelet Scores." *Journal of College Student Development* 47, no. 5 (2006) 550–63.

Pocock, Barbara, et al. "Work, Life and Workplace Flexibility: The Australian Work and Life Index 2009." Centre for Work + Life, University of South Australia, 2009.

Stone, Catherine, and Sarah E. O'Shea. "Time, Money, Leisure and Guilt—the Gendered Challenges of Higher Education for Mature-Age Students." *Australian Journal of Adult Learning* 53, no. 1 (2013) 90–110.

TEQSA. "Risk Assessment Framework." http://www.teqsa.gov.au/regulatory-approach/risk-assessment-framework.

Tinto, Vincent. *Leaving College: Rethinking the Causes and Cures of Student Attrition.* Chicago: University of Chicago Press, 1987.

Whannell, Robert. "Predictors of Attrition and Achievement in a Tertiary Bridging Program." *Australian Journal of Adult Learning* 53, no. 2 (July 2013) 280–301.

Wong, Arch Chee Keen. "What Factors Help Seminary Students Continue in Their Academic Programs? A Qualitative Case Study." *Journal of Adult Theological Education* 11, no. 2 (2014) 150–64.

18

The Contributors to Spiritual Formation in Theological Education

What the Students Say

Ian Hussey

Abstract

This chapter reports on research into the contribution of various aspects of a student's experience of theological education to their spiritual formation in a Baptist theological college in Queensland, Australia. Students were invited to participate in a survey and focus groups to identify and explore which aspects of their theological college experience were contributing most to their spiritual formation. This chapter reports on these findings and discusses the implications for theological education at the college. It also integrates the findings with current theories about spiritual formation in theological education to develop an enhanced model of spiritual formation. The findings and the conclusions regarding spiritual formation are suggestive for other theological training institutions.

Introduction

MALYON COLLEGE IS THE Baptist theological training college in Queensland, Australia, offering degrees from diplomas to doctorates. It is composed of about 250 students and fifteen faculty and staff. About half of the students are training to be pastors, many of them on a part-time basis while employed by a church. The other students are "lay" people, largely from Queensland Baptist churches. About 40 percent of the units (subjects) offered by Malyon College are in distance (off-campus) mode.

Recently Malyon College has developed a greater awareness of the concept of "spiritual formation" of students. However, "spiritual formation" is a highly contextual term. The definitions vary significantly depending on the tradition in which an institution or individual stands. In the case of Malyon College, the understanding has been largely shaped by the conservative, male, evangelical, "action-oriented" nature of the denomination it serves and its rejection of what is perceived as liberal or catholic theology. Many may find the denomination's understanding of spiritual formation as underdeveloped, but it remains the context in which the college serves and this research must function.

Cronshaw defines spiritual formation as "the process of the character and person of Christ being formed in a person."[1] This understanding of spiritual formation is one that would be widely affirmed amongst Queensland Baptists. Spiritual formation is both an inward, fundamental change, and a change visible to others. It is both intrinsic and behavioral.

In previous research,[2] I attempted to develop an instrument to measure spiritual formation so that an objective assessment of the college's role in the spiritual formation of students could be undertaken. The research reported in this chapter seeks to build on this research by identifying the aspects of the theological college's experience which are most helpful for spiritual formation.

There is a rich complexity of traditions of spirituality and spiritual formation in Christianity.[3] However, at some points in Christian history, the idea of withdrawal from the world (for example, into a monastery) in order to develop spirituality has been prominent.

Although this withdrawal is often an individual endeavor, the idea of community has also featured strongly, for example, in the writings of

---

1. Cronshaw, "Reenvisioning Theological Education and Missional Spirituality," 14.
2. Hussey, "Spiritual Formation in an Australian Baptist Theological College."
3. Zschiele, *Cultivating Sent Communities: Missional Spiritual Formation*, 8.

Bonhoeffer.[4] Pettit in his introduction to a book titled "Foundations of Spiritual Formation: A Community Approach to Becoming Like Christ," goes as far as to say, "change for the Christian does not normally involve change that occurs in isolation from others."[5]

Hence, within the context of theological education, Adam[6] suggests that spiritual formation is fostered by community (shared values and experiences, activities, meals and space), chapel (worship, prayer, Bible, sacrament), and faculty (counselling, mentoring, talking, models of life and ministry). Such an approach focuses on the college facility as the locus of formation.

However, as important as Christian community is to formation, engagement with non-Christians has also been recognized as important: "So the Christian, too, belongs not in the seclusion of a cloistered life but in the thick of foes. There is his commission, his work."[7] The idea of missional spirituality, which is developed in actual engagement with the world, has recently emerged.[8] It advocates that "spiritual transformation occurs within the emerging Christian community *and* in relationship with nonbelieving others."[9]

Although the "monastic" model has strongly influenced models of spiritual formation in theological colleges in Australia, there has been a recent "reenvisioning" of theological education in the light of the notion of missional spirituality.[10] Banks and Cronshaw argue that missional spirituality happens best when it cultivates inner contemplation and outer engagement, and when it relates faith to everyday life and local contexts.

Hence, spiritual formation calls not only for a rhythm of both "being together" and "being alone," but also one of "being with believers" and "being with non-believers."

Malyon College has been characterized by the "college-focused" model described by Adams. However, the increasing proportion of students

---

4. Bonhoeffer, *Life Together*.

5. Pettit, *Foundations of Spiritual Formation: A Community Approach to Becoming Like Christ*, 19.

6. Adam, "Education and Formation for Ministry in Theological Education Today," 2.

7. Bonhoeffer, *Life Together*, 17.

8. Helland and Hjalmarson, *Missional Spirituality: Embodying God's Love from the Inside Out*.

9. Zschiele, *Cultivating Sent Communities: Missional Spiritual Formation*, 8.

10. Banks, *Reenvisioning Theological Education: Exploring a Missional Alternative to Current Models*; Cronshaw, "Reenvisioning Theological Education and Missional Spirituality."

studying part-time and an emphasis on reflective practice through the fieldwork subjects has meant that the college has come to a broader understanding of spiritual formation. The college has recognized that students are formed by God in every context of their lives, not just when they are in lectures. The role of the college is then to be the *facilitator* of spiritual formation throughout the student's life (rather than sole *provider*), whether that be in class, on a short-term mission trip, or anywhere in-between. With this background in mind, the research looked to focus on the broader "Malyon College experience," recognizing that spiritual formation is achieved by far more than simply lecture attendance.

Methodology

The methodology for this research[11] is case study.[12] Although this methodology lacks breadth, and therefore generalizability, it allows for the development of profound theory within a given context because it explores a case in depth. The developed theory is substantiated through multiple data sources from within the case. Although the developed theory explains the phenomenon in the specific context, in terms of generalizability, it is suggestive rather than prescriptive.

Under the case study methodology, this research used surveys and focus groups. A survey was developed (see Appendix 1) and offered to all students online and in paper form at the end of 2014 and 2015. It began by defining spiritual formation:

> The idea of spiritual formation/growth comes from verses like Romans 8:29:
> "For those God foreknew he also predestined to be conformed to the likeness of his Son, that he might be the firstborn among many brothers." (NIV)

Students were then asked to identify how satisfied they were with their spiritual formation/growth and what role Malyon College had played in that formation:

How satisfied are you with your spiritual formation/growth this year? (Please circle one):

---

11. The research was approved and monitored by the Malyon College Ethics Committee.

12. Johansson, "Case Study Methodology."

| Not at all Satisfied | A Little Satisfied | Moderately Satisfied | Satisfied | Very Satisfied |

How much has your Malyon College experience contributed to your spiritual formation/growth this year? (Please circle one):

| Not at All | To a Small Degree | To a Moderate Degree | To a Considerable Degree | To a Great Degree |

Students were then asked to select the four (or less) items which made the greatest contribution to their spiritual formation through Malyon College from a list of thirty items generated by the college faculty and ordered alphabetically. Students were also given the option of nominating an "Other" item, but few did, suggesting the exhaustiveness of the list. The forced choice approach compelled participants to identify the most helpful aspects of the college experience.

In 2016 two focus groups were conducted to verify and augment the data generated by the surveys. The first group was composed of three women and six men. The second group was composed of four women and five men. The participants were asked three questions as stimulants to discussion:

1. How much has your Malyon College experience contributed to your spiritual formation/growth this year?
2. We did a survey over a couple of years asking what aspects of the Malyon experience contributed to spiritual formation. What would you say are the biggest contributors to your personal spiritual formation?
3. Students nominated the following as making a great contribution to their spiritual formation. Can you please explain how each of these things contribute?

The discussions were recorded and transcribed. Fourteen pages of text was generated and analyzed with a view to developing themes. The findings from the two surveys and the two focus groups are presented in the next section.

Findings

Out of a total college enrollment of about 250 students, 97 responded to the 2014 survey and 51 to the 2015 survey. Just over half were full-time students while 30 percent had, or were, studying online (distance). The largest segment was aged 21 to 30 (35–39 percent) and almost exactly one third were women.

When asked how satisfied they were with their spiritual formation 63.9 percent (2014) and 72.6 percent (2015) were satisfied or very satisfied. Most (59.8 percent in 2014 and 70.5 percent in 2015) identified that the Malyon experience had contributed a considerable or great degree to their spiritual formation/growth during the year. However, the survey indicated that about a quarter of the students were less than satisfied with their spiritual formation, even though they were studying at a theological college.

The two variables ("satisfaction with growth" and "contribution of Malyon") were moderately correlated (Pearson's $r=0.495$ $p < 0.001$). In other words, the majority of students who were satisfied with their spiritual growth/formation also indicated that Malyon had made a considerable contribution to that growth. The satisfaction was the same for on campus and off campus students, but the contribution of Malyon was slightly lower (0.2 on a 5-point scale) for off campus students. This was not surprising, but the significance of the difference was smaller than initially expected. It suggests that the mode of study was not a significant determinant of spiritual formation. Such findings have been previously suggested by Nichols.[13]

The responses to the question: "Which of the following have made the greatest contribution to your spiritual formation through Malyon College?" are in Table 1:

Item	2014	2015
Researching and writing essays	44%	41%
In-class discussions	35%	37%
Faculty input in class	31%	29%
Informal discussions with other students	24%	22%
Private reading related to study	20%	24%
Learning Guide content	22%	24%
A particular unit of study	20%	41%

Table 1: Greatest Contributors to Spiritual Formation

The most nominated contributor, "Researching and writing essays," was nominated by less than half of the students. This would suggest there is

13. Nichols, "A Comparison of the Spiritual Participation of On-Campus and Theological Distance Education Students," 121–36; "A Comparison of Spiritual Formation Experiences."

no "silver bullet" for spiritual formation, but rather, a range of contributors are needed to cater for the diverse preferences of students.

As would be expected, off campus students were far less likely to nominate "In-class discussions" and "Faculty input in class" as major contributors, but otherwise the responses were largely consistent, regardless of mode of study. Given that three of the major contributors, "Researching and writing essays," "Private reading related to study" and "Learning Guide[14] content" are solitary activities, their value for off campus students is not surprising. What is surprising is that so many on campus students also nominated these "solitary" contributors.

The "Particular unit of study" nominated varied significantly indicating that many different subjects, whether biblical, theological or practical were able to be spiritually formative for different students.

As significant as the identification of these major contributors to spiritual formation are, the perceived low value of others is equally significant. In-class activities, formal discussions with faculty, Guided Spiritual Formation[15] journaling activities and readings, online interaction with faculty and other students and reflection on field education experiences were only major contributors for less than 5 percent of the students. Other activities like chapel worship, field education and meetings with field education mentors, study tours and even prayer meetings were major contributors to spiritual formation for less than 10 percent of the students. Clearly, for a majority of students, many of the activities that the college assumed were *major* contributors to spiritual formation, are not.

The focus groups confirmed a diversity of opinion regarding the amount of spiritual formation and the contribution of the college towards it. When asked, "How much has your Malyon College experience contributed to your spiritual formation/growth this year?" one participant said, "Not a huge amount, but significant," while another said, "I feel I've come a long way in the last six months. I've grown an enormous amount." They did agree that the approach was holistic: "I think that Malyon does a really good job of incorporating spiritual formation into every facet of life at Malyon."

---

14. Learning Guides are enhanced lecture notes which guide students through the learning materials available on the learning management system (Moodle). These Learning Guides are made available to all students regardless of study mode.

15. Guided Spiritual Formation (GSF) is a unit (subject) offered by the college which involves students participating in weekly seventy-five minute groups with up to twelve others, facilitated by a faculty member, and the submission of a reflective journal at the end of semester. Students need to complete four semesters to pass the unit. It focuses on the integration of the college experience with ministry, family and person.

However, even amongst those students who did report significant growth, their experience of college life was inconsistent: "It can be very spiritually forming and it is very spiritually forming and helps a lot with my relationship with God. I find some assignments spiritually nourishing and others very draining and can interfere with my relationship with God."

A number of students indicated that the benefits of the biblical and theological subjects came some time after the lecture or assignment rather than during the process. "There is sort of a period of time. You have to do the head knowledge but once it's on-board it's a foundation, but later on you can absorb it."

When asked what was the biggest contribution of the Malyon experience to their spiritual formation, a number of themes emerged. One was the concept of the "mini-sermon" during the lectures: "I love it when [the lecturer] gets inspired and gives a mini-sermon." "[Lecturer] has a mini-sermon at the end of every lecture. That's what makes it real. You can grasp it. It suddenly brings it into today's context. It takes the academic side off." The application of the biblical content to contemporary life in the "mini-sermons" was a key feature:

> I think the most spiritually forming experience at college has been listening to the content of both Old and New Testament and how it applies to us today because people who have been Christians for a long time, and in the habit of reading their Bibles, don't actually get much out of it because you are just reading along. But it just seems to come alive in the lecture especially when it has personal application to us today.

Chapel also strongly emerged as an unprompted contributor in one focus group even though only 15 percent (2014) and 5 percent (2015) nominated "Chapel Sermons" as formative in the survey. They said: "The messages in Chapel have spoken to me." "Chapel does play a big role."

Similarly, the Guided Spiritual Formation groups were strongly valued by one of the focus groups even though it did not emerge strongly in the survey. "I don't want to just come [to college] and consume content but I want to be reflective, and I think for me GSF has been great in terms of just hearing people's thoughts and challenges and their own walk—they help me to reflect on my own life and on the aspects of becoming more Christlike."

When participants in the focus groups were told that the survey had indicated that "Researching and writing essays" was the greatest contributor to spiritual formation they were initially surprised. One extravert said, "Who filled this survey in? They were lying to you! I'm telling you now. Sure if I am reading some beautiful book and I am sitting here and nothing is due, absolutely, but not a day before it's due and I am typing away—no way."

However, as they thought about it, they warmed to the idea: "Yes, actually that makes sense." One said, "Spiritually, even though it is an academic book God still works really powerfully through that. One of the assignments actually triggered a reunion with my dad who I hadn't spoken to for seven years." When asked how it was that researching and writing essays was formative, they indicated that the process helped them to develop new knowledge: "The covenant essay helped me to learn a lot about God. It was very important for my relationship with God. I could see how God's relationship with the Israelites applied into my life." Another said, "The fact that you haven't thought about it before. Unless you are forced to look at it you wouldn't think about it. It becomes like this little treasure chest of amazing information. Things you didn't realize before." "It is that the whole thing is about being forced to think outside the box."

However, the formative benefits of this new knowledge sometimes emerged not at the time of researching and writing, but subsequently as they engaged with everyday life:

> It's not like in that moment you see the benefits of the essay. Like, I've never felt I've gone to another spiritual plain while I've been slogging away at an assignment. You do all that and it lays the foundations for afterwards when you are worshipping or praying or whatever you just reflect on that hard work and the knowledge bears fruit later on.

Another said, "I think the doing the essay part of it is like the theoretical side of it and when you get to Chapel, and GSF, and any ministry, or wherever you are, those kind of things you learn within those studies play out in life. So I think they kind of book-end each other."

The participants also indicated that researching and writing essays was formative because it developed acceptance of others: "They make me think and understand how other people think about an issue. Instead of arguing or trying to impose your point of view on them, just seeing how they get there. It involves extending grace to others. Assisting in the process of being patient and kind and exercising self-control. Gives you empathy." "It helps you know your place—amongst believers who have thoughts and opinions different to you."

This idea of developing acceptance of others as students engaged with other people's ideas also came through in the exploration of the next major contributor—"In-class discussion." One participant said: "You get the opportunity to hear where somebody else is on that [subject] and the reasoning behind it." "People have different ideas which makes us ask, 'Why do I even think that?'" Another said: "I feel like I grow a lot when I am challenged by other people's views. When I go, 'No that's not right—that's not what I have come to understand.' So then I reflect through, 'What of that was good? What of my own thoughts was good?' and 'Where is the commonality?'" The encounter with diverse ideas both in the research process and in the class discussions emerges as highly formative.

One graduate student had come to change his view of the value of in-class discussion at Malyon:

> I always thought that I wanted a really good orator to speak well at me for a couple of hours. I used to love that. The best classes are where the person teaching is an excellent speaker and can just communicate things really well. But I find it totally opposite now. I thought I would like that, and I do I guess, but the less they talk and the more we get to talk—I get so much more out of that. And I always thought "I want my money's worth: I want the best person who can communicate well." But that has changed. I would rather someone who can facilitate the group to learn. I find that way more powerful.

Another student described how in-class interaction had helped her grow more confident to ask questions:

> But I also think it is beneficial for life after college to be in a position, no matter where you are. That it is all right to ask questions and all right to clarify things and have discussions with people who say, "What do you think about whatever?" I think that is going to be spiritually formative for the rest of your life. Being in a safe place. I didn't grow up where it was okay to ask questions in church, it was just, "This is what you believe" and "That is what is right." For me especially, it is just good to be able to be safe to ask questions and then everybody just bounces off each other.

Another highlighted how in-class discussion changed his understanding of Jesus:

> Whatever discussion you're having, if that ends up leading towards a better revelation of Jesus, that is what forms you. It could be through anything, though: a conversation at the lunch table, through something you have talked about in class, whatever ends up leading you to know him better ends up being the most formative stuff. And that is all over the place, how can you pin that down? It happens everywhere in various ways but it also

THE CONTRIBUTORS TO SPIRITUAL FORMATION 251

mushes together, and you worship and you go to him and you say "I see you differently now."

But the in-class discussion needs to be well facilitated:

> I really appreciate class discussion, but I sometimes get frustrated with going off topic and people talking for a long time when we haven't really learned a lot about what we're talking about. I want a comprehensive understanding and a detailed explanation about it so that we can have a formative discussion.

The process whereby the next major contributor, "Faculty input in class," contributed to formation was less clear. For some the helpful input was in application: "The questions they ask in lectures can help you be reflective. 'What are your worthless idols?'" For others it was example: "Seeing the zeal and excitement of lecturers even though they have been teaching the same content for twenty to thirty years is inspiring." For others the "mini-sermons" were important: "Some of the most formative times for me last semester were when [Lecturer] went off on a tangent and had a little mini-preach session, and all of a sudden I knew something more about God I didn't know before . . ."

When discussing how "Informal discussions with other students" contributed to formation, participants indicated that it gave them the venue to process the material presented in the lectures: "Gives time and scope to talk through the issues raised during the class time. You can focus on the things that are really important to you which you don't have time for in class." This also informs the process whereby in-class discussions can be formative.

However, the informal discussions with other students are also formative in another way: "It can be frustrating too. I don't know if they are the most helpful all the time. Sometimes it can be banter and agenda and I don't always find them most helpful. But I think they are helpful learning patience! Are they healthy for your spiritual formation then? I think so."

The process whereby informal discussion with faculty is formative is quite different: "Just being able to have spiritual conversations with faculty is spiritually forming. It doesn't matter what the content is about, it is just a matter of being able to have them which is spiritually forming. It breaks down the academic wall. You see other believers—no us and them." "You feel the investment—the relational aspect which is a huge part of spiritual formation." It would appear that it is not the content of the discussions that is formative but the values of the faculty they reflect. As one student said:

> The value in Malyon has been in those informal conversations. I think the spirit, and the atmosphere, and the culture that is

created here from the faculty, and the fact that they are really open to actually share, talk and discuss . . . and it is not just about assessments. They are actually about building leaders for the next generation. That speaks heaps to me. I have learnt tons from those small conversations. That is quite different to a university.

As suggested by the survey, the individual units (subjects) of study which contributed to a student's formation, varied from student to student. Some discussed how the practical nature of a subject like "Theology for Everyday Life" was helpful, whereas others found the content of subjects like Church History formative: "The Eucharist assignment was really formative for me." It would appear that the unit content is not the determinant of formative value, but the way it is learnt.

Conclusions

The findings of this research are clearly contextual, but they are also suggestive. Other theological colleges would be wise to reevaluate their strategy with regard to spiritual formation of their students. The contribution of traditional formative activities like formal and informal faculty input, chapel, reflection groups and lecture notes is affirmed. However, the emergence of activities such as researching and writing essays, private reading related to study, class discussions and informal discussions with other students suggests that spiritual formation is a far more complex matter than many have thought.

The surprising contribution of researching and writing essays to spiritual formation should be considered. Not all essay topics are obviously formative. However, some students indicated that the benefits were a delayed reaction as what seemed disconnected knowledge found formative value as they subsequently engaged with their worlds. With this in mind, one could conclude that essay topics need not *aim* to be formative in order to be formative. However, the insight from this research suggests that if essay topics are set with spiritually formative outcomes in mind they can be extremely effective. To do this, however, students need to learn to think, reflect and live theologically in light of their theological learning. These skills of theological reflection should be taught, not assumed, because they are the crucial link between a theoretical essay and spiritual formation.

The focus groups also highlighted that researching and writing essays is formative because they caused the students to engage with a variety of views. Faculty should be encouraged to expose students to a variety of opinions on a topic rather than just asking them to research the "right" one (held, of course, by the lecturer.) Such an approach is not only in step with postmodern thinking but is also spiritually formative, as students learn acceptance and humility as they comprehend the plethora of well-informed ideas contrary to their own.

Faculty also need to reflect on the potential value of in-class discussions for spiritual formation. As students hear the opinions of others they not only develop acceptance but they have the space to reflect on, and apply, theoretical learning. Lecturers have sometimes argued that there is too much content to be delivered to allow time for in-class discussion. Such an approach is not only at odds with the benefits of a "flipped classroom"[16] approach to learning but sacrifices the opportunity for spiritual formation.

Of course, the students in this research were only able to comment on the spiritually formative activities that the college is undertaking. The brief literature review at the beginning of this chapter concluded that to be spiritually formative the college experience needs to aim for a rhythm of both "being together" and "being alone," but also one of "being with believers" and "being with non-believers." The college needs to provide students with both solitary (e.g. essay research and writing) and communal formative activities (e.g. in-class discussions). But it also needs to facilitate engagement with other believers (e.g. informal discussions with faculty and students) and with the non-Christian world. It is certainly here, in the last dimension of spiritual formation, that the most glaring hole exists in the Malyon College strategy. The college offers a weeklong "Week of E" which includes exposure to ministries to the non-churched and the opportunity to be involved in evangelism. However, only 5 percent (2014) and 2 percent (2015) of students identified it as a major contributor to their spiritual formation. "Week of E" and, potentially, other activities which engage theological students with those they are called to missionally serve, need to be enhanced in order to produce more spiritually formed graduates.

The diversity of the contributors to spiritual formation in this research suggests that it is definitely not a "one-size-fits-all" activity. Each student is unique and colleges should provide a variety of formative activities for their students in each of the four dimensions (solitary, communal, church, non-church).

Some activities which were thought to be *the* major contributors to spiritual formation, (in-class activities, formal discussions with faculty, online interaction with faculty and other students, reflection on field

16. Hantla, "The Effects of Flipping the Classroom on Specific Aspects of Critical Thinking in a Christian College: A Quasi-Experimental, Mixed-Methods Study"; Mangan, "Inside the Flipped Classroom."

education experiences, field education and meetings with field education mentors, study tours and prayer meetings) need to be reevaluated. Theoretically, these activities should be effective. Their delivery needs to be reviewed to fulfill their potential. Each should be examined through the lens of the question, "How does this activity contribute to spiritual formation as we have defined it."

In contrast, highly formative activities like "mini-sermons" (where the lecturer draws personal spiritual implications from content), specifically formative assessment tasks, well facilitated in-class discussion and informal engagement with faculty, should be actively promoted at Malyon College and considered by others.

Appendix 1—Survey Instrument

We want to know a bit about your Malyon College experience.

Please fill in the anonymous survey below as honestly as you possibly can. If you would like to talk to someone as a result of participating in this survey, please contact any member of the faculty. Thanks.

How many units have you completed at Malyon College?	☐ 0–7		☐ 8–15		☐ 16–23		☐ 24 or more
Are you a full-time or part-time student?	☐ Full-time		☐ Part-time		☐ Both (at some stage)		
What has been, or is, your primary mode of study?	☐ On campus		☐ Online/ Distance		☐ Both (in equal amounts)		
How old are you?							
☐ 20 or younger	☐ 21–30	☐ 31–40	☐ 41–50	☐ 51–60	☐ 61–70	☐ 71+	
What is your gender?	☐ Male	☐ Female					

Contributors to Your Spiritual Formation

The idea of spiritual formation/growth comes from verses like Romans 8:29:

> For those God foreknew he also predestined to be conformed to the likeness of his Son, that he might be the firstborn among many brothers. (NIV)

THE CONTRIBUTORS TO SPIRITUAL FORMATION 255

How satisfied are you with your spiritual formation/growth this year? (Please circle one):

Not at all Satisfied	A Little Satisfied	Moderately Satisfied	Satisfied	Very Satisfied

How much has your Malyon College experience contributed to your spiritual formation/growth this year? (Please circle one):

Not at All	To a Small Degree	To a Moderate Degree	To a Considerable Degree	To a Great Degree

Which of the following have made the greatest contribution to your spiritual formation through Malyon College? (Please choose four (4) or less)

Please tick up to four (4) only
- ☐ A particular unit of study (Please nominate: _____)
- ☐ Chapel guest speakers
- ☐ Chapel sermons
- ☐ Chapel worship
- ☐ In-class discussions
- ☐ In-class activities
- ☐ Conversation/online interaction with the college tutors
- ☐ Example of faculty and staff
- ☐ Faculty input in class
- ☐ Faculty testimonies
- ☐ Formal feedback on assessment
- ☐ Formal discussions with faculty
- ☐ Guided Spiritual Formation (PC444/644) guest speakers
- ☐ Guided Spiritual Formation journaling activities
- ☐ Guided Spiritual Formation mentoring groups
- ☐ Guided Spiritual Formation readings
- ☐ Informal discussions with faculty
- ☐ Informal discussions with other students
- ☐ Meeting with my Field Ed ministry mentor
- ☐ Learning Guide content
- ☐ My Field Education experiences
- ☐ Online interaction with faculty (e.g. forums)
- ☐ Online interaction with other students (e.g. forums)

- ☐ Practical aspects of assessment requirements
- ☐ Prayer meetings
- ☐ Private reading related to study
- ☐ Reflection on Field Education experiences
- ☐ Researching and writing essays
- ☐ Study tours
- ☐ Week of E
- ☐ Other: _____

Bibliography

Adam, Peter. "Education and Formation for Ministry in Theological Education Today." (2009). www.actheology.edu.au/general%20files/Education_and_formation.pdf.

Banks, Robert. *Reenvisioning Theological Education: Exploring a Missional Alternative to Current Models.* Grand Rapids: Eerdmans, 1999.

Bonhoeffer, Dietrich. *Life Together.* New York: Harper & Row, 1954.

Cronshaw, Darren. "Reenvisioning Theological Education and Missional Spirituality." *Journal of Adult Theological Education* 9, no. 1 (2012): 9-27.

Hantla, Bryce F. "The Effects of Flipping the Classroom on Specific Aspects of Critical Thinking in a Christian College: A Quasi-Experimental, Mixed-Methods Study." Southeastern Baptist Theological Seminary, 2014.

Helland, Roger, and Leonard Hjalmarson. *Missional Spirituality: Embodying God's Love from the inside Out.* Downer's Grove: IVP, 2011. Kindle Edition.

Hussey, Ian. "Spiritual Formation in an Australian Baptist Theological College: A Survey-Based Case Study." *Journal of Adult Theological Education* 12, no. 2 (2015): 137-52.

Johansson, Rolf. "Case Study Methodology." *A key note speech at the International Conference "Methodologies in Housing Research" organised by the Royal Institute of Technology in cooperation with the International Association of People–Environment Studies, Stockholm, 22–24 September 2003* (2003). http://www.psyking.net/HTMLobj-3839/Case_Study_Methodology-_Rolf_Johansson_ver_2.pdf.

Mangan, Katherine. "Inside the Flipped Classroom." *Chronicle of Higher Education* 60, no. 5 (2013): B18-B21.

Nichols, Mark. "A Comparison of Spiritual Formation Experiences between on-Campus and Distance Evangelical Theological Education Students." PhD Diss., University of Otago, 2014.

———. "A Comparison of the Spiritual Participation of on-Campus and Theological Distance Education Students." *Journal of Adult Theological Education* 12, no. 2 (2015): 121-36.

Pettit, Paul. *Foundations of Spiritual Formation: A Community Approach to Becoming Like Christ.* Grand Rapids: Kregel Publications, 2008.

Zscheile, Dwight J. *Cultivating Sent Communities: Missional Spiritual Formation.* Grand Rapids: Eerdmans, 2012.

Part IV

Future Directions

19

The Utilization of Telecommuting Staff in Australian Theological Education

Nathain Secker

Abstract

Telecommuting, the utilization of technology to enable non-proximal staff members to work as employees of an organization in roles that have traditionally been undertaken in a physically present fashion, is on the increase in higher education circles. Lecturing previously undertaken in a face-to-face mode is seeing new expressions with academic staff undertaking roles as online unit coordinators. Formally on-site student services staff may now be manning off-site virtual help desks. Harnessing the contributions of these non-proximal staff members, particularly in relation to organizational direction and culture, represents an important task for those organizations wanting to make full use of this increasingly common staffing method.

Introduction

IN FEBRUARY 2016, AFTER decades utilizing telecommuting staff, IBM announced it was ending its remote work policy for marketing employees.[1] In March 2016, Zapier, an IT company utilizing remote teams, announced a relocation assistance package aimed at helping its remote workforce, many of who lived in the expensive San Francisco Bay area, to relocate further afield.[2] IBM had just experienced nineteen consecutive quarters of declining sales.[3] Zapier had risen from its inception in 2012 to over 600,000 users by 2015.[4] Both are making strategic changes in their approaches to telecommuting with the aim of improving their business, yet who has it right?

Preparing a strategic approach to managing the telecommuting human resources of a theological institution requires knowledge of the issues faced by the industry, an understanding of telecommuting in the higher education sector, and the specific opportunities and challenges for telecommuting in theological education.

IBM changing what doesn't seem to work for them anymore seems to make sense. So too does Zapier's doubling down on telecommuting given their experience of growth. These differences are a salient reminder that simple formulas to achieve strategic telecommuting do not exist. That said there are some clear actions that can be taken, and limitations avoided, when putting a strategic human resource management (SHRM)[5] telecommuting policy together.

---

1. Kessler, "IBM, Remote-Work Pioneer, is Calling Thousands of Employees Back to the Office."

2. The initiative seeks to help employees improve their standard of living by reducing housing costs. See Foster, "De-Location Package: Keep Your Career and Live Beyond the Bay Area."

3. Hustle Newsletter, 23 March 2017.

4. See Turnbull, "How Zapier Went from Zero to 600,000+ Users in Just Three Years."

5. Strategic human resource management (SHRM) represents the organizational approach to managing staff from recruitment through to their engagement in the satisfactory delivery of the organizational mission. Specific SHRM policies exist for different aspects of SHRM. Policies for recruitment, review, remuneration, and intellectual property contribute to the organization's overall SHRM plan. If an organization utilized telecommuting staff then a telecommuting SHRM policy would be an appropriate governance practice.

Rationale for Telecommuting Staff Members

The rise of telecommuting in the Australian higher education sector has been facilitated by casualization, eLearning developments, and government initiatives.[6] Clear financial benefits are evident too. In the Australian Institute of Management white paper on managing in a flexible work environment, Burgmann says institutions that facilitate flexible telecommuting arrangements will be able to attract the best of those staff opting for partial retirement, offering an increased pool of talent to draw from.[7]

A number of elements in telecommuting may also be attractive for staff. Flexibility of location for lifestyle, reduced commuting and associated travel costs are evident. So too are less tangible aspects such as greater opportunity for alignment of personal values and frameworks for the staff member with the institution. Opportunities are also present for a specialist staff member to serve a number of institutions that would not normally be able to justify hiring such a specific specialty.

In theological education experience is a valuable resource, not simply within a person's discipline but also in terms of industry and organizational history. Given the small size of staff teams in Australian theological colleges, turnover, particularly at the executive level, represents a substantial risk. If instead of a key staff member leaving due to their spouse taking a role in another city their role was converted to telecommuting then significant advantages in maintaining corporate knowledge could be delivered, as well as alleviating the financial cost of replacement and the potential cost of misaligned recruitment.

Generic Issues Related to Telecommuting Staff

Burgmann's comments about the ability of telecommuting to attract quality staff are evident. However, attracting quality staff is only one aspect of the equation; effectively utilizing those staff, harnessing their experience and insight, and connecting this to the organizational strategy in a way that continues to keep them engaged and motivated is required if the model is to deliver to its fullest.

6. In March 2011, the Australian Minister for Broadband, Communications and the Digital Economy set a goal of raising teleworking participation from its current 6 percent to 12 percent of workers by 2020; see Nankervis et al, *Human Resource Management: Strategies and Processes*, 208. Federal proposals in connection to the 2014 budget increasing the age of retirement also exert influence.

7. Burgmann, "Managing in a Flexible Work Environment: White Paper November 2012."

Substantial SHRM literature exists regarding telecommuting workers, particularly from organizational culture and social exchange theory perspectives.[8] However, in practice, business and employee representative groups have adopted these insights in their formal policy documents to a limited degree.[9] The focus at the formal level often remains on implications, such as cost reduction and basic productivity, rather than progressing to consider the fulfillment of the psychosocial contract (those cognitive assumptions, expectations, and values within the transactional nature of employment) with telecommuting staff. This contrasts with the plethora of SHRM literature that supports the importance of the psychosocial contract for telecommuting staff. A possible reason for this discrepancy is the notoriously difficult nature of perceiving the fulfillment of psychosocial contracts.[10]

This missing or limited SHRM element in formal policy development represents an opportunity and productivity loss that deserves increased focus and intentional solutions.

Burgmann argues that the case for flexibility in the workplace requires identifying how this either avoids pain or achieves gain.[11] Maintaining the social contract, essentially the intangible relational elements of the employment agreement between employer and employee, is a significant challenge for telecommuting. Ameliorating issues exacerbated by perceived isolation for those telecommuting makes strategic sense for an organization, particularly once the initial benefit of flexibility for both the employer and employee has worn off. This then incorporates traditional HRM concepts of job design, enlargement, and enrichment.[12]

The literature identifies a number of specific SHRM issues that the telecommuting model may, if not accounted for, impact in regard to the psychosocial contract for telecommuting staff. These include:

---

8. Hylmö and Buzzanell, "Telecommuting as Viewed through Cultural Lenses," 329–56; Hornung and Glaser, "Employee Responses to Relational Fulfilment and Work-Life Benefits," 73–92.

9. European Trade Union Confederation, Union of Industrial and Employers' Confederations of Europe, European Association of Craft Small and Medium-Sized Enterprises, and European Centre of Employers and Enterprises Providing Public Services, 2002; Department of Communications, "Teleworkers are Vital to Australia's Workforce Challenges."

10. Coyle-Shapiro and Kessler, "The Employment Relationship in the U.K. Public Sector," 213–30.

11. Burgmann, "Managing in a Flexible Work Environment: White Paper November 2012," 16.

12. Härtel et al., *Human Resource Management*, 275–7.

- Retardation of promotion due to the "out-of-sight, out-of-mind" function,[13] or lack of informal networking opportunities for remote staff[14]
- Time management issues, including extremes of procrastination and workaholism, due to the paucity of boundaries[15]
- Interruptions and intrusions, particularly childcare and eldercare[16]
- Loss of productive commuting time and transitioning opportunities provided[17]
- Telecommuting exacerbation of work intensification[18]
- Uncertainty (Nankervis et al. do not develop beyond this single phrase; concepts of self-management, prioritization, and general limitation of feedback would fit well under this heading)[19]
- Difficulties establishing common ground and developing teamwork.[20] Limitations regarding informal learning, interpersonal networking, and mentoring opportunities[21]
- The limited ability to contribute to core directional framing of the organization.[22]

---

13. Kurland and Bailey, 1999, Mallia and Ferris, 2000, and Perlow, 1998, in Hylmö and Buzzanell, "Telecommuting as Viewed through Cultural Lenses," 329–56; Cooper and Kurland, 2002, McCloskey and Igbaria, 1998, in Ng, "Academics Telecommuting in Open and Distance Education Universities," 1–16; Department of Communications, "The Telework Kit: Making Telework a Success."

14. Burgmann, "Managing in a Flexible Work Environment: White Paper November 2012," 16; Cooper and Kurland, 2002, in Ng, "Academics Telecommuting in Open and Distance Education Universities," 1–16.

15. Nankervis et al, *Human Resource Management*; Ng, "Academics Telecommuting in Open and Distance Education Universities," 1–16.

16. Ng, "Academics Telecommuting in Open and Distance Education Universities," 1–16.

17. Salomon and Salomon, "Telecommuting: The Employee's Perspective," 15–28.

18. Burgmann, "Managing in a Flexible Work Environment: White Paper November 2012"; Department of Communications, "The Telework Kit: Making Telework a Success."

19. Nankervis et al, *Human Resource Management*.

20. Ibid.

21. Cooper and Kurland in Ng, "Academics Telecommuting in Open and Distance Education Universities," 1–16.

22. Burgmann, "Managing in a Flexible Work Environment: White Paper November 2012."

Failing to address these issues from no more than the fiscal benefit of employee satisfaction and retention represents a significant opportunity loss for organizational mission and limitation of the effective sustainability of current telecommuting frameworks. Burgmann argues that restricting the flexible worker's access to opportunities impacts the employee's career and the organization misses out on their insight, skills, and experience.[23] He argues intentional arrangements should be made to engage with off-site workers which include promoting flexible workers to managerial roles, utilizing short, frequent phone calls to replace incidental contact, and remote staff scheduling time when on-site to provide informal networking. Hartman et al. observed a positive correlation between telecommuter satisfaction and increased levels of technical and emotional supervisor support.[24] Similarly, Hornung and Glaser demonstrated a positive correlation between social exchange and organizational citizenship behavior for telecommuting workers.[25]

Issues Related to Telecommuting Staff in Higher Education

While technological platforms to support telecommuting staff of higher education institutions are both affordable and sufficiently advanced in terms of delivering communication and collaboration over distance, there is little evidence of strategic thought about telecommuting staff from a policy point of view.

Cheuk Fan Ng argues that there is very little research that focuses on telecommuting in post-secondary institutions.[26] Currently 30,188 articles are listed in the Macquarie University MultiSearch database for the search term "eLearning," rising from 2,771 articles in 2014. For the same period only 1,309 articles are listed for the search "telecommuting academics," rising previously from 350.[27] The growth of knowledge between these two areas is not keeping pace and an already evident gap is extending.

---

23. Ibid.

24. Hartman et al., "An Investigation of Selected Variables Affecting Telecommuting Productivity and Satisfaction," 207–25.

25. Hornung and Glaser, "Employee Responses to Relational Fulfilment and Work-Life Benefits," 73–92.

26. Ng, "Academics Telecommuting in Open and Distance Education Universities," 1–16.

27. Figures from March 28, 2017 and May 4, 2014.

In higher education, the development of ICT and telecommuting has seen mixed results. The University of Phoenix, a strong utilizer of telecommuting academics, provides a recruitment and mentoring phase for staff members utilizing ICT for shadowing online classes, with mentors providing weekly evaluations and support.[28] Ng however, notes expectations of research for staff in open and distance institutions are often unclear, and cites the work of Yick regarding the centrality of research for institutional credibility and faculty's professional growth.[29]

Telecommuting for staff within Australian theological colleges has generally not been as widely adopted as elsewhere in the Australian higher education sector. Theological education in Australia has in its recent history experienced implicit barriers that have had an impact on the utilization of telecommuting staff. Examples include the debate regarding the possibility of student formation in a non-face-to-face mode (as addressed by Hockridge in 2011[30], 2013[31], and 2015[32]), which has a correlative impact on the consideration of the efficacy of telecommuting staff to participate in institutional enculturation activities. Until recently, procedural barriers (lifted in 2012) that limited flexible delivery for some significant Australian College of Theology courses also represented a similar implicit barrier.

The challenges for theological education in this regard are the same as the ones faced by business generally, yet with additional cognitive hurdles. Both need to answer: how do we bring people's experience and creativity to the point where it impacts on the organization's direction and their workers?

Specific Issues Related to Telecommuting Theological Institution Staff: A Timothy Partnership Case Study

The Timothy Partnership is a joint venture between Youthworks College and Presbyterian Youth NSW to provide ACT advanced diploma, diploma, and certificate level studies that are delivered online and in a flexible format. As a manager directly responsible for the PY NSW team members where 50

28. Wildavsky et al., *Reinventing Higher Education*; K. Sparrow, Customer Services Officer at University of Phoenix [Personal Communication, May 23, 2014].

29. Yick, 2005, in Ng, "Academics Telecommuting in Open and Distance Education Universities," 1–16.

30. Hockridge, "What's the Problem? Spiritual Formation in Distance and Online Theological Education," 25–38.

31. Hockridge, "Challenges for Educators Using Distance and Online Education to Prepare Students for Relational Professions," 142–60.

32. Hockridge, "Learning Design for Formational Learning in Non-Campus-Based Learning Contexts," 237.

percent of these staff telecommute, harnessing the full SHRM capacities of the psychosocial contract in this circumstance is significant.

Limited opportunity to input to core direction and issues relating to uncertainty and teamwork are some of the SHRM telecommuting issues listed above that can be seen within my organization. While these are embryonic (predominantly due to the start-up nature of the organization, commencing classes in Semester 1, 2010) and have less impact due to the "novelty" of flexibility that telecommuting offers still present, to continue without addressing these will result in the substantial loss of opportunity described. Given that the average age for my telecommuting staff is fifty-five, with an average of twenty years teaching or administrative experience, this is untenable.

The organization's internal staff review process utilizes Herzberg's two-factor model to shape the staff review process.[33] The model enables staff to effectively critique the organization's limitations in hygiene factors (elements required for a person to undertake their role that once delivered to the required level sate desire), and motivators (elements that enliven the staff member to their role). While the psychosocial contract can operate in both areas, it has strongest traction in the motivational aspect. Coyle-Shapiro and Kessler, reviewing the relationship between the psychological contract and motivation in organizational commitment and citizenship behavior for UK public servants, found that organizational support (where the employer demonstrates interest in and support for the employee) and employee involvement in decision-making and influencing organizational direction represented a significant path for fulfilling relational obligations that were often difficult to perceive.[34] Considering the relationship revealed by Coyle-Shapiro and Kessler and the limitations of the telecommuting model,[35] adopting steps to ameliorate or circumvent these relational limitations would seem prudent for maintaining employee motivation and obtaining strategic benefit from the insights.

Nankervis et al. as part of their SHRM model suggest a twenty-two-point outline of key questions that HRM is concerned with resolving. Relevant to the psychosocial contract they include:

1. How can well-chosen employees be kept productive, satisfied and motivated to contribute to organizational growth and development?

33. Herzberg, "One More Time: How Do You Motivate Employees?" 5–16.
34. Coyle-Shapiro and Kessler, "The Employment Relationship in the U.K. Public Sector," 213–30.
35. Burgmann, "Managing in a Flexible Work Environment: White Paper November 2012."

2. What methods are appropriate to maintain effective relationships between employees, jobs, work environment and management?[36]

Given the team's capacity for critiquing the organization's engagement with hygiene factors and motivators, "From a virtual/remote staff member perspective" was added to these questions and circulated to relevant staff.

Within the PY NSW team members of the Timothy Partnership, six telecommuting staff members were surveyed. Two of these were non-instructional staff who delivered student services and prepared study materials, and four were instructional staff responsible for the preparation and delivery of online units of study. All were on permanent part-time contracts and had been with the organization for four years prior to the survey. The two non-instructional staff members had worked extensively on-site with one basing their telecommuting experience on a six-month placement in the UK, and the other on the aspects of their role conducted off-site. Other remote and virtual staff members were utilized by the organization at the time, often as developers or tutors, however, they were not included in the survey as these were casual arrangements resulting in temporary rather than permanent staffing.

In relation to the first question, team members surveyed felt that it was important for staff members to be able to influence the overall goals of the organization and work as a team rather than just on their individual disciplines. Respondents indicated that without this, competent people would not be able to connect with the organization's objectives. This desire for involvement extended to learning design, with participants suggesting an increased commitment would develop from personal involvement. These findings support the insights of Burgmann.

Respondents indicated that these needs would likely be met by spending time together discussing design and organizational direction. One respondent outlined that sharing the heart was more effective than promulgating new policies. Communication and feedback on tasks undertaken was also listed as important.

Non-instructional staff surveyed mostly addressed practical issues in their comments. This is not necessarily indicative, however, as both non-instructional staff members had spent substantial time working on-site and may have thought that they had already had substantial opportunity to engage with design and vision aspects.

In summary, discussing and evaluating the vision of the organization and the design of the learning materials is a vital part of producing

---

36. Nankervis et al, *Human Resource Management*, 38.

productive, satisfied, and motivated remote and virtual staff members. Respondents indicated that these aspects were being addressed through retreats and professional development, but that more could be done to improve the involvement in design and vision development.

Addressing the second question regarding the maintenance of effective relationships, a number of off-line suggestions such as retreats, social interactions, and performance reviews were combined with on-line methods, both synchronous, such as Skype meetings and teleconferences, and asynchronous, such as Facebook.

Respondents again indicated that while improvement was possible, the organization was already helping to address these aspects. However, it was noted that isolation could reduce the sense of contribution to the bigger picture and that there could be a failure to engage with and see the overall finished product and those using the products. One respondent expressed that having tasks placed within a broader context made them more satisfying to complete.

In summary, it would seem that not only is the provision of opportunity for engagement important but also that engagement focuses at the integrated and organizational shaping level rather than simply the informational or skills-based level. This integration enables competent people to commit to the organizational objectives that they can influence. These findings fit substantially with the SHRM concerns for telecommuting staff outlined above.

Mitigating the Issues

The case study indicates that mitigating issues raised by the use of a telecommuting model may not require the adoption of entirely new approaches to management. Lessons learnt from existing practices may go a long way to engaging with these if they are intentionally applied to this context.

Burgmann supports this suggesting that SHRM in this environment calls upon current skills of managers such as supervising, appraising and supporting staff, and communicating with teams and colleagues. However, he also indicates that any deficiencies in management are magnified in the flexible work environment.[37]

In terms of transferable skills, the eLearning community has a number of capacities in relation to student support that can be leveraged to assist telecommuting staff. Capacities for learning management systems (LMS) for

---

37. Burgmann, "Managing in a Flexible Work Environment: White Paper November 2012."

building online communities of practice and repositories of asynchronous reflection, together with potentiality for platform support of team projects are also significant crossover areas. Ng argues that, "To promote a sense of belonging, open and distance education institutions should explore the use of the same tools and technologies used to build communities as we do for our students."[38] However, Burgmann's warning regarding the exasperation of deficiencies is also applicable.

The disconnect between an academic consideration of eLearning and the limited consideration of telecommuting academic staff already noted in the growing literature is underscored in practice. Surveying the members of the eLearning panel of the Australian College of Theology, my organization's accrediting body, which is responsible for sixteen institutions across Australia, no member was able to supply material regarding telecommuting SHRM policy or procedure for either academic or non-instructional staff across the consortia.[39] It would seem while many institutions in the consortia are engaged in eLearning, telecommuting of staff is either not widespread and/or the SHRM considerations of staff telecommuting has not been substantially engaged with.

It seems possible that it is not a specific focus on the psychosocial contract for telecommuting workers that is needed but rather a general consideration of how managers can translate the higher order aspects of SHRM into the rapidly expanding, off-site virtual telecommuting and flexible workplace environment.

Organizations that address the higher-order aspects of SHRM for teleworkers will reap substantial benefits, not only attracting the best telecommuting talent, but getting the most from them. Clear opportunities exist given the demonstrated research and practice gaps. For the theological institution seeking to develop in this area, engagement with the implicit limitations from our discipline's history will also be important.

Conclusions and Recommendations for Colleges Considering Telecommuting Staff

Productivity without creativity, with creativity defined as the ongoing making of the organization and its values through its human interactions, is in the long term unfulfilling and unsustainable. If managers of theological

---

38. Ng, "Academics Telecommuting in Open and Distance Education Universities," 10.

39 Requests were made to members of the ACT eLearning panel in April 2014.

institutions engage in telecommuting without mechanisms to ensure this form of creativity occurs substantial human resources will be wasted.

Although it begins here, difficulties in achieving this reside not philosophically, but operationally. For this to occur, we need to build the systems that support these inputs. Systems are needed that reduce the trend to see on-site staff as core, and telecommuting staff as periphery. Intentional steps need to be developed to overcome the out-of-site, out-of-mind inertia that may occur. Importantly, this is not simply about making the hub more accepting of telecommuting staff, it is also about assisting telecommuting staff to remain engaged and to understand their responsibility in the creative process.

Four clear areas of focus emerge for the institution intentionally seeking to build effective approaches to help develop the longer-term benefits of managing and supporting telecommuting staff while avoiding the pitfalls for both institution and employee.

The first would be the development of a vision for the ceremonial and intentional aspects of how telecommuting staff engage with the organization. This would include expectations of, and systems for, telecommuting staff's engagement with the setting of organizational direction and design. This would ameliorate communication, collaboration, aspects of uncertainty, and teamwork difficulties.

The second would be developing a vision for integration. Meeting the psychosocial needs of telecommuting staff requires the engagement of staff across the entire enterprise. Helping proximal staff engage with telecommuters facilitates the integration of telecommuters and improves the organization's overall engagement with objectives. This also delivers a tighter focus for networking, and facilitating engagement with organizational direction and learning design. These steps begin to ameliorate issues related to communication, collaboration, uncertainty, and teamwork difficulty.

The third and most difficult aspect is maintaining realistic expectations of telecommuting staff in regard to directional inputs. Organizational direction and design faces a number of pressures.[40] Management's role is to be cognisant of these forces and optimize for the organization in light of this. However, these pressures also limit the scope of management in setting the organizational direction and design. Partnerships with other organizations, denominational pressures, regulation and accreditation processes, and changes in government policy all provide parameters. Inviting contribution to organizational objectives and designs solicits new and creative approaches, yet an employee's lack of wider organizational perspectives

---

40. Porter, 1980, in Robbins et al., *Management*.

may render many suggestions inoperable. Explaining non-implementation to proximal staff can be beneficial as they have the opportunity to directly observe results, but the telecommuting staff member who battles a sense of isolation may be left with the perception that the offer of input from management is disingenuous. Burgmann's comments about levering existing management tools,[41] even with the warning that faults are magnified when applied to telecommuting, is not enough as the challenges here are greater. Intentional policy that delivers the context that is gained informally by proximal staff members is required for telecommuting staff members.

While all three aspects impact the psychosocial contract, it seems likely that addressing the collaboration for productivity and effectiveness element will meet immediate needs in this regard. Such priorities will necessitate the development of greater collaborative work platforms, such as Google docs, and existing Moodle wikis, together with the processes for using them. Improving communication through regular teleconferences, as well as the formalizing of existing professional development and assessment review retreats would also be beneficial.

The three aspects outlined above could be applicable to any telecommuting workplace, however, the utilization of telecommuting in a higher education environment, particularly for academics, introduces a fourth specific visionary aspect: the maintenance and propagation of the academy. Engagement within the academy requires community, peer collaboration, and mentoring emerging academics, together with publishing and debating advancements, discoveries, and new applications.[42] Any vision for meeting the psychosocial needs of telecommuting staff in a theological higher education setting needs to account for this responsibility, not simply for reasons of economics or sentimentality, but for sustainability, effectiveness, and achievement of mission objectives.[43]

Designing a plan of approach to achieve this vision requires addressing these aspects from a clear process perspective.[44] Workman's research indicated that tightly controlled virtual teams performed better.[45] This research

---

41. Burgmann, "Managing in a Flexible Work Environment: White Paper November 2012."

42. Magnuson, 2002, in Ng, "Academics Telecommuting in Open and Distance Education Universities."

43. Yick, 2005, in Ng, "Academics Telecommuting in Open and Distance Education Universities"; Hornung and Glaser, "Employee Responses to Relational Fulfilment and Work-Life Benefits," 73–92.

44. Pinsonneault and Boisvert, 1996, in Ng, "Academics Telecommuting in Open and Distance Education Universities."

45. Workman, "Virtual Team Culture and the Amplification of Team Boundary

also indicated a need for the explicit management of telecommuting staff in terms of their supports and in-group processes, as well as higher levels of policy and process regulation to reduce the acceptable levels of ambiguity that are usually found in proximal settings. Theological institutions would do well to leverage their growing competencies in eLearning student support to facilitate the higher order needs of telecommuting staff. However, an honest engagement with the implicit limitations is also required for full progress to be made.

Bibliography

Burgmann, Lucy. "Managing in a Flexible Work Environment: White Paper November 2012." North Sydney: Australian Institute of Management NSW & ACT Training Centre Limited, 2012.

Coyle-Shapiro, Jacqueline A-M., & Ian Kessler. "The Employment Relationship in the U.K. Public Sector: A Psychological Contract Perspective." *Journal of Public Administration Research and Theory* 13, no. 2 (2003) 213–30. http://eprints.lse.ac.uk/832/.

Department of Communications. "The Telework Kit: Making Telework a Success: A Guide for Leaders, Managers and Employers." http://apo.org.au/node/36237.

———. "Teleworkers are Vital to Australia's Workforce Challenges." http://www.communications.gov.au/news/media_centre/teleworkers_are_vital_to_australias_workforce_challenges.

European Trade Union Confederation, Union of Industrial and Employers' Confederations of Europe, European Association of Craft Small and Medium-Sized Enterprises, and European Centre of Employers and Enterprises Providing Public Services. "Framework agreement on Telework." http://www.ueapme.com/docs/joint_position/Telework%20agreement.pdf.

Foster, Wade. "De-Location Package: Keep Your Career and Live Beyond the Bay Area." https://zapier.com/blog/move-away-from-sf-get-remote-job/.

Härtel, Charmine, et al. *Human Resource Management: Transforming Theory into Innovative Practice*. Frenchs Forest, NSW: Pearson Prentice Hall, 2007.

Hartman, Richard I., et al. "An Investigation of Selected Variables Affecting Telecommuting Productivity and Satisfaction." *Journal of Business and Psychology* 6, no. 2 (1991) 207–25.

Herzberg, Frederick. "One More Time: How Do You Motivate Employees?" *Harvard Business Review*, 65, no. 5 (1987) 5–16. http://www.facilitif.eu/user_files/file/herzburg_article.pdf.

Hockridge, Diane. "Challenges for Educators Using Distance and Online Education to Prepare Students for Relational Professions." *Distance Education* 34, no. 2 (2013) 142–60.

———. "Learning Design for Formational Learning in Non-Campus-Based Learning Contexts." *Teaching Theology in a Technological Age* 34, no. 2 (2015) 237.

Permeability on Performance," 435–58.

———. "Making the Implicit Explicit: Exploring the Role of Learning Design in Improving Formational Learning Outcomes." In *Learning and Teaching Theology: Some Ways Ahead*, edited by Les Ball and James R. Harrison, 131–45. Morning Star, 2014.

———. "What's the Problem? Spiritual Formation in Distance and Online Theological Education." *Journal of Christian Education* 54, no. 1 (2011) 25–38.

Hornung, Severin, and Jürgen Glaser. "Employee Responses to Relational Fulfilment and Work-Life Benefits: A Social Exchange Study in the German Public Administration." *International Journal of Manpower* 31, no. 1 (2010) 73–92.

Hustle Newsletter, 23 March 2017. https://thehustle.co/daily.

Hylmö, Annika, and Patrice M. Buzzanell. "Telecommuting as Viewed through Cultural Lenses: An Empirical Investigation of the Discourses of Utopia, Identity, and Mystery." *Communication Monographs*, 69, no. 4 (2002) 329–56.

Kessler, Sarah. "IBM, Remote-Work Pioneer, is Calling Thousands of Employees Back to the Office." https://qz.com/924167/ibm-remote-work-pioneer-is-calling-thousands-of-employees-back-to-the-office/.

Nankervis, Alan, et al. *Human Resource Management: Strategies and Processes*. 8th ed. Melbourne, VIC: Cengage Learning Australia, 2014.

Ng, Cheuk F. "Academics Telecommuting in Open and Distance Education Universities: Issues, Challenges, and Opportunities." *International Review of Research in Open and Distance Learning* 7, no. 2 (2006) 1–16.

Robbins, Stephen P., et al. *Management*. Frenchs Forest, NSW: Prentice Hall, 2000.

Salomon, Ilan, and Meira Salomon. "Telecommuting: The Employee's Perspective. *Technological Forecasting and Social Change* 25, no. 1 (1984) 15–28.

Turnbull, Alex. "How Zapier Went from Zero to 600,000+ Users in Just Three Years." https://www.groovehq.com/blog/zapier-interview-with-wade-foster.

Wildavsky, Ben, et al. *Reinventing Higher Education: The Promise of Innovation*. Cambridge, MA: Harvard Education Press, 2011.

Workman, Michael. "Virtual Team Culture and the Amplification of Team Boundary Permeability on Performance." *Human Resource Development Quarterly* 16, no. 4 (2005) 435–58.

20

The Current Environment of Theological Education in Australia

MARK HARDING

Abstract

This chapter first reviews briefly the major changes in theological education of the last forty years noting increases in student enrollments, the diversification of modes of delivery and the wide range of intentions for studying that mark the experience of most providers today. Focus then turns to the regulatory and social environment in which providers find themselves and the ways in which providers have experienced changes and are being challenged. The impact of the provision of FEE-HELP and the advent of the Tertiary Education Quality and Standards Agency (TEQSA) are considered, followed by concise observations about the cost of theological education, the challenge of student-centered learning, and the need for sound, publicly accountable corporate governance. Finally, regarding the current social environment, I exhort theological colleges to devise strategies needed to encourage women to enroll in research degrees and to support women in this costly enterprise in the interest of increasing the talent pool of applicants for academic staff positions. In addition, I argue that it is essential for employer stakeholders and colleges to work collaboratively and intentionally to subvert and finally eradicate abusive cultures and behaviors, and implement transparent cultures which unequivocally and undeniably reflect Christian values. The chapter concludes with brief observations about the need to build bridges between communities of faith and society with respect to training and formation.

Then and Now

WHEN I BEGAN FORMAL theological education in 1975 all but one of my class of twenty-five or so was male. Almost all were under thirty. All were studying full time. Most of us were enrolled in the Australian College of Theology's (ACT's) Bachelor of Theology degree, a new degree. All but two of us were seeking ordination or were candidates for cross-cultural work in Australia or overseas. One of the two was the sole woman student: I was the other. But by the time I had completed first year I too was an ordination candidate. Most theology students of that time were youngish, male, studying in full-time and in on-campus mode, and intending to work full time in churches or in cross-cultural agencies. Unless a student was a candidate for ordained ministry, they had to pay tuition fees up front. The provision of Austudy was still seventeen years away; FEE-HELP would emerge thirty years hence.

Now, more than forty years later, most ACT students are studying in part-time mode. Women make up 40 percent of the student body across the ACT—a figure reportedly higher in other providers. Degrees in theology—rare in 1975—are now ubiquitous. About half of the graduates of the ACT find work in full-time ministry of one sort or another. But the *range* of these ministries would have been hard to anticipate forty years ago. Those preparing for ordination or for accreditation with churches or in church or cross-cultural agencies represent a smaller proportion of the current total student body than in 1975.

And there are more students studying theology than ever before. The student load of the ACT has increased by about 50 percent in the last decade. The average age of incoming students across the ACT is thirty-five, with a significant number of students returning to study in middle age.

Many enroll in theology courses out of an interest in the Christian tradition. They know they can continue their duties as a homemaker or a professional or a caregiver, and study theology part-time. Many colleges offer courses that are taught in the evenings or in intensive mode or, increasingly, in off-campus mode through the internet thereby facilitating students' preferences for study. This is highly commendable in my view. Student-centered learning is the defining mark of the current Australian higher education landscape.[1]

There certainly was minimal regulation of theology providers in 1975. However, approval to offer degrees—first achieved by the then Melbourne College of Divinity (now the University of the Divinity[2]) and later by the ACT—has brought steadily increasing regulatory scrutiny in company with prestige, standing and increasing enrollments. Approval implied that the degrees of non-university higher education providers (NUHEPs) were demonstrably assessed, resourced, quality assured and centrally managed to a standard equivalent to that operating in the universities. With regard to the ACT, accreditation approvals were renewed by the NSW higher education regulator, and later by other state regulators, every five years. New degrees at undergraduate, masters and doctoral levels were steadily added to the ACT's suite of courses. Regulators held the governing body of the ACT responsible for academic oversight, the generation of a single set of academic policies, and the operation of a quality assurance framework with which all affiliated colleges were required to comply. Colleges, once loosely related to the ACT office and governing body and preparing candidates for ACT external examinations, now submit annual financial and academic reports, comply with all ACT academic policies, furnish data when required by the ACT office and regulators, receive regular formal visits by the Dean and CEO of the ACT, and sign affiliation agreements. Regulators have placed the ACT Ltd on notice that its model of affiliated colleges organized on a national basis and delivering the ACT's courses on behalf of the company must maximize its operation as a single provider with many delivery points. Consequently, the challenge for each affiliated college, on the one hand, is to find ways of differentiating itself in the marketplace and maintaining its ethos and, on the other, to satisfy its obligations with respect to the ACT Ltd as provider. But increased regulation of all providers in the one higher education sector also provides opportunities. Accordingly, the ACT has endeavored to put itself in a position to realize a long-held institutional aspiration, namely, to be approved as a specialized university provider whereby all affiliated colleges would become colleges of the ACT Ltd as a university of theology.

1. The Tertiary Education and Quality Agency, the national higher education regulator, defines its role as safeguarding "the interests of all current and future students studying within Australia's higher education system." See http://www.teqsa.gov.au/regulatory-approach.

2. The Melbourne College of Divinity (MCD), established by a 1910 Act of the Victorian Parliament (unique in Australia among non-university theological colleges), has been known as the University of Divinity since 2011.

But theology providers have changed and have been changed in other ways since 1975. Two areas of change will be discussed here: the regulatory environment and the social environment.

Government Higher Education Policy and Theological Education

FEE-HELP and Commonwealth Funding

The most remarkable change in education policy of the last generation has been the introduction of FEE-HELP. The scheme is enshrined in the Higher Education Support Act (HESA) 2003.[3] Eligible students enrolled in an approved course provided by a duly registered higher education provider are able to borrow up to 100 percent of their tuition fees and defer payment until their taxable income reaches a certain threshold, currently about $54,000. Since the FEE-HELP scheme began operating in January 2005, NUHEPs have experienced steadily increasing enrollments. Another benefit of FEE-HELP is that the non-university providers can now charge tuition fees that more closely approximate the actual costs of tuition.

All NUHEP theology providers, including the ACT Ltd with its affiliated colleges, now find themselves highly dependent on FEE-HELP. Federal governments have shown no inclination to remove FEE-HELP. Nevertheless, successive departments of education have been taking steps to ensure that providers are held more accountable for their management of FEE-HELP funds—it is tax payers' money after all. There have been widely reported scandals in the vocational education and training (VET) sector where a small number of unscrupulous providers have enrolled large numbers of ineligible students under the VET FEE-HELP scheme only for it to be revealed that very few of their students actually graduate. However, these revelations have not appeared to undermine the esteem with which the non-university higher education sector is perceived. The federal government is reportedly considering recouping unpaid tuition loans from deceased estates and reducing the taxable income threshold at which loans begin to be repaid, but as yet no change in policy has been enacted.[4] Theological

---

3. HELP stands for Higher Education Loan Program. The role of the Council of Private Higher Education (COPHE) under its then Chair, Dr. Brian Millis (Principal of Christian Heritage College) and Adrian McComb (Executive Officer of COPHE) was crucial in shaping the political will that saw the passage of the HESA.

4. With regard to possible amendments ("reform") of higher education funding, the following news report urging caution appeared in the Sydney Morning Herald on 24 January 2017: http://bit.ly/2jKLcoE. At the time of writing (27 January 2017), the

college governing bodies have a responsibility to ensure that ACT admission criteria are upheld, monitor retention, attrition, and graduation rates, and, with respect to these, take immediate steps to address disappointing data. Were the problems that currently affect some VET providers to infect any NUHEP, even one, the loss of reputation to the sector, not to mention the particular provider, would erode public and government confidence in the ability of all NUHEPs to manage tax payers' money. FEE-HELP brings greater accountability as its price.

FEE-HELP debt per student will be capped at $100,879 in 2017.[5] This amount should be sufficient to fund seven years' full-time theological education for a student enrolled in ACT courses. Just a few ACT students have reached the limit of what they can borrow under the FEE-HELP scheme. In time, given trends in tuition fee increases, it is likely that more students will reach the FEE-HELP cap in less than seven years' ACT study. Theological college governing bodies should therefore ensure that tuition costs are kept as low as possible without sacrificing current commitments to employing predominantly full-time, highly credentialed academic and professional staff and maintaining plant and resources that meet student needs.

But while we can celebrate the provision of FEE-HELP, at the heart of the higher education funding system is an inequity by which students enrolled at a university in the same degrees provided by NUHEPs are effectively subsidized by the Commonwealth through the Commonwealth Grants Scheme (CGS). Eligible students enrolling in a university degree attract government funding in the form of a Commonwealth Supported Place (CSP), reducing the tuition fee which is either paid up front or, as is usually the case, deferred by a loan under what is called the Higher Education Contribution Scheme (HECS).

This directly impacts on NUHEPs that offer degrees in theology. For most of the twentieth century, theological education was the province of non-university providers.[6] However, from the 1990s a number of universities, among them Charles Sturt, Murdoch, and Flinders, began offering degrees in theology in partnership with established non-university theological colleges in Canberra, Perth, and Adelaide respectively. In 2016, a full-time Bachelor of Theology student at a university attracts a commonwealth sub-

---

definitive details of the government's reform package have not been released.

5. This is the limit for all courses with the exception of students in medicine, dentistry and veterinary science where the FEE-HELP limit increases to $126,101.

6. The first Australian universities intentionally excluded the teaching of theology, and only allowed it in "halls of residence" (i.e. residential colleges) established by churches on campuses. See also Piggin, "A History of Theological Education in Australia," 24–43.

sidy worth $5,539 to the university with the student either paying the HECS amount of no more than $6,256 up front or taking out a loan. But if the student were to enroll in the same course at a theology NUHEP, there is no CSP. They would either have to pay the full tuition fee up front or, more likely, take out a FEE-HELP loan for the full amount, which in almost every case will exceed the capped CSP tuition fee of $11,795, which is the sum of the subsidy and the HECS amount, let alone the HECS amount of $6,256. The inequity of this funding policy is clear.

In the context of Higher Degrees by Research (HDRs), the inequity of Commonwealth funding policy is even more stark. Full-time doctoral candidates enrolled at the universities receive a tuition scholarship under the Research Training Scheme (RTS). These candidates can also compete for a tax-free stipend worth about $25,000 annually. It is reported that about 20 percent of candidates are successful. However, NUHEPs with a research load and publication output do not have access to the RTS despite representations to the Department of Education and Training for access to be granted.[7] As a result, doctoral candidates are more likely to enroll with those several universities that provide research degrees in theology than with a NUHEP, thus vitiating and potentially undermining providers' research profiles and, therefore, their institutional aspirations which largely depend on maintaining a healthy research load. Even federal governments that are more naturally supportive of free enterprise and competition baulk at extending the RTS to NUHEPs with proven research load and output.

The Council of Private Higher Education (COPHE) and the NUHEPs have argued that the CGS should be extended to the non-university sector. Some NUHEPs do have access to CSPs if they are delivering teacher-training and nursing courses.[8] Currently, only the University of Divinity has been included in the RTS.

How might NUHEPs, especially those providing courses in theology, respond? Enrollments in NUHEPs have been growing at a faster rate than in the universities.[9] However, in 2015 only about 8.5 percent of Australian

---

7. In March 2012, the ACT Ltd submitted an extensive application based on the university compact template to the Department of Education and Training for consideration of the college as an institution approved for accessing and competing for Research Training Scheme Funding. The application was shelved by the Department.

8. These NUHEPs are listed on pages 70–71 of the Commonwealth Supported Places (CSP) and the Higher Education Loans Program (HELP) Handbook for 2016. The handbook can be accessed at http://bit.ly/2kqgDEj.

9. For 2015 student summary data (the most recent national data available), see http://bit.ly/2jDbHLI. In 2015, there was an increase of 9.9 percent in student enrollments in non-university higher education institutions compared with a 2.2 percent increase in enrollments in the "public universities."

higher education EFT is enrolled in NUHEPs.[10] A majority of students in courses in theology are enrolled in NUHEPs. In time, the current marginalization of the NUHEPs should be harder to maintain as EFT continues to increase at a higher rate than in the universities. NUHEPs often outperform the universities in measures relating to student satisfaction. The recently inaugurated federally-funded surveys known as Quality Indicators for Learning and Teaching (QILT) is publicly accessible, and provides the evidence when NUHEP data is compared with the universities.[11]

Ongoing lack of access to the RTS for NUHEPs is a much harder challenge because not all have a research load. Moreover, theology NUHEPS with research doctoral and masters' candidates will struggle to extend the proportion of their HDR load to the 6–7 percent of total EFT achieved by university humanities departments, albeit sustained by long-standing benefit of access to the RTS. Accordingly, theology NUHEPs must have generous scholarship systems in place to attract research candidates away from the universities. Attracting academic staff with proven publishing and supervision records is also crucial. Pleasingly, the ACT has experienced the benefit of a scholarship provision over the last few years in attracting HDR candidates. In addition, affiliated colleges are increasingly employing proven researchers thus potentially attracting quality candidates away from the universities. I also note that theological colleges are realizing that their focus on ministry training can happily coexist with and be enhanced by a developing research training and publication profile.

Political will is required to extend equitable funding to the NUHEP sector, although there are members of parliament and departmental officials who understand the need to correct anomalies and inequities in the funding system in the interests of treating all higher education students fairly.[12] For their part NUHEPs must do all that is possible to continue demonstrating that they are part of a unified Australian higher education system in terms of their compliance with regulation, publicly accountable quality assurance mechanisms, participation in the QILT, and the intent to fearlessly implement evidence-based improvements in learning and teaching.

10. See http://bit.ly/2jDbHLI.

11. See https://www.qilt.edu.au. The website allows comparisons between institutions on a range of 2015 student experience data. Theology has been included in the study area of Humanities, Culture and Social Science.

12. The one-time federal Labor member for Lowe, the Hon. John Murphy MP, gave a speech supportive of the ACT's aspirations to access the RTS to the parliament in June 2013. The text of his speech can be found at http://bit.ly/2k962jW.

Tertiary Education Quality and Standards Agency (TEQSA)

In mid 2011, the federal government established the Tertiary Education Quality and Standards Agency (TEQSA) by an act of Parliament thus establishing a national higher education regulator replacing state higher education bodies. Section 13 of the TEQSA Act specifies the following basic principles for regulation.

> [TEQSA] must comply with the following principles when exercising a power under this Act in relation to a regulated entity: (a) the principle of regulatory necessity; (b) the principle of reflecting risk; and (c) the principle of proportionate regulation.[13]

By these principles TEQSA is bound not to overburden the "entity" (i.e. the provider), has regard to any risk that relates to the entity's current and future financial capacity, student experience, resourcing, and quality assurance strategies, and exercises its power in proportion to any non-compliance or the risk of future non-compliance. To this end TEQSA has developed threshold standards[14] and a risk assessment framework.[15]

Section 15 of the Act requires TEQSA to take account of each "entity's" history, its scholarship, teaching and research, its student's experiences, its financial status and capacity, as well as its compliance with the Threshold Standards including its quality assurance mechanisms. Consequently, each provider submits annual financial, academic, and student data to TEQSA and receives a report analyzing the data with respect to TEQSA's risk indicator thresholds and containing a determination of the provider's risk ratings for each risk category. The governing body of each provider is under an obligation to engage with its TEQSA Risk Report, and to take steps to mitigate elevated risks.

TEQSA expects the ACT Ltd to ensure that its affiliated colleges also comply with the Threshold Standards and TEQSA's risk framework. The ACT Ltd manages and mitigates educational and corporate risk across its network. Compliance in all respects is not an option if access to FEE-HELP, provider registration, and accreditation of higher education awards are to

---

13. The Act can be accessed at http://bit.ly/2kyZThG.

14. There are four standards that comprise the Higher Education Standards Framework. The four are (1) Provider Registration Standards, (2) Provider Category Standards, (3) Provider Course Registration Standards, and (4) Qualification Standards. The latest version of the Standards Framework was made on 7 October 2015 under subsection 58(1) of the TEQSA Act 2011. The standards can be accessed at http://bit.ly/2jWRtOo.

15. The details of TEQSA's risk assessment framework can be accessed at http://bit.ly/2kqiARt.

be protected. The ACT Ltd and affiliated colleges must continue to work collegially in a context of interdependence and mutual trust to demonstrate compliance with statutory obligation.

A key component of TEQSA's risk assessment is student experience. In the previous decade, the Australian Universities Quality Agency (AUQA) challenged the higher education sector to provide evidence for claims made by providers about matters such as their standing in the community, their endorsement by employer stakeholders, the quality of student experience, and student satisfaction. The inauguration of QILT surveys in 2015 enables students considering enrollment in like or identical courses to compare satisfaction rates across university and non-university providers, thus facilitating informed decision-making and transparency on performance for the benefit of institutional governing bodies and stakeholders. The realization of the ACT's institutional aspirations depends in large part on the ACT Ltd and its affiliated colleges satisfying TEQSA and the Minister for Education that the consortium is financially viable, its management of risk is robust, it perpetuates a commitment to continuous quality improvement, and records high levels of student satisfaction and engagement.

The Cost of Theological Education

In 1975, theological and Bible colleges faced no competition for student enrollments from the universities. Students enrolled in the theological college of their denominational affiliation or in a Bible college if seeking to embark on cross-cultural ministry. Moreover, the cost of compliance with regulation was minimal. Since then costs have increased dramatically to meet student-focused educational needs, to provide resources for academic staff research and the delivery of HDRs, and to comply with regulation—all this in a highly competitive sector in which denominational loyalties have largely broken down. College governing bodies bear a significant responsibility for the oversight and management of the cost of education.

One of the strategic goals of the ACT Ltd's Strategic Plan (2014–2016) was to investigate ways of taking costs out of theological education. In discussions with affiliated college principals, examples of the kind of savings colleges might consider were amalgamation with another college, the sharing of academic staff, and divestment of plant that is costly to maintain and refurbish. I am aware that some affiliates have set about implementing cost-saving measures. College governing bodies need to consider such options regularly.

For NUHEPs competing with university providers, which, as we saw above, are able to offer cheaper tuition to students enrolled in the same courses, there is a temptation to cut costs by employing more casual staff, reducing full-time staff, and increasing staff load. However, the affiliated colleges of the ACT have maintained their commitment to employing permanent full-time academic staff. This greatly assists colleges to establish viable communities of learning on their campuses and in the online environment, which is one of the great added values colleges have always striven to provide.

Student-Centered Learning

The Australian higher education context is increasingly one in which learning is student-centered. In 2015, the ACT completed an extensive project that resulted in the approval of student learning outcomes for all ACT courses and units of study. It was undertaken in response to a ministerial requirement issued to all providers mandating course learning outcomes for all courses. The ACT has also required that learning outcomes be incorporated into all student assessments. This represents a culture change not only in course and unit design but also in assessment centered on student learning outcomes.

The great increase in delivery in off-campus mode study has revolutionized education in Australia. Beginning in 2004, the entire ACT Bachelor of Ministry degree and up to one-third of the Bachelor of Theology and the Master of Divinity could be offered in off-campus mode. In 2012, after a thorough year-long process, restrictions on the amount of a course that could be delivered in this mode were removed. This change was driven by student need and choice. For example, relocation to a major or capital city to undertake theological education is a costly and disruptive choice. Some colleges find the removal of these limits regrettable because it weakens the formation on one campus of a whole-of-student-body cohort. Rather than deliver units in off-campus mode, some colleges have chosen to increase the number of units taught face-to-face in intensive mode. The opening of regional campuses is another option gaining traction across the ACT consortium, though these have the potential to compromise compliance with the Threshold Standards which mandate student learning outcomes to be equivalent wherever the unit is delivered and in whatever mode. Delivery of units and courses in other than full attendance mode challenges classic educational paradigms, but diversity of delivery modes contributes to raising the level of theological education in churches and in regional and remote communities at a time when sensitive engagement with popular and intellectual culture is needed.

Given the clear commitment of the higher education sector and the national regulator, TEQSA, to student-centered learning there is a necessity for NUHEPs to embrace all measures and initiatives that underscore engagement with student-centered learning. Failure to do so risks the charge that we are not committed to student welfare.

Governance

The governance arrangements for all providers have long been the subject of regulatory scrutiny, especially with respect to ensuring that governing bodies have external members and members with higher education and financial expertise. Indeed, the reform of the ACT's academic and corporate governance structures was strongly recommended by the NSW higher education regulator in early 2006 if the college was to be considered for any future higher education approvals. Among the risks faced by companies, and theological colleges as a subset of these, is the breakdown of sound governance through an ill-disciplined CEO, or an out-of-touch chair, or lack of a clear understanding of the division of responsibilities of the board and the CEO.

All governing bodies should embark on a rigorous review of governance, preferably in association with an external expert with primary sources such as the Australian Stock Exchange's Principles,[16] the Christian Management Association's (CMA's) Essential Standards of Ministry Governance,[17] and the Corporations Act. Moreover, governing bodies should ensure that there is an annual review of compliance with the principles of good governance and that funds are set aside annually for the professional development of board members. We should not underestimate the witness of good governance in a society that sees plentiful evidence that governing bodies fail to declare or manage conflicts of interest, perpetuate behaviors protective of bullying or abusive cultures, and oversee destructive human relations.

---

16. http://www.asx.com.au/documents/asx-compliance/cgc-principles-and-recommendations-3rd-edn.pdf

17. http://www.cma.net.au/governance/index.php

Social Setting

Having considered in detail the effect of regulation on providers, I turn to reflect briefly on the setting of theological education in Australian society and three of the challenges that lie before the ACT in this regard.

Representation of Women as Academic Staff

A major contrast between theological education of 1975 and now is the number of women studying theology, including those enrolled in HDRs, now standing at about 40 percent of the total students of the ACT. But over half of Australian tertiary students and academic staff are women.[18] Unfortunately, markedly at variance with the tertiary sector, the proportion of women employed as academic staff across the affiliated colleges of the ACT in 2016 is 23.4 percent. Among full-time ACT academic staff, only 11 percent are women.[19] In time a growing number of women ACT HDR graduates should swell this proportion beyond the disappointing levels now in evidence. This will not be easy: women accounted for only 13 percent of ACT HDR graduates between the years 2008 and 2015. College governing bodies would do well to consider the strategies needed to encourage women to enroll in research degrees and to support them in this costly enterprise. Unsurprisingly, ACT affiliated colleges find themselves attracting comparatively few ACT-trained women applicants for academic staff positions. The talent pool would be immeasurably enriched if more women were qualified.

Safe Ministry

Sections of Australian society and the media are increasingly hostile to the churches. It is impossible to deny the damage that has resulted from revelations of the abuse of the vulnerable, children especially, at the hands of clergy and other church workers, in many cases protected by the hierarchy. The challenge for theological and Bible colleges is acute. They train the majority of future church and denominational leaders. The colleges trained and supposedly formed the generation of leaders who protected the abusers—abusers who were themselves trained at the same colleges. As a matter

---

18. In 2015, 55.4 percent of all tertiary students were women. See https://docs.education.gov.au/node/41696. In the same year, 56.7 percent of academic staff members were women. See https://docs.education.gov.au/node/38385.

19. For additional data and analysis, see the chapter by Kara Martin, Megan Powell du Toit, Jill Firth, and Moyra Dale in this volume.

of urgency, therefore, all college personnel and governing body members should know how they contribute to safe ministry and safe cultures in the college, and, at a greater remove, in supporting churches, denominations, and para-church agencies. The emphasis on whole-of-person formation (rather than merely focusing on educating the ministry candidate) and the insistence on psychological assessment for candidates for ministry are steps in the right direction. It is also essential for employer stakeholders and colleges to work collaboratively and intentionally to subvert and finally eradicate abusive cultures and behaviors, and implement transparent cultures which unequivocally and undeniably reflect Christian values.

Mission-Oriented Training

The theological and Bible colleges continue to train large numbers of educational, hospital and prison chaplains, as well as clergy and other church, community and cross-cultural workers. Their undoubted contribution is often undervalued or unrecognized. Given the growing disconnect between churches and wider society much can be said for theological education which assumes that all Christian workers are being prepared for cross-cultural mission wherever they will serve. Strategies designed to build bridges between communities of faith and society should be a major focus of the educational goal the colleges pursue with respect to training and formation.

Bibliography

Piggin, Stuart. "A History of Theological Education in Australia." In *The Furtherance of Religious Beliefs: Essays on the History of Theological Education in Australia*, edited by Geoffrey, R. Treloar, 24–43. Sydney: Centre for the Study of Australian Christianity for the Evangelical History Association of Australia, 1997.

21

The Challenges for Theological Education in Australia

Brian Harris

Abstract

Taking the title of the paper literally, this chapter systematically explores three areas of challenge facing theological educators in Australia, namely the theological challenge, the educational challenge, and the Australian challenge. It argues that the changed context in which we theologize necessitates theological educators equipping their students to counter claims that the Christian faith is intellectually vacuous, morally suspect and experientially empty, and proposes that theologians need to do theology not only for the church but also for the marketplace, to help ensure that the Christian faith is not marginalized in society. In exploring educational challenges, it is suggested that an area of increasing complexity is finding ways to form students for Christian ministry in an increasingly online environment where face-to-face contact is often limited.

Australian challenges discussed include training students for pastoral ministry in an increasingly post-denominational era, the challenge of adequately funding theological education and the opportunity provided by the increasing number of new immigrants who are enrolling in our colleges.

Introduction

THE WRITER OF ECCLESIASTES is clearly correct in asserting that there is nothing new under the sun.[1] The insight is worth remembering when we consider the challenges facing theological education in Australia. There are certainly challenges ahead, but has there ever been a time when this was not true? And would we want to live at a time when all was certain and every potential problem was already solved? Probably not.

I start this way to reassure readers that what follows is not a lament or whine about how difficult our future is likely to be. We live at an interesting time in history, and while our role is to promote theological education at a time when skepticism about the Christian faith is growing, this simply requires us to be especially diligent about what we do. The stakes are high and the outcome matters. If theological educators are not able to assist the church work towards a clearer understanding of how to respond to the many pressing challenges of our time, who will? Hopefully the seriousness of our setting will make us better than we might have been if complacency had been a realistic option.

The title of this paper implies three kinds of challenge—the theological challenge, the educational challenge and the Australian challenge. I will look at each in turn.

The Theological Challenge

While not at the coalface of direct pastoral ministry, theological educators prepare (amongst others) those who are.

The church in Australia faces a hardening secularism. Census trends are clear. A significantly smaller percentage of Australians are willing to identify with the Christian faith than was previously the case.[2] More disturbingly, whilst failure to identify with Christianity in the past usually reflected indifference, increasingly it is now accompanied by an active hostility. This has been clearly demonstrated in the rise of New Atheism. Probably the key factor that differentiates New Atheism from the old is the level of antagonism towards faith. The title of Christopher Hitchen's book says it all, *God is Not Great: How Religion Poisons Everything*.[3] The old atheists

---

1. Ecclesiastes 1:9.

2. For a wealth of information on religious affiliation, church attendance and related matters, see http://www.mccrindle.com.au/the-mccrindle-blog/church_attendance_in_australia_infographic.

3. Hitchens, *God Is Not Great: How Religion Poisons Everything*.

might not have believed that God exists, but were often willing to concede that belief in God served a societal good. This is now rarely the case, and faith is increasingly seen to be inherently poisonous.[4]

Essentially the Christian faith is being confronted with three key accusations, being that it is:

1. intellectually vacuous
2. morally suspect
3. experientially empty.

How can theological educators help train future practitioners who face this groundswell of discontent and cynicism?

In the first instance they need to recognize how important the shift is. If students are trained with the assumption that their ministry can operate with a Christendom mind-set, they have been set up to fail.[5] In other words, no longer can students assume that the broader society will view their vocational choice as noble and sacrificial. Being a member of the clergy now wins neither trust nor respect. Nor does it grant an automatic voice in the public square.

In spite of these changes (and perhaps especially because of these changes), theological educators need to take seriously their mandate to do theology not only for the church, but also for the marketplace—after all, the gospel is good news not just for the church, but for the world. Historically, Christianity has helped to drive the social agenda of society. It has been an active (frequently a dominant) contributor to the public debate on whatever the issues of the day happen to be. Often it has been the church who has brought otherwise unnoticed issues to public attention, and championed causes which could have been overlooked.[6]

Today we run the risk of retreating into a ghetto—and theologizing only for the faithful. There are reasons for this. Since the demise of Christendom, the default mood, which used to be in favor of the church, has

---

4. For a fuller discussion of this, and an analysis of both the merits and weaknesses of this claim, see my book, *When Faith Turns Ugly: Understanding Toxic Faith and How to Avoid It*. There are some who believe the New Atheists have overplayed their hand and that we now have the new new atheists who are allegedly more nuanced in their assessment of the role of faith in society. See https://www.spectator.co.uk/2013/04/after-the-new-atheism/.

5. For an excellent examination of the implications of ministry in a post-Christendom era, see the Paternoster series, *After Christendom*. See especially Murray, *Post-Christendom; Church After Christendom*.

6. For a helpful overview of the contribution of Christianity to human flourishing, see Schmidt, *Under the Influence: How Christianity Transformed Culture*.

decisively shifted. Whereas it was once considered that the church would automatically participate in and largely shape all public debate, contemporary participation is at best reluctantly accepted and often met with fierce hostility. This is especially so if those who represent the church adopt a position at variance with the wider society. It has never been easy to have a prophetic voice in society, but the barriers to that voice have been raised significantly. Our graduates need to be alert to this shift and to become wise and winsome in the way in which they reengage the broader society with the Christ story and its implications.

How we engage in the discussion is important. Too often the church is noted only for its opposition to whatever new innovation is being proposed. Increasingly the church is seen as a brake on moral progress, and unwilling to budge on long-held moral positions, regardless of what new evidence might come to light. This is deeply unhealthy, and will hasten the marginalization of the church.

This situation places a special responsibility on those engaged in theological education. Elsewhere I have written: "It is only stating the obvious to note that if the seminary, which employs those who are the best educated in the insights of the Christian faith, says nothing about the major issues of our day, people will conclude that it is because the Christian faith has nothing to say."[7]

Regardless of their area of specialization, given the challenges of our day, I would argue that all who teach in theological colleges need to be equipped as apologists, ethicists and missiologists. To quote from a paper I wrote on this topic:

> Rather than only speak at theological conferences, we should prepare ourselves to present papers at conferences on education, philosophy, business ethics, public policy ... the list goes on and on. George Marsden speaks supportively and enthusiastically of "the outrageous idea of Christian scholarship" and we should be willing to support this quest.[8] It should not be limited to conference participation. Why should theologians only teach theology students? Should we not raise our hand to teach courses in ethics, and philosophy or to participate in class debates about the care of the environment, the eradication of poverty and the appropriate use of wealth? Belief in the Christian God makes a significant difference to the way in which each of these subjects is handled, and if we do not make ourselves available to

---

7. Harris, "Faithful Thinking: The Role of the Seminary in Promoting a Thoughtful Christian Faith."

8. Marsden, *The Outrageous Idea of Christian Scholarship*.

explore this difference, who will? As we contribute relevantly in this arena, it is only a matter of time until we will be invited to contribute in yet wider arenas. Why should the new atheists be the only ones who get a public hearing?[9]

The difficulty of doing this should not be underestimated. A key issue is that there is usually very little agreement amongst theologians as to how issues should be approached. The debate within the theological academy often reflects a similar range of perspectives to those without. Christianity has many tribes, and they often see things in decidedly different ways. A unified view on global warming, gay marriage, genetic engineering or an appropriate political agenda is improbable. This being the case, perhaps our contribution can be in the manner in which the debate is both hosted and conducted. Instead of shrilly trying to score points off opposing perspectives, perhaps we can train our students to genuinely listen, to accurately represent alternate ideas and most of all, to actually hear the concerns which lie behind perspectives we disagree with—no matter how strong the disagreement. Producing graduates able to do this would be a significant contribution in itself. Naturally it will start with what we model, and theological colleges should be places of lively, but always charitable, debate.

Underlying this is another issue. Do we intend our graduates to essentially present orthodox views of the Christian faith, or can we as theological educators be a little more ambitious, aiming to produce graduates who embrace three essential "orthos"—orthodoxy (right thinking and belief), orthopraxy (right practice) and orthopathy (right feeling). This trio of "orthos" is essential if we are to regain trust and credibility in the wider arena. The task of producing graduates who think, live and empathize well—and who do so in a manner that clearly reflects the impact of the Christ story on their lives, is no easy task, but it is one that theological educators, at their best, embrace.

The earlier recognition that there is sometimes little agreement amongst theologians as to how an issue should be approached signals another issue for theological educators, that of academic freedom. Again, this is nothing new under the sun. Almost all theological colleges with a history longer than a decade or two would, at some time or another, have had to decide what to do about the views of a member of their academic staff which were at significant variance to the official views of their sponsoring body.

Some colleges have championed the cause of academic freedom, and have insistently upheld the right of academic staff to teach the truth as they

---

9. Harris, "Faithful Thinking: The Task Ahead for Christian Higher Education," 243.

see it, encouraging them to follow it regardless of where it might lead. Others have been significantly more controlling, and a change of view on the part of an academic staff member has sometimes necessitated a change of place of employment. Some whose views have changed have found themselves unemployable within a church-sponsored context.

This second approach, where employment at a theological college requires an ongoing commitment to a prescribed confessional standpoint, is likely to prove increasingly problematic in the future and could be viewed as a discriminatory employment practice. Likewise, lifestyle requirements made of academic staff members could prove difficult to enforce—and indeed, to even require.

This is a complex issue. Church denominations are confessional bodies, and they usually require of their clergy clear and affirming convictions that support the major tenants of the denominations' understanding of the Christian faith. This in turn needs to be supported by a lifestyle which is in accordance with these convictions. Theological colleges around the world are grappling with the legal complexity of ensuring they can retain the right to employ staff of their choosing and to dismiss them for offences they (but not necessarily the wider society) deem serious, whilst not running afoul of anti-discrimination and academic freedom legislation.

Behind this debate lies the issue of what academic freedom means in a confessional context. The fact that the context is confessional immediately signals awareness that all are not in agreement with the approach and stance of the institution. The ecclesiology taught in a Baptist college is unlikely to win the warm approval of an Anglican college, and the reverse is equally true. Again, the way forward probably lies in the manner in which the conversation takes place. Theological educators, regardless of their personal persuasion, should be committed to ensuring that alternate views are fairly presented, and that our students are not allowed to get away with villainizing caricatures of opponents. Genuine understanding of the "what," "why," and social context of other positions is an important building block of academic credibility.

Not far from this issue is that of the prophetic responsibility of theological educators. On the one hand, most theological colleges exist to provide a steady stream of graduates for their sponsoring bodies. But there is a deeper call for all those engaged in theological education, and that is the responsibility to serve as a prophetic voice to those bodies when they need to change or modify their practice. The church is always at risk of falling captive to the idols of the time. Be it a quick route to church growth, or a downplaying of the call of Christ, the temptation to bow at the altar of power, success and privilege is ever-present. Speaking with prophetic courage is not comfortable, and can be risk-ridden when a college is financially dependent on those they must speak against, but it is part of the reason theological colleges exist. We must assess the practice of the church in the light of the mandate found in Scripture, the tradition of the church, and the particular call of our time and context. Our colleges are places of deep thought and reflection. That thought should shape not just the lives of our graduates, but also the practice of the church and parachurch bodies they serve.

The Educational Challenge

Like all involved in higher education, theological educators face a changed environment. Higher education has become increasingly democratized, and is no longer the preserve of the elite. The second recommendation of the Bradley review into higher education is that by 2020, 40 percent of Australians between the ages of 25 to 34 should have at least a first degree—and this influential review suggests steps the country could take to make this possible.[10]

While the increased number of students participating in higher education is itself a challenge, what actually takes place in institutions for higher education is changing rapidly. Previously the university was seen as the repository of knowledge, the place students attended to unearth information that would otherwise have been unavailable. With the average phone now providing access to more information than the average university of only a decade ago, this situation is forever changed. Today's student will do a quick Google fact check on information provided during a lecture, and is unlikely to attend any timetable slot that is essentially just a lecture. If a lecture is simply a collation of pieces of information around a selected topic (as lectures so often are), students will increasingly opt to glean the relevant data in the comfort of their own home. Consequently, the lecture room is becoming a venue for flipped learning—flipped because it is now the venue for discussion and exploration of ideas already explored by the student, with them now being analyzed, clarified, and applied in a small group setting.

Historically, the dilemma of those in higher education has been to find enough lecturers sufficiently expert in their field to pass on their insights to an up-and-coming generation. Today, professional expertise must be supplemented with educational expertise, and it is likely that in the foreseeable future those who teach in higher education will need to supplement the qualifications they hold in their discipline with additional qualifications in education. It will no longer be enough to be an expert in molecular

---

10 Bradley et al., "Review of Australian Higher Education," 21.

biology—lecturers will also need to be experts in assessment, learning styles and pedagogy. They will also face ruthless evaluation by their students, who will assess them not only on their knowledge of their discipline, but also on their enthusiasm for it, their time management skills and the quality of the feedback they provide on work assessed. Management is likely to pay as much attention to feedback from students as it is to the list of recent publications a lecturer can claim credit for, especially as student satisfaction rates are now likely to impact the financial bottom line.

These changes have seen the occupation of university lecturer change from one assumed to be essentially scholarly and leisurely, to one that is becoming increasingly pressurized and with clear and demanding output expectations. It is now common to differentiate between those who teach in higher education and those who conduct research in a higher education environment—and staff often have to choose where their focus will be, teaching or research.

These changes impact all who are engaged in higher education, and theological educators are in essentially the same boat as everyone else as they face them.

One difference is that theological education has always claimed a special interest in the formation of its students. Academic brilliance is not a clear predictor of success in pastoral ministry. Congregants expect their pastor to relate compassionately and insightfully with others whilst living a credible—even exemplary—personal life. They often pay more attention to this than to their pastor's theological position. Theological educators are well aware of this, and so have been reluctant to train students in an entirely online environment, where face-to-face contact with students can be minimal, and the ability to engage meaningfully with the wider life of the student can be limited.

Given that an increasing number of students are now studying theology in an entirely online environment, it is not surprising that research into the online formation of students is now a topic of both serious and urgent study. It will probably result in new forms of cooperation between the theological college and the local church, with the local church often being the hub where formational issues can be unpacked and grounded. This will be especially important when the college's physical location is hundreds of kilometers away from the student's residence. Whilst noting this, we should not underestimate the potential for formation to take place in an entirely online environment. Technological advances will continue to transform the range of options open to us, and we must creatively engage in this space.

The Australian Challenge

What then are some of the specifically Australian challenges being faced by theological educators?

While it is always tempting to assume our situation is unique, most themes are similar to those faced elsewhere. Almost all theological educators are feeling the financial pinch. Often this links to the demise of denominations which were previously willing to fund seminaries under their jurisdiction.

A post-denominational era also leaves seminaries with no guaranteed supply of students. A Baptist student will not necessarily opt to study at a Baptist college, and the same is true of Lutherans, Methodists and Pentecostals. Indeed, many students no longer claim any denominational allegiance, and might pragmatically decide on a denomination for reasons of employment, rather than as a result of theological conviction. It is now not uncommon for students to have no church allegiance at all, sometimes having what Alan Jamieson terms a "churchless faith."[11] While such students might have a keen interest in theology, and even a vibrant faith in Jesus, they are often disillusioned and suspicious of anything that appears to resemble the institutional church. Some are committed to finding new and fresh expressions of church, and will look to their lecturers to guide them in this quest.

There are some specific Australian issues. The introduction of FEE-HELP—a government funded low interest loan scheme to assist students studying at private institutions for higher education to pay their fees—has greatly improved access for students wishing to study theology, and indeed, has seen the number of students studying theology increase dramatically. However, whilst not under any immediate threat, its future should not be assumed to be secure. Nor should it be assumed that theological education is equitably funded in Australia, for it is not—with theological educators in the government funded university sector receiving a substantially better deal than those in the private sector—and it is in the private sector that most theological education takes place.[12]

Whilst consortium arrangements have worked well for private theological providers in Australia, the growth of online degrees in theology is leading to fresh challenges. Colleges which previously worked collegially now compete with other colleges within the same consortium for online students. Online study collapses geographic boundaries, introducing an

---

11. Jamieson, *A Churchless Faith: Faith Journeys Beyond Evangelical, Pentecostal and Charismatic Churches*.

12. For a much fuller discussion of this, see Mark Harding's excellent chapter in this volume.

element of rivalry that was not present when large distances separated colleges. This is a recent development, and it is too early to pick its outcome. Ideally colleges will rise to the opportunities presented by an online environment (not least being the option of employing adjunct staff located anywhere in the world), and will work collaboratively to ensure optimal outcomes for students—but we cannot assume that this will be the case. Perhaps an online environment will see theological training outsourced to countries which can provide it both cheaply and credibly.

The shape of the church in Australia is also changing rapidly. Whilst in retreat in many sectors, other parts are thriving. In particular, the arrival of immigrants from Asia and Africa is seeing the rapid growth of churches with a focus on particular cultural and linguistic groups. Too often theological colleges have adopted a "one size fits all" model of theological education, and the naivety of this is becoming apparent. A growing number of our students come from the cultural group they plan to minister to, and a traditional theological training shaped by the assumptions and issues faced by the "Western world" is not necessarily the most appropriate. This is an important shift, and one which invites creative engagement. In addition, the number of international students studying at our colleges is increasing. Again, the relevance of our training for the settings to which they will return, must be carefully thought through.

Nothing New Under the Sun

There is nothing new under the sun, and theological educators continue to face challenges. This is how it has ever been, and will ever be. In essence, the challenges continue to revolve around issue of prophetic relevance, effective formation of students and threats to funding. They are accompanied by real opportunities for greater collaboration, ingenuity and reach if we can overcome minor differences and work together to introduce theology to the increasing number of students studying in the higher education sector, regardless of the mode in which they study.

Bibliography

Bradley, Denise, et al. "Review of Australian Higher Education." Canberra: DEEWR, 2008.

Harris, Brian. "Faithful Thinking: The Role of the Seminary in Promoting a Thoughtful Christian Faith." *The Pacific Journal of Baptist Research* 8, no. 1 (2013): 27–35.

———. "Faithful Thinking: The Task Ahead for Christian Higher Education." In *Vose Seminary at Fifty: From 'Preach the Word' to 'Come Grow'*, edited by Nathan Hobby, John Olley and Michael O'Neil, 233–44. Preston: Mosaic, 2013.

———. *When Faith Turns Ugly: Understanding Toxic Faith and How to Avoid It*. Milton Keynes: Paternoster, 2016.

Hitchens, Christopher. *God Is Not Great: How Religion Poisons Everything*. New York: Twelve, 2007.

Jamieson, Alan. *A Churchless Faith: Faith Journeys Beyond Evangelical, Pentecostal and Charismatic Churches*. Wellington: Philip Garside, 2000.

Marsden, George. *The Outrageous Idea of Christian Scholarship*. New York: Oxford University Press, 1997.

Murray, Stuart. *Church After Christendom*. Carlisle: Paternoster, 2004.

———. *Post-Christendom*. Carlisle: Paternoster, 2004.

Schmidt, Alvin J. *Under the Influence: How Christianity Transformed Culture*. Grand Rapids: Zondervan, 2001.

Conclusion

THEOLOGICAL EDUCATION TODAY IS a multifaceted phenomenon, which faces a variety of challenges and opportunities as it seeks to support the mission of the church. Looking towards the future, one thing is certain: the sector will continue to change. It is quite likely that theological education in the Australian context—and probably in any number of other contexts also—will be substantially different to its form today in a generation from now. As Mark Harding's chapter in this volume observes, theological education in Australia, reflecting parallel developments in many other countries, has seen not one but many substantial changes since the mid-1970s. Many of these changes have in fact occurred not just in the last forty years, but in the last twenty years. The pace of change in relation to developments has accelerated since the mid-1990s. For example, in Australia, government loan funding, together with all of the developments that have flowed from it, has been in place for only around fifteen years. The very substantial expansion in the range of degrees, courses and study pathways available through most Australian providers, described by Les Ball and Geoff Treloar, has also occurred in a similar space of time. The increase in part-time, online, and female students, and other aspects of diversification has occurred in less than a generation. These developments have been driven in large measure by changes in the social and cultural characteristics of Christianity in the Australian context, societal attitudes and practices regarding formal study and training, and institutional and structural factors. Given that changes in these domains look set to continue at a considerable rate, and often with unpredictable effects, we should expect that theological education itself will continue to evolve considerably in Australia and beyond for the foreseeable future. In light of this, we might sum up the perspectives offered in this volume in the following way. If the trajectory of theological education is understood as a journey—which involves rapid and sometimes bewildering twists and turns—then the Bible itself is the path along which we walk. The histories which this volume and others articulate are the lampposts along the way illuminating various key insights and landmarks to remember, and the reflections upon both practical questions and future perspectives are a flickering light which gives us a glimpse of where we are at currently and a short distance ahead.

However, in the midst of ongoing change, some essential features of theological education will stay the same. A number of chapters in this volume have made the case that certain critical elements *should* remain unchanged if seminaries and theological educators are to serve the church and the community in a changing world. Of first importance in this regard is the importance of theological training remaining wedded to and captivated by Scripture, in terms of curricular content and as the epistemological foundation of all of the sub-disciplines which find a place in theological education. Also, the Scriptures ought to shape the goals, pedagogy, and practice of theological education more broadly, particularly for any and all who would claim the Bible as their supremely authoritative guide. As Foord's chapter points out, the biblically-defined nature of the church's ministry and its leadership demands training that will necessarily incorporate certain foundations, goals and elements, if seminaries are to fulfill their mission in any time or place. More specifically, the pedagogical principles and practices which guide teaching and learning in each subject area should be guided by the convictions which we draw from the Scriptures. Beginning with the Old and New Testaments, as Kit Barker and David Starling point out we must allow what the Scriptures teach about themselves, and Christians and churches as readers, to shape how we teach them, including in academic contexts such as seminaries. As is illustrated in several places in the historical studies section of this volume, the very best of theological educators in former times have given this kind of fundamental, guiding role to Scripture in their educational practice, as they sought to facilitate the personal formation of students by the Scriptures. Reflecting upon the task today, the chapters by Peter Francis, Brian Harris, and Ian Hussey are a reminder of the continuing importance for today of biblical training landing in personal formation and transformation.

Alongside the unchanging place of the unchanging Scriptures, many contributions to this volume underline the importance of theological education being appropriately responsive to the evolving needs of its context.

The task of faithfully passing on the deposit given once and for all to the saints—and equipping the saints to live and speak their faith into their part of the world—in new ways and even new institutional settings which are effective in training participants for life and ministry in their time and place, is vitally important if Christianity is not to become marginalized and irrelevant. Supporting the mission of the church today in post-Christian settings may require new solutions for some in training, such as the ACT's new Master of Missional Leadership course discussed by Karina Kreminski and Michael Frost. For others, it may involve the introduction of new subject units, for others, integrating what is newly-important with existing elements of the curriculum, and for others still relocating the seminary in terms of its physical geography, online "location," or its orientation towards the ambient culture. In some cases, it might be elements beyond the formal curriculum that provide a critical part of the mix: in relation to an Australian example, Anthony Brammall has highlighted that at SMBC the non-accredited "internal" training offered has played this role over many years.

As Martin Foord and David Starling remind us, theological education must be tied closely to the needs of the local church not only to be effective but even to have a biblical shape. At times of great change in society and the church, where new forms of theological education develop these can have much value in their own time and significance for the future, as we see in the examples of both late antiquity and the sixteenth century discussed by Andrew Bain and Graeme Chatfield respectively. Even in contexts where the scale of social or ecclesiastical change may not be quite as revolutionary as in these periods, more subtle developments alongside changes in the educational landscape can, and perhaps should, still call forth new forms appropriate to the local context such as Rhys Bezzant describes occurring at the turn of the nineteenth century in the United States.

However, responding to the needs of the local church in a particular place or time is no easy matter: as Ian Hussey points out, not only are students diverse and unsuited to a one-size-fits-all approach, but the assumptions of theological teachers about what is most effectively formative are often incorrect when considered alongside the views of the students themselves. Theological educators wishing to equip Christians to better serve in their context would also do well to remember, as Diane Hockridge points out, that there are limits to what seminaries can do in isolation, and that strong partnerships with local churches are essential particularly in seeing deeply formational outcomes realized.

On maintaining and strengthening the relevance of theological education as we head into the future, Brian Harris highlights a number of key areas in relation to the Australian context, one of which is to ensure that theological training is responsive to levels of immigration and ethnic diversity which continue to grow. This reflects the wider challenge for theological education of globalization in its various forms, which is relevant to the sector in virtually every part of the world. To take an example, Australian theological education is still almost entirely comprised of locally-based institutions, as is the case in many other countries. Will the recent phenomenon of universities establishing campuses in foreign countries, and forming international collaborative partnerships in greater numbers, start to more commonly spill over into the theological education sector? The growing regulatory and corporate-governance demands highlighted by Mark Harding, along with the ever-increasing impetus towards academic rigor and engagement, tend to require that institutional resources also increase. Such pressures will likely push seminaries towards greater collaboration domestically in Australia and some other countries and for some raise the prospect of consolidation within the sector, and may provide an impetus for an increase in transnational ventures even in relation to well-established first world theological education sectors such as Australia's.

The old tension for theological education of seeking to simultaneously serve the church and relate to the academy tends to most commonly come to the surface in Australia today as it does in some other countries in relation to questions around accreditation and other state-driven requirements parallel to those in place for the universities. Increasingly, requirements in this area concern not only matters of academic standards and basic fiduciary duties, but broader issues around corporate governance, the form and structuring of qualifications, and community expectations regarding matters such as equity. Seminaries and bodies such as the ACT are expected to have in place an array of policies which they would not have imagined implementing even a decade ago, in order to meet not only the formal requirements of governments but also to keep pace with community expectations of how a variety of fee-paying students will be supported as they study. In Australia, the increasing application of the Australian Qualifications Framework (AQF) to many aspects of theological education is an example of how state expectations in the area of qualifications can drive substantial change in the sector, for good or for ill. The challenge for those involved in theological education is to seek to harness such government and community demands so as to drive improvements in how well we perform our ministry, while keenly watching that acceptance of some incremental changes do not slowly and subtly undermine faithfulness to biblical norms. Closer application of standards placed on related institutions such as universities has the potential to support our mission-in-context by aligning practices with legitimate community expectations and promoting stronger relationships with other social institutions: provided it does not detract from the biblical shape of the mission itself.

Looking to the future, there are a number of areas this volume has identified where theological education in Australia could make improvements, which may also be relevant to the Australian sector's relatives in other countries. The good news presented here is that it appears that ways forward to strengthen theological education are available. The editors' chapter on the reflections of ACT graduates on the applicability to ministry of their training indicates that the basic foundation in the classical disciplines of biblical studies, systematic theology, and church history continues to be appreciated by graduates in practice as well as being theologically appropriate. Where the graduates would have appreciated more help was primarily in the area of taking this training and relating it to people in their churches and communities: and the research does suggest ways in which this can be achieved. Likewise, Phillip Scheepers' discussion of theological training in relation to mission identifies several readily-applicable constructive steps that can be taken, as does Martin, Powell du Toit, Firth and Dale's analysis of female involvement in Australian theological education. Attrition rates as discussed by Delle Matthews have been a significant and growing problem for theological colleges and seminaries, and in this area also it appears that there are effective steps that can be taken to drive improvement.

Theological education, in Australia and beyond, continues to face both particular issues and questions as well as the ever-present challenge of providing biblically-faithful training for continually-changing contexts. In this respect, the story of theological education today continues that of times past. As we have seen, theological educators from late antiquity to the Reformation to the early United States to other periods in Australian history have taken hold of the opportunity to offer the training needed for the mission of the church in changing and challenging circumstances. It is our prayer that the readers of this volume will be inspired to do the same, in the power of the Holy Spirit and the confidence that comes from a knowledge of the biblical foundations, historical lampposts and exciting future possibilities presented.

Andrew M. Bain
Ian Hussey
Brisbane, 2017

Index

academic freedom, 291–92
attrition (student), 228–240, 278, 302

culture, 5, 10, 25, 40, 57, 148–59, 178, 185, 216–20, 223–25, 300

denominations (and theological education), xv–xvi, xx, 27, 66, 78, 84–85, 91, 97, 99–100, 108, 111–12, 124, 127–28, 129–30, 140, 142, 146, 202, 242, 270, 282, 292, 295
diversity, 27, 49, 123, 168, 217n8, 219, 283–84, 301

FEE-HELP, xx, 113, 114n50, 116, 275, 277–79, 295
field education, 95–96, 142, 145, 146, 186, 191–92, 212, 247, 253–54
finance (challenges and limitations), 98, 107, 125, 261, 281, 282, 294, 295
flipped learning, 293

innovation, 94, 95–97, 99, 114–15, 289–90

leadership, 34–37, 51–52, 77–78, 114–15, 144, 146, 164, 167, 169–70, 177–79, 183
Learning Outcomes, 13n23, 114, 184, 221, 283–84

mission, 21, 25, 40, 68, 71, 79–80, 84, 94–95, 115–16, 120–21, 124, 126, 131–32, 176–78, 183–85, 217–20, 222–23, 225, 243, 286, 300
multiculturalism, 108, 217, 218

new atheism, the, 288–89

online learning, 42, 51, 182, 204, 206, 207–208, 246, 283, 294, 295–96

reflection (in theological education), 21, 56, 85, 155, 158, 180, 182, 184, 190–99, 207–208, 210, 212–13, 218–19, 223, 243–44, 247n15, 248, 251

spiritual formation, 13n22, 25–27, 50–51, 55–58, 84–86, 110, 111–12, 123–24, 131, 136, 178, 180–81, 182, 184–85, 188–89, 201–213, 217, 221–23, 235, 242–54, 265, 283, 286, 294, 299

TEQSA (the *Tertiary Education Quality and Standards Agency*, of Australia), 98, 114, 116, 204, 229, 281–82, 284
theological orthodoxy, 23, 53, 82, 85, 126–28, 291
trends (theological education), 98–100, 161–64, 224, 278–79, 285–86, 288, 293–96

women (in theological education), 90–91, 125, 161–72, 233–34, 275, 285

www.ingramcontent.com/pod-product-compliance
Lightning Source LLC
Chambersburg PA
CBHW050619300426
44112CB00012B/1573